Pedagogy and
the Politics of Hope

THE EDGE: CRITICAL STUDIES IN EDUCATIONAL THEORY

Series Editors   Joe L. Kincheloe, Peter McLaren, and Shirley R. Steinberg

---

Pedagogy and the Politics of Hope

Theory, Culture, and Schooling

A Critical Reader

Henry A. Giroux

WestviewPress

A Division of HarperCollins*Publishers*

The Edge: Critical Studies in Educational Theory

Copyright © 1997 by Westview Press, A Division of HarperCollins Publishers, Inc.

Published in 1997 in the United States of America by Westview Press, 5500 Central Avenue, Boulder, Colorado 80301-2877, and in the United Kingdom by Westview Press, 12 Hid's Copse Road, Cumnor Hill, Oxford OX2 9JJ

Library of Congress Cataloging-in-Publication Data
Giroux, Henry A.
    Pedagogy and the politics of hope : theory, culture, and schooling
: a critical reader / Henry A. Giroux.
        p.   cm.—(The edge, critical studies in educational theory)
    Selection of author's essays previously published over past
fifteen years.
    Includes bibliographical references and index.
    ISBN 0-8133-3273-7(hc).—ISBN 0-8133-3274-5(pb)
    1. Critical pedagogy.   2. Postmodernism and education.
3. Politics and education.   I. Title.   II. Series.
LC196.G573   1997
370.11´5—dc21   96-39884
                                                                                        CIP

The paper used in this publication meets the requirements of the American National Standard for Permanence of Paper for Printed Library Materials Z39.48-1984.

10   9   8   7   6   5   4   3   2

For the children

Contents

Series Editors' Foreword

As editors of Westview's series The Edge: Critical Studies in Educational Theory, we asked Henry Giroux to put together a series of his most definitive essays from the past fifteen years so that education and cultural studies scholars could gain a sense of the roots and progression of his work. *Pedagogy and the Politics of Hope* is the product of that request. Giroux's work is so prodigious and multidimensional that the effort to select a manageable but comprehensive sampling of it became a frustrating chore: "How can we leave out the essay on the Frankfurt School?" or "I don't understand why the essay on the critique of reproduction theory was deleted" became common questions and observations in our deliberations. To do justice to the variety of discourses that Giroux has drawn upon or the various theoretical advances he has offered in his relatively short career would require a Quintilianesque multivolume set. We yielded to the demands of practicality; *Pedagogy and the Politics of Hope* is the result of our conferences. We hope that readers will find the work included here as compelling and insightful as we do. As this volume illustrates, Giroux is undoubtedly one of the most creative educational thinkers of the last third of the twentieth century, and his innovative scholarship and influence will continue into the twenty-first century and beyond.

Giroux's passion and genius revolve around the struggle for a radical democracy both in the United States and in the world at large. *Radical democracy,* as he uses the term, involves the effort to expand the possibility for social justice, freedom, and egalitarian social relations in the educational, economic, political, and cultural domains that locate men, women, and children in everyday life. Thus, *Pedagogy and the Politics of Hope* documents the development of Giroux's trademark language of critique and possibility and the ways he deploys it in the effort to expose the forces that undermine education for a critical democracy. In the context of recent U.S. history such forces have flourished in the cocoon of Reaganism; indeed, it is in this environment that Giroux's insurgent analyses take shape. In the Age of Reagan, Giroux's introduction of Frankfurt School critical theory into the discourse of educational scholarship struck a responsive chord with those offended by duplicitous right-wing proclamations of an oppression-cleansed history of American education. Giroux's ability to name the ever-so-subtle ways in which power operated to undermine the dignity and mobility of marginalized students was unprecedented in educational scholarship. Deftly deploying critical theory with its nondogmatic discourse of social transformation, emancipation, and perpetual self-critique, Giroux in his early work demonstrated the power of social theory in generating transempirical understanding of sociopolitical and educational processes. Via the application of critical theory's immanent critique and dialectical thought, Giroux unmasked forms of domination for educators of all ideological stripes.

He understood that somewhere in the relationship among power, ideology, and schooling the crisis of historical consciousness was exacerbated. Isolating what he labeled the *culture of positivism,* Giroux delineated its irrational rationality characterized by an emphasis on prediction and technical control. When combined with the rejection of the interpretive dynamics of hermeneutics, this culture of positivism transmogrified into a dominant ideological form. Although he was consistently clear on the issue, many of Giroux's readers were unable to appreciate the distinction between the culture of positivism as ideological form and positivism as a specific philosophical movement. Such a distinction is crucial to the understanding of Giroux's unique contribution to educational critique and analysis. In the culture of positivism education becomes a form of social regulation that guides humans toward destinies that preserve the status quo. Reflection on the formation of subjectivity or analysis of "what is" vis-à-vis "what should be" is dismissed from the positivistic culture. In other words, consciousness of historical forces and their relationship to everyday life has no place in the technocratic rationality of the culture of positivism.

Thus, as Giroux observed schooling through the prism of Frankfurt theory in the late 1970s and early 1980s, he came to understand the conceptual corner into which radical critics had painted themselves. Though they understood that schools were sites of oppression in which race, class, and gender inequities were perpetuated, they were able to appreciate neither how student and teacher subjectivities were constructed nor the self-determination (agency) such constructions made possible. At the same time, of course, Giroux was acutely aware of the inability of mainstream educational critics to understand how ideological and structural forces influence the nature of educational experience. Viewed in this context, Giroux's theoretical innovation became more apparent: Agencies of socialization (in particular, schools) do not undermine the possibility of a radical democracy merely by preparing students for vocations that help sustain the dominant mode of economic production; at the same time, schools and other agencies of socialization are never autonomous from dominant economic and other social (white supremacy and patriarchy, for example) structures. Appreciating the emerging poststructuralist contribution to social theory, Giroux understood that the forces that subvert radical democracy always exist in a dynamic, ever-shifting relationship with those that support it—indeed, he insisted, the nature of their connection is historically specific. If educators are ever to make sense of education and its relation to the vicissitudes of the democratic struggle, they will have to develop a complex apprehension of how individuals *receive* the messages sent by the forces of domination and, in particular, how they *mediate* the ideological representations and material practices that formulate their lived experiences. Respecting individuals' agency, Giroux wanted to know how individuals and groups produce meaning on extant social, economic, and political terrains and how such production relates to the struggle for radical democracy.

By the early 1980s Giroux's theoretical infrastructure was taking shape. Throughout the decade, as his familiarity with the emerging postmodern critique deepened, Giroux fine-tuned his insights concerning modes of reception and mediation and their relation to the construction of consciousness and the production of subjectivity. His early fascination with British cultural studies—especially the work of Raymond Williams, Richard Johnson, and Stuart Hall—led Giroux to connect his study of subjectivity, power, and pedagogy to issues of language, discourse, and desire. He made use of the best of twentieth-century educational scholarship—including the progressivism of John Dewey, the transgressive pedagogy of Paulo Freire, and the insights of the curricular reconceptualists—to transcend the notion that power is merely the distribution of political and economic resources. Employing and extending this battery of theoretical sensibilities, Giroux conceptualized power as a concrete set of practices that produces social forms through which distinct experiences and subjectivities are shaped—a position that emphasized again the receptive and mediative dimensions of the process. Such dimensions, he understood, pointed to the importance of pedagogy not only in educational theory but in social theory in general; this finding would become increasingly relevant to students of education, sociology, and cultural studies in the 1990s.

In this context, Giroux analyzed the relation between the critical postmodern feminist theory that began to emerge in the mid-1980s and his theoretical project. Recognizing in the work of Jane Flax, Seyla Benhabib, Cora Kaplan, Meaghan Morris, Linda Nicholson, Nancy Fraser, Linda Hutcheon, and many others a means of traversing the conceptual minefield formed by the binary opposition between modernism and postmodernism, Giroux listened carefully to the feminist conversation.

In their attempt to develop a political voice the postmodern feminists had adeptly freed themselves from the modernist-postmodernist binarism. On the one hand, they pledged a modernist allegiance to equality, justice, and freedom; on the other, like critical postmodernists, they exposed modernism's exaltation of the universal over historically and culturally specific ways of seeing, and they raised doubts about its scientific claims to objectivity and truth. This synthesis, when combined with Giroux's interpretation of critical theory, Deweyan progressivism, British cultural studies, Freirian liberation, curricular reconceptualization, and the domain of pedagogy, set the stage for a radical democratic praxis that was contextually sensitive and politically transformative. At this point Giroux was theoretically equipped to make use of the post-colonial critiques of the Eurocentric position that Western culture was the barometer of civilization and produced a transhistorical educational canon. Thus, buoyed by postmodernist feminist theory, Giroux began to contemplate the means and methods of producing new academic discourses and unprecedented knowledge forms.

In addition to shedding light on the social and political silences in school discourses, knowledge, and materials; the refusal to include various disciplinary perspectives; the denial of human agency; and the common tendency to legitimate dominant power relations, Giroux by his theoretical innovations generated new ways of viewing education and schooling. The result was an ever-evolving critical pedagogy—a critical postmodern and multicultural pedagogy. Such a "critped" viewed teachers as intellectuals who were empowered to create and participate in a radical democracy. Consistently refusing to offer a simple blueprint of how to institute a critical pedagogy in schools around the world, Giroux emphasized the contextual specificity of each application of the process over the presence of common themes. Expanding this postmodern insight, Giroux's evolving critical pedagogy began increasingly to focus on issues of difference in a politically transformative frame. Vitally concerned with the complex ways that race, class, and gender identities of student and teacher are constructed, he connected them to larger public struggles. The postmodern concern with historical and social specificity moved Giroux to focus on the pedagogical terrain of power, knowledge production and transmission, identity/subjectivity formation, and socialization in relation to the referent of a radical democracy. He understood that the pedagogical process was expanding into new cultural spaces created by technology, necessitating new modes of analyzing the politics of education. In this context the process of representation—by which the world is delineated, depicted, schematized, and inscribed with meaning—was increasingly taking place around the domain of pleasure, accompanied by affective and emotional investments.

At this juncture Giroux joined forces with cultural studies scholars in the effort to legitimize popular culture as an academic concern. As a primary producer of pleasure, popular culture is a powerful pedagogical agent for representing the world in ways that both disempower and empower. Frankfurt School critics had long maintained that culture is a political entity; operating on that assumption, Giroux set out to bring cultural studies insight into the analysis of *popular* culture as a pedagogical/political locale. Refusing to merely mimic cultural studies' emphasis on the popular, Giroux has refocused cultural studies around his long-time concern with radical democracy. He thereby moved to the center stage of cultural studies, as his innovative work within the field raised larger questions of justice, liberty, and equality. Using the interdisciplinary and transdisciplinary tools of cultural studies to translate theory into democratic practice, Giroux continues to expand the intellectual envelope in his search for new modes of academic enterprise. In this way, his work in the 1990s has provided new understandings of the pedagogical process, new insight into pleasure, new maps of desire, and fresh interpretations of the relation among reason, emotion, and domination. Ironically, Giroux has thus helped return cultural studies to its pedagogical roots—as exemplified by Raymond Williams's studies of adult education and the roles of democracy and social change in the academic process.

It is this reestablishment of the study of pedagogy that this book, as well as Giroux's work in general, addresses. If pedagogy involves the production and transmission of knowledge, the construction of subjectivity, and the learning of values and beliefs, then educational scholarship over the past half-century has typically been nonpedagogical. As Giroux reinserts pedagogy into educational studies, he incorporates it into the cultural studies agenda. Examining how people learn, make emotional investments, and negotiate the world around them, pedagogy is central to any discipline that studies educational and cultural processes vis-à-vis the making of meaning. Pedagogical study may be even more important to political activists, dedicated to self- and social empowerment, the creation of community, and the establishment of principles of justice and democracy. As Giroux conceptualizes it within the theoretical frames of political modernism, critical postmodernism, and postmodern feminism, pedagogy becomes an indispensable tool in the struggle for a radical democracy. Indeed, without an understanding of how power is viewed by men, women, and children in specific settings, our understanding of social change remains crude, clumsy, and prone to essentialist simplification. The production, transmission, and reception of knowledge is always problematic; to assume otherwise, to dismiss the study of pedagogy and its political ramifications, is to turn one's back on the conditions under which human identity is constructed. Until Giroux's insight into pedagogy is understood and employed by scholars and students of cultural studies, a major piece of the educational puzzle will be missing. *Pedagogy and the Politics of Hope* provides readers with a map to the missing piece as well as an archaeology of its theoretical evolution.

Joe L. Kincheloe
Peter McLaren
Shirley R. Steinberg

PART ONE

Theoretical Foundations for Critical Pedagogy

Schooling and the Culture of Positivism: Notes on the Death of History

There is no neutral material of history. History is not a spectacle for us because it is our own living, our own violence and our own beliefs.[1]

I

One of the more fundamental questions raised by educators in recent years focuses on how public school classroom teachers might develop an orientation to curriculum development and implementation which acknowledges the important underlying ethical and normative dimensions that structure classroom decisions and experiences. The absence of such an orientation has been well noted.[2] For example, in different ways both phenomenological and neo-Marxist perspectives on educational thought and practice have pointed to the atheoretical, ahistorical, and unproblematic view of pedagogy that presently characterizes curriculum development particularly in the social sciences.

Some phenomenological critics have charged that teaching practices are often rooted in "common sense" assumptions that go relatively unchallenged by both teachers and students and serve to mask the social construction of different forms of knowledge. In this view the focus of criticism is on the classroom teacher who appears insensitive to the complex transmission of socially based definitions and expectations that function to reproduce and legitimize the dominant culture at the level of classroom instruction.[3] Teachers and other educational workers, in this case, often ignore questions concerning how they perceive their classrooms, how students make sense of what they are presented, and how knowledge is mediated between teachers (themselves) and students.

On the other hand, some neo-Marxist critics have attempted to explain how the politics of the dominant society are linked to the political

3

character of the classroom social encounter. In this perspective the focus shifts from an exclusive concern with how teachers and students construct knowledge to the ways in which the social order is legitimated and reproduced through the production and distribution of "acceptable" knowledge and classroom social processes.[4] Thus, neo-Marxist educators are not simply concerned with how teachers and students view knowledge; they are also concerned with the mechanisms of social control and how these mechanisms function to legitimate the beliefs and values underlying wider societal institutional arrangements.

Both views have led to a greater appreciation of the hermeneutic and political nature of public school pedagogy. Unfortunately, neither view has provided a thorough understanding of how the wider "culture of positivism," with its limited focus on objectivity, efficiency, and technique, is both embedded and reproduced in the form and content of public school curricula. While it is true that some phenomenologists have focused on the relationship between the social construction of classroom knowledge and the major tenets of positivism, they have generally ignored the forms and social practices involved in its transmission. On the other hand, while neo-Marxist critiques have emphasized the ideological underpinnings of classroom social practices, they have done so at the cost of providing an in-depth analysis of how specific forms of knowledge are produced, distributed, and legitimated in schools.[5]

While it is clear that the hermeneutic and political interests expressed by both groups must be used in a complementary fashion to analyze the interlocking beliefs and mechanisms that mediate between the wider culture of positivism and public school pedagogy, the conceptual foundation and distinct focus for such an analysis need to be further developed. This paper attempts to contribute to that development by examining the culture of positivism and its relationship to classroom teaching through the lens of a recently focused social and educational problem, the alleged "loss of interest in history" among American students and the larger public. This issue provides a unique vehicle for such an analysis, because it presents a common denominator through which the connection between schools and the larger society might be clarified.

II

Within the last decade a developing chorus of voices has admitted to the public's growing sense of the "irrelevance" of history. Some social critics have decried the trend while others have supported it. For instance, the historian, David Donald, believes that the "death of history" is related to the end of the "age of abundance." History, in Donald's view, can no longer provide an insightful perspective for the future. Voicing the de-spair of a dying age, Donald resigns himself to a universe that appears unmanageable, a sociopolitical universe that has nothing to learn from history. Thus, he writes:

> The "lessons" taught by the American past are today not merely irrelevant but dangerous. . . . Perhaps my most useful function would be to disen-thrall (students) from the spell of history, to help them see the irrelevance of the past,. . . (to) remind them to what a limited extent humans control their own destiny.[6]

Other critics, less pessimistic and more thoughtful, view the "death of history" as a crisis in historical consciousness itself, a crisis in the abil-ity of the American people to remember those "lessons" of the past that illuminate the developmental preconditions of individual liberty and social freedom. These critics view the "crisis" in historical conscious-ness as a deplorable social phenomenon that buttresses the existing spiritual crisis of the seventies and points to a visionless and politically reactionary future. In their analyses the "irrelevance of history" argu-ment contains conservative implications, implications which obscure the political nature of the problem: the notion that history has not be-come irrelevant, but rather that historical consciousness is being sup-pressed. To put it another way, history has been stripped of its critical and transcendent content and can no longer provide society with the historical insights necessary for the development of a collective critical consciousness. In this view the critical sense is inextricably rooted in the historical sense. In other words, modes of reasoning and interpreta-tion develop a sharp critical sense to the degree that they pay attention to the flow of history. When lacking a sense of historical development, criticism is often blinded by the rule of social necessity which parades under the banner of alleged "natural laws." The assault on historical sensibility is no small matter. Marcuse claims that one consequence is a form of false consciousness, "the repression of society in the formation of concepts . . . a confinement of experience, a restriction of meaning."[7] In one sense, then, the call to ignore history represents an assault on thinking itself.

While it is true that both radicals and conservatives have often drawn upon history to sustain their respective points of view, this should not obscure the potentially subversive nature of history. Nor should it ob-scure the changing historical forces that sometimes rely upon "history" to legitimate existing power structures. Historical consciousness is ac-ceptable to the prevailing dominant interest when it can be used to but-tress the existing social order. It becomes dangerous when its truth con-tent highlights contradictions in the given society. As one philosopher writes, "Remembrance of the past might give rise to dangerous insights, and the established society seems to be apprehensive of the subversive content of memory."[8]

The suppression of history has been accurately labeled by Russell Jacoby as a form of "social amnesia." "Social amnesia is a society's repression of its own past . . . memory driven out of mind by the social and economic dynamic of this society."[9] Jacoby's analysis is important because it situates the crisis in history in a specific sociohistorical context. If Jacoby is right, and I think he is, then the "crisis" in historical consciousness, at least its underlying ideological dimensions, can be explained in historical and political terms. This perspective can be put into sharper focus if we begin with an explanation of the changing nature of the mechanisms of social control over the last sixty years in the United States. To do this, we will have to turn briefly to the work of the late Italian theorist, Antonio Gramsci.

Gramsci was deeply concerned about what he saw as the changing modes of domination in the advanced industrial societies of the West. He claimed that with the rise of modern science and technology, social control was exercised less through the use of physical force (army, police, etc.) than through the distribution of an elaborate system of norms and imperatives. The latter were used to lend institutional authority a degree of unity and certainty and provide it with an apparent universality and legitimation. Gramsci called this form of control "ideological hegemony," a form of control which not only manipulated consciousness but also saturated and constituted the daily experiences that shaped one's behavior.[10] Hence, ideological hegemony referred to those systems of practices, meanings, and values which provided legitimacy to the dominant society's institutional arrangements and interest.

Gramsci's analysis is crucial to understand how cultural hegemony is used by ruling elites to reproduce their economic and political power. It helps us to focus on the myths and social processes that characterize a specific form of ideological hegemony, particularly as it is distributed through different agencies of socialization such as schools, families, trade unions, work places, and other ideological state apparatuses.[11] Thus, the concept of cultural hegemony provides a theoretical foundation for examining the dialectical relationship between economic production and social and cultural reproduction.[12] At the core of this perspective is the recognition that advanced industrial societies such as the United States inequitously distribute not only economic goods and services but also certain forms of cultural capital, i.e., "that system of meanings, abilities, language forms, and tastes that are directly and indirectly defined by dominant groups as socially legitimate."[13] This should not suggest that primary agencies of socialization in the United

States simply mirror the dominant mode of economic production and function to process passive human beings into future occupational roles. This over-determined view of socialization and human nature is both vulgar and mystifying. What is suggested is that the assumptions, beliefs, and social processes which occur in the primary agencies of socialization neither "mirror" wider societal interests nor are they autonomous from them. In other words, the correspondences and contradictions that mediate between institutions like schools and the larger society exist in dialectical tension with each other and vary under specific historical conditions.[14]

It is within the parameters of the historically changing dialectical relationship between power and ideology that the social basis for the existing crisis in historical consciousness can be located. Moreover, it is also within this relationship that the role schooling plays in reproducing this crisis can be examined. Underlying the suppression of historical consciousness in the social sphere and the loss of interest in history in the sphere of schooling in the United States at the present time are the rise of science and technology and the subsequent growth of the culture of positivism. It is this historical development that will be briefly traced and analyzed before the role that public school pedagogy plays in reproducing the crisis in historical consciousness is examined.

With the development of science and new technology in the United States in the early part of the twentieth century, both the pattern of culture and the existing concept of progress changed considerably. Both of these changes set the foundation for the suppression of historical consciousness. As popular culture became more standardized in its attempt to reproduce not only goods but also the needs to consume those goods, "industrialized" culture reached into new forms of communication to spread its message. Realms of popular culture, formerly limited to dance and dime store novels, were now expanded by almost all of the media of artistic expression.[15] The consolidation of culture by new technologies of mass communication, coupled with newly found social science disciplines such as social psychology and sociology, ushered in powerful, new modes of administration in the public sphere.[16]

Twentieth century capitalism gave rise to mass advertising and its attendant gospel of unending consumerism. All spheres of social existence were now informed, though far from entirely controlled, by the newly charged rationality of advanced industrial capitalism. Mass marketing, for example, drastically changed the realms of work and leisure and, as Stuart Ewen has pointed out, set the stage for the contestation and control over daily life.

> During the 1920's the stage was set by which the expanding diversity of corporate organization might do cultural battle with a population which was

in need of, and demanding, social change. The stage was in the theatre of daily life, and it was within the intimacies of that reality—productive, cultural, social, psychological—that a corporate piece-de-theatre was being scripted.[17]

While industrialized culture was radically transforming daily life, scientific management was altering traditional patterns of work. For instance, the integration of skill and imagination that had once characterized craft production gave way to a fragmented work process in which conception was separated from both the execution and experience of work. One result was a fragmented work process that reduced labor to a series of preordained and lifeless gestures.[18]

Accompanying changes in the workplace and the realm of leisure was a form of technocratic legitimation based on a positivist view of science and technology. This form of rationality defined itself through the alleged unalterable and productive effects the developing forces of technology and science were having on the foundations of twentieth century progress. Whereas progress in the United States in the eighteenth and nineteenth centuries was linked to the development of moral self-improvement and self-discipline in the interest of building a better society, progress in the twentieth century was stripped of its concern with ameliorating the human condition and became applicable only to the realm of material and technical growth.[19] What was once considered humanly possible, a question involving values and human ends, was now reduced to the issue of what was technically possible. The application of scientific methodology to new forms of technology appeared as a social force generated by its own laws, laws governed by a rationality that appeared to exist above and beyond human control.[20]

Inherent in this notion of progress and its underlying technocratic rationality is the source of logic that denies the importance of historical consciousness. Moreover, this form of rationality serves to buttress the status quo by undermining the dialectic of human potential and will. As a mode of legitimation, this form of rationality has become the prevailing cultural hegemony. As the prevailing consciousness, it celebrates the continued enlargement of the comforts of life and the productivity of labor through increasing submission of the public to laws that govern the technical mastery of both human beings and nature. The price for increased productivity is the continued refinement and administration of not simply the forces of production but the constitutive nature of consciousness itself. For example, in spite of its own claims, positivist rationality contains a philosophy of history that "robs" history of its critical possibilities. Thomas McCarthy writes that this philosophy of history "is based on the questionable thesis that human beings control their destinies to the degree to which social techniques are applied, and that human destiny is capable of being rationally guided to the extent of cybernetic control and the application of these techniques."[21] If critical consciousness, in part, represents an ability to think about the process as well as the genesis of various stages of reflection, then this notion of history contains few possibilities for its development as a critical and emancipatory force.

This form of rationality now represents an integral part of the social and political system of the United States and, as noted previously, can be defined as the culture of positivism. If we are to understand its role in suppressing historical consciousness, the culture of positivism must be viewed through its wider function as a dominant ideology, powerfully communicated through various social agencies. The term "positivism" has gone through so many changes since it was first used by Saint-Simon and Comte that it is virtually impossible to narrow its meaning to a specific school of thought or a well-defined perspective. Thus, any discussion of positivism will be necessarily broad and devoid of clear-cut boundaries. However, we can speak of the culture of positivism as the legacy of positivistic thought, a legacy which includes those convictions, attitudes, techniques, and concepts that still exercise a powerful and pervasive influence on modern thought.[22]

"Culture of positivism," in this context, is used to make a distinction between a specific philosophic movement and a *form* of cultural hegemony. The distinction is important because it shifts the focus of debate about the tenets of positivism from the terrain of philosophy to the field of ideology. For our purposes it will be useful to indicate some of the main elements of "positivism." This will be followed by a short analysis of how the culture of positivism undermines any viable notion of critical historical consciousness.

The major assumptions that underlie the culture of positivism are drawn from the logic and method of inquiry associated with the natural sciences.[23] Based upon the logic of scientific methodology with its interest in explanation, prediction, and technical control, the principle of rationality in the natural sciences was seen as vastly superior to the hermeneutic principles underlying the speculative social sciences. Modes of rationality that relied upon or supported interpretative procedures rated little scientific status from those defending the assumptions and methods of the natural sciences. For instance, Theodore Abel echoed a sentiment about hermeneutic understanding that still retains its original force among many supporters of the culture of positivism.

> Primarily the operation of Verstehen (understanding human behavior) does two things: It relieves us of a sense of apprehension in connection with behavior that is unfamiliar or unexpected and it is a source of

"hunches," which help us in the formulation of hypotheses. The operation of Verstehen does not, however, add to our store of knowledge, because it consists of the application of knowledge already validated by personal experience; nor does it serve as a means of verification. The probability of a connection can be ascertained only by means of objective, experimental, and statistical tests.[24]

Given the positivist emphasis on technical control and coordination, it is not surprising that the role of theory in this perspective functions as a foundation to boost scientific methodology. At the heart of this perspective is the assumption that theory plays a vital role in manipulating certain variables to either bring about a certain state of affairs or to prevent its occurrence.[25] The basis for deciding what state of affairs is to be brought about, or the interests such state of affairs might serve, are not questions that are given much consideration. Thus, theory, as viewed here, becomes circumscribed within certain "methodological prohibitions."[26] It was August Comte who laid the foundation for the subordination of theory to the refinement of means when he insisted that theory must be "founded in the nature of things and the laws that govern them, not in the imaginary powers that the human mind attributes to itself, erroneously believing itself to be a free agent and the center of the universe."[27] What is missing from Comte's perspective can be seen when it is instructively compared to the classical Greek notion of theory. In classical thought, theory was seen as a way men could free themselves from dogma and opinions in order to provide an orientation for ethical action.[28] In other words, theory was viewed as an extension of ethics and was linked to the search for truth and justice. The prevailing positivist consciousness has forgotten the function that theory once served. Under the prevailing dominant ideology, theory has been stripped of its concern with ends and ethics, and appears "unable to free itself from the ends set and given to science by the pre-given empirical reality."[29] The existing perspective on theory provides the background for examining another central tendency in the culture of positivism: the notion that knowledge is value free.

Since theory functions in the interest of technical progress in the culture of positivism, the meaning of knowledge is limited to the realm of technical interests. In brief, the foundation for knowledge is drawn from two sources: "the empirical or natural sciences, and the formal disciplines such as logic and mathematics."[30] In this scheme knowledge consists of a realm of "objective facts" to be collected and arranged so they can be marshalled in the interest of empirical verification. Knowledge is relevant to the degree that it can be viewed ". . . as description and explanation of objectified data, conceived—a priori—as cases of instances of possible laws."[31] Thus, knowledge becomes identified with scientific methodology and its orientation towards self-subsistent facts whose law-like connections can be grasped descriptively. Questions concerning the social construction of knowledge and the constitutive interests behind the selection, organization, and evaluation of "brute facts" are buried under the assumption that knowledge is objective and value free. Information or "data" taken from the subjective world of intuition, insight, philosophy and nonscientific theoretical frameworks is not acknowledged as being relevant. Values, then, appear as the nemeses of "facts," and are viewed at best, as interesting, and at worst, as irrational and subjective emotional responses.[32]

The central assumption by which the culture of positivism rationalizes its position on theory and knowledge is the notion of objectivity, the separation of values from knowledge and methodological inquiry alike. Not only are "facts" looked upon as objective, but the researcher himself is seen as engaging in value free inquiry, far removed from the untidy world of beliefs and values. Thus, it appears that values, judgments, and normative-based inquiry are dismissed because they do not admit of either truth or falsity. It seems that empirical verification exacts a heavy price from those concerned about "the nature of truth."[33]

The severance of knowledge and research from value claims may appear to be admirable to some, but it hides more than it uncovers. Of course, this is not to suggest that challenging the value-neutrality claims of the culture of positivism is tantamount to supporting the use of bias, prejudice, and superstition in scientific inquiry. Instead, what is espoused is that the very notion of objectivity is based on the use of normative criteria established by communities of scholars and intellectual workers in any given field. The point is that intellectual inquiry and research free from values and norms is impossible to achieve. To separate values from facts, social inquiry from ethical considerations is pointless. As Howard Zinn points out, it is like trying to draw a map that illustrates every detail on a chosen piece of terrain.[34] But this is not just a simple matter of intellectual error; it is an ethical failing as well. The notion that theory, facts, and inquiry can be objectively determined and used falls prey to a set of values that are both conservative and mystifying in their political orientation.

While it is impossible to provide a fully detailed critique of the assumptions that underlie the culture of positivism, it is appropriate to focus on how these assumptions undermine the development of a critical historical consciousness and further serve to diminish public communication and political action. Consequently, it is important to look briefly at how these assumptions function as part of the dominant ideology. Functioning both as an ideology and a productive force in the interest of a ruling elite, the culture of positivism cannot be viewed as simply a set of beliefs, smoothly functioning so as to rationalize the existing society. It is more than that. The point here is that the culture of positivism is not just a set of ideas, disseminated by the culture industry; it is also a material force, a set of material practices that are embedded in the routines and experiences of our daily lives.[35] In a sense, the daily rhythm of our lives is structured, in part, by the technical imperatives of a society that objectifies all it touches. This is not meant to suggest that there are no contradictions and challenges to the system. They exist, but all too often the contradictions result in challenges that lack a clear-cut political focus. Put another way, challenges to the system often function as a cathartic force rather than as a legitimate form of protest; not infrequently, they end up serving to maintain the very conditions and consciousness that spurred them in the first place. Within such a posture, there is little room for the development of an active, critical historical consciousness.

The present crisis in historical consciousness is linked to the American public's deepening commitment to an ever-expanding network of administrative systems and social control technologies. One consequence of this has been the removal of political decisions from public discourse by reducing these decisions to technical problems answerable to technical solutions. Underlying this crisis are the major assumptions of the culture of positivism, assumptions which abrogate the need for a viable theory of ideology, ethics, and political action.

Silent about its own ideology, the culture of positivism provides no conceptual insight into how oppression might mask itself in the language and lived experiences of daily life. "Imagining itself valuable only to the extent that it escapes history,"[36] this form of rationality prevents us from using historical consciousness as a vehicle to unmask existing forms of domination as they reproduce themselves through the "facts" and common-sense assumptions that structure our view and experience of the world. The flight from history is, in reality, the suppression of history. As Horkheimer writes, "Again and again in history, ideas have cast off swaddling clothes and struck out against social systems that bore them."[37] The logic of positivist thought suppresses the critical function of historical consciousness. For underlying all the major assumptions of the culture of positivism is a common theme: the denial of human action grounded in historical insight and committed to emancipation in all spheres of human activity. What is offered as a replacement "is a form of social engineering analogous to the applied physical sciences."[38] It is this very denial which represents the essence of the prevailing hegemonic ideology.

Instead of defining itself as an historically produced perspective, the culture of positivism asserts its superiority through its alleged suprahistorical and supracultural posture. Theory and method are held to be historically neutral. By maintaining a heavy silence about its own guiding interest in technical control, it falls prey to what Husserl once called the fallacy of objectivism.[39] Unable to reflect on its own presuppositions, or to provide a model for critical reflection in general, it ends up uncritically supporting the status quo and rejecting history as a medium for political action.

As the fundamental dominant myth of our time, the positivist mode of rationality operates so as to undermine the value of history and the importance of historical consciousness in other significant ways: First, it fosters an undialectical and one-dimensional view of the world; second, it denies the world of politics and lacks a vision of the future; third, it denies the possibility that human beings can constitute their own reality and alter and change that reality in the face of domination.[40]

Wrapped in the logic of fragmentation and specialization, positivist rationality divorces the "fact" from its social and historical context and ends up glorifying scientific methodology at the expense of a more rational mode of thinking. Under these conditions the interdependence of knowledge, imagination, will, and creativity are lost in a reduction of all phenomena to the rule of the empirical formulation.

Rather than comprehending the world holistically as a network of interconnections, the American people are taught to approach problems as if they existed in isolation, detached from the social and political forces that give them meaning. The central failing of this mode of thinking is that it creates a form of tunnel vision in which only a small segment of social reality is open to examination. More important, it leaves unquestioned those economic, political, and social structures that shape our daily lives. Divorced from history, these structures appear to have acquired their present character naturally, rather than having been constructed by historically specific interests.

It seems clear that the mode of reasoning embedded in the culture of positivism cannot reflect upon meaning and value, or, for that matter, upon anything that cannot be verified in the empirical tradition. Since there is no room for human vision in this perspective, historical consciousness is stripped of its critical function and progress is limited to terms acceptable to the status quo. Yet, as Horkheimer points out, it is the contradiction between the existent society and the utopian promise of a better life that spurs an interest in both history and historical progress.[41] The suppression of mankind's longing for justice and a better world are the motive forces that usurp the meaningfulness of history and an historical consciousness. These forces are an inherent part of the logic of positivist rationality.

The culture of positivism rejects the future by celebrating the present. By substituting what is for what should be, it represses "ethics" as a category of life and reproduces the notion that society has a life of its own, independent of the will of human beings. The neutralization of ethics effectively underscores the value of historical consciousness as well as public discourse on important political issues. Instead, we are left with a mode of reasoning that makes it exceptionally difficult for human beings to struggle against the limitations of an oppressive society.[42]

Finally, inherent in this perspective is a passive model of man. The positivist view of knowledge, "facts," and ethics has neither use nor room for an historical reality in which man is able to constitute his own meanings, order his own experience or struggle against the forces that prevent him from doing so. Meaning, like "time and memory," becomes objectified in this tradition and is eliminated as a radical construct by being made to exist independently of human experience and intention. In a society that flattens contradictions and eliminates evaluative and intellectual conflict, the concept of historical consciousness appears as a disturbing irrationality. Marcuse puts it well:

> Recognition and relation to the past as present counteracts the functionalization of thought by and in the established reality. It militates against the closing of the universe of discourse and behavior; it renders possible the development of concepts which de-stabilize and transcend the closed universe by comprehending it as historical universe. Confronted with the given society as object of its reflection, critical thought becomes historical consciousness; as such it is essentially judgment.[43]

I have argued so far that the loss of interest in history in the public sphere can only be viewed within the context of existing sociopolitical arrangements; and that what has been described as a marginal problem by some social critics, in essence, represents a fundamental problem in which the dominant culture actively functions to suppress the development of a critical historical consciousness among the populace.[44] This is not meant to imply a conscious conspiracy on the part of an "invisible" ruling elite. The very existence, interests, and consciousness of the dominant class is deeply integrated into a belief system that legitimizes its rule. This suggests that existing institutional arrangements reproduce themselves, in part, through a form of cultural hegemony, a positivist world view, that becomes a form of self delusion, and in addition, leaves little room for an oppositional historical consciousness to develop in the society at large. In other words, the suppression of historical consciousness works itself out in the field of ideology. In part this is due to an underlying "self-perpetuating" logic that shapes the mechanisms and boundaries of the culture of positivism. This logic is situated in a structure of dominance and exists to meet the most fundamental needs of the existing power relations and their corresponding social formations.[45] It appears to be a logic that is believed by the oppressed and oppressors alike, those who benefit from it as well as those who do not.

III

I now want to examine how the culture of positivism has influenced the process of schooling, particularly in relation to the way educators have defined the history "crisis" and its relationship to educational theory and practice at the classroom level. I will begin by analyzing how the nature of the loss of interest has been defined by leading members of the educational establishment.

Unlike critics such as Lasch and Marcuse, American educators have defined the "loss of interest" in history as an academic rather than political problem. For instance, the Organization of American Historians published findings indicating that history was in a crisis, and that the situation was "nationwide, affecting both secondary schools and higher education in every part of the country."[46] According to the OAH report, the value of history is being impugned by the growing assumption on the part of many educators that history is not a very practical subject. What is meant by practical appears problematic. For example, the Arizona Basic Goals Commission urged teachers to make history more practical by placing a stress on ". . . positive rather than negative aspects of the American past, eschew conflict as a theme, inculcate pride in the accomplishments of the nation and show the influence of rational, creative, and spiritual forces in shaping the nation's growth."[47]

For other educators, making history practical has meant reversing the growing divisions and specializations in history course offerings at all levels of education. This group would put back into the curriculum the broad-based history courses that were offered in the 1950s. In this perspective, the loss of interest in history among students has resulted from the fragmented perspective provided by specialized offerings in other disciplines. Warren L. Hickman sums this position up well when he writes:

> The utility of history is perspective, and that is in direct opposition to specialization at the undergraduate level. History's position in the curriculum, and its audience, have been eroded steadily as specialization, fragmentation, and proliferation of its offerings have increased.[48]

Both of these responses view the loss of interest in history as a purely academic problem. Severed from the socio-economic context in which they operate, schools, in both of these views, appear to exist above and beyond the imperatives of power and ideology. Given this perspective, the erosion of interest in history is seen in isolation from the rest of society and the "problem" is dealt with in technical rather than political terms, i.e., history can be rescued by restructuring courses in one way or another. These positions, in fact, represent part of the very problem they define. The loss of interest in history in schools is due less to the changes in course structure and offerings, though these have some effect, as much as it is due to the growing effect of the culture of positivism on the process of schooling itself, and in this case, particularly the social studies field. It is to this issue that we will now turn.

Classroom pedagogy in varying degrees is inextricably related to a number of social and political factors. Some of the more important include: the dominant societal rationality and its effect on curriculum thought and practice; the system of attitudes and values that govern how classroom teachers select, organize and evaluate knowledge and classroom social relationships; and, finally, the way students perceive their classroom experiences and how they act on those perceptions. By focusing on these limited, but nonetheless, important areas we can flesh out the relationships between power, ideology, and social studies pedagogy.

As I have pointed out, within the United States the social sciences have been modeled largely against the prevailing assumptions and methods of the natural sciences.[49] In spite of recent attacks on this mainstream perspective, the idea of social science conceived after the model of the natural sciences exerts a strong influence on contemporary educational thought and practice. Historically, the curriculum field, in general, has increasingly endeavored to become a science. That is, it has sought to develop a rationality based on objectivity, consistency, "hard data," and replicability. As Walter Feinberg writes, "The social scientists and policy makers who laboured in the field of education in this century were born under the star of Darwin, and . . . this influence was to have a profound impact upon the direction of educational theory."[50]

Moreover, in the seventies, as financial aid to education has decreased and radical critics have dwindled in number, the positivist orientation to schooling appears to be stronger than ever. Calls for accountability in education, coupled with the back-to-basics and systems management approaches to education have strengthened rather than weakened the traditional positivist paradigm in the curriculum field. As William Pinar and others have pointed out, the field is presently dominated by traditionalists and conceptual-empiricists, and while both groups view curriculum in different ways, neither group steps outside of the positivist or technocratic world view.[51]

These two groups must be viewed in something other than merely descriptive, categorical terms. Both the assumptions they hold and the modes of inquiry they pursue are based upon a world view that shapes their respective educational perspectives. Moreover, these world views precede and channel their work and influence the development of public school curricula.[52] This suggests that, whether adherents to these positions realize it or not, their theoretical frameworks are inherently valuative and political; thus, they share a relationship to the wider social order. Thomas Popkewitz captures the essence of this when he writes:

> . . . educational theory is a form of political affirmation. The selection and organization of pedagogical activities give emphasis to certain people, events and things. Educational theory is potent because its language has prescriptive qualities. A theory "guides" individuals to reconsider their personal world in light of more abstract concepts, generalizations and principles. These more abstract categories are not neutral; they give emphasis to certain institutional relationships as good, reasonable and legitimate. Visions of society, interests to be favored and courses of action to be followed are sustained in history.[53]

One way of looking at the political and valuative nature of educational thought and practice is through what Thomas Kuhn has called a "paradigm." A paradigm refers to the shared images, assumptions, and practices that characterize a community of scholars in a given field. In any specific field one can find different paradigms; thus, it is reasonable to conclude that any field of study is usually marked by competing intellectual and normative perspectives. As Kuhn has written: "A paradigm governs, in the first instance, not a subject matter but a group of practitioners."[54]

The concept of paradigm is important not merely because it guides practitioners in their work, it also illustrates that paradigms are related to the nexus of social and political values in the larger society. That is, the genesis, development, and effects of a given paradigm have to be measured against wider social and cultural commitments. In a simple sense, a paradigm might be viewed as in opposition or in support of the dominant ideology, but it cannot be judged independently of it. Educational workers in public education are not only born into a specific historical context, they embody its history in varying ways both as a state of consciousness and as sedimented experience, as a felt reality. To what degree they critically mediate that history and its attendant ideology is another issue. Thus, educational practitioners can be viewed as not only products of history but as producers of history as well. And it is this dynamic process of socialization that links them and the schools in which they work to the larger society.[55] Finally, it is important to stress that acknowledging the social and cultural basis of the character of different modes of pedagogy is important but incomplete. This approach must be supplemented by analyzing the assumptions embedded in a given educational paradigm against larger social and political interests. Questions which arise out of this type of analysis might take the following form: What interest do these assumptions serve? What are their latent consequences? What are the material and intellectual forces that sustain these assumptions and their corresponding paradigm?

Both the traditionalists and conceptual-empiricists in the curriculum field share the basic assumptions of the culture of positivism. Furthermore, these assumptions shape their view of social science knowledge, classroom pedagogy, as well as classroom evaluation and research. In brief, both groups support a form of positivist rationality in which it is assumed that: (1) The natural sciences provide the "deductive-nomological" model of explanation for the concepts and techniques proper for social science. (2) Social science ought to aim at the discovery of lawlike propositions about human behavior which are empirically testable. (3) Social science modes of inquiry can and ought to be objective. (4) The relationship between theory and practice in the social science domain is primarily a technical one, i.e., social science knowledge can be used to predict how a course of action can best be realized. (5) Social science procedures of verification and falsification must rely upon scientific techniques and "hard data," which lead to results that are value free and intersubjectively applicable.[56]

At the core of this social science paradigm is a preoccupation with the instrumental use of knowledge. That is, knowledge is prized for its control value, its use in mastering all dimensions of the classroom environment. In this perspective, technical rationality eschews notions of meaning that cannot be quantified and objectified. This becomes clear when we examine the relationship between theory and practice in the culture of positivism as it affects the curriculum field in general. For instance, traditionalists in the curriculum field like Robert Zais, Glen Nass, and John McNeil, whose influence on public school pedagogy is no small matter, view theory as secondary to meeting the existing needs and demands of social practitioners. In this case, theoretical formulations used in the shaping of curriculum development, design, and evaluation are guided by assumptions that bend to the dictates or exigencies of administrators and teachers in the "real" world of public school education. In this perspective, the "iron link" between knowledge and practical needs dissolves theory into utility.[57]

While the traditionalists may be viewed as atheoretical, the conceptual-empiricists acknowledge the importance of theory in curriculum work, but limit its meaning and importance by subordinating it to technical interests. The conceptual-empiricists have developed an approach to curriculum which "celebrates" rigorous and systematic research. Theory is used to generate and accumulate "hard data" and knowledge. Theory, in this sense, is linked to forms of explanation that are subject only to the criteria of empirical verification or refutation. Theory, as used in this paradigm, capitalizes upon one type of experience. As Habermas writes: "Only the controlled observation of physical behavior, which is set up in an isolated field under reproducible conditions by subjects interchangeable at will, seems to permit intersubjectively valid judgments of perceptions."[58]

Central to this form of rationality in the curriculum field is the notion of objectivity and neutrality. Guided by the search for reliability, consistency, and quantitative predictions, positivist educational practice excludes the role of values, feelings, and subjectively defined meanings in its paradigm. Normative criteria are dismissed either as forms of bias or are seen as subjective data that contribute little to the goals of schooling. Criticism of this sort is often couched in calls for more precise methods of pedagogy. W. James Popham, a leading spokesman for systems analysis methods, illustrates this position when he writes:

> I believe that those who discourage educators from precisely explicating their educational objectives are often permitting, if not promoting, the same kind of unclear thinking that has led to the generally abysmal quality of education in this country.[59]

More guarded critics such as George Beauchamp acknowledge that normative based curriculum theories have their place in the field, but, true to the spirit of his own view, he reminds us that "we" need to "grow up in the use of conventional modes of research in curriculum before we can hope to have the ingenuity to develop new ones."[60] In both Popham's and Beauchamp's arguments, the underlying notion of the superiority of efficiency and control as educational goals are accepted as given and then pointed to as a rationale for curriculum models that enshrine them as guiding principles. The circularity of the argument can best be gauged by the nature of the ideology that it thinly camouflages.

Missing from this form of educational rationality is the dialectical interplay among knowledge, power and ideology. The sources of this failing can be traced to the confusion between objectivity and objectivism, a confusion which, once defined, lays bare the conservative ideological underpinnings of the positivist educational paradigm. If objectivity in classroom teaching refers to the attempt to be scrupulously careful about minimizing biases, false beliefs, and discriminating behavior in rationalizing and developing pedagogical thought and practice, then this is a laudable notion that should govern our work. On the other hand, objectivism refers to an orientation that is atemporal and ahistorical in nature. In this orientation "fact" becomes the foundation for all forms of knowledge, and values and intentionality lose their political potency by being abstracted from the notion of meaning. When objectivism replaces objectivity, the result, as Bernstein points out, "is not an innocent mistaken epistemological doctrine."[61] It becomes a potent form of ideology that smothers the tug of conscience and blinds its adherents to the ideological nature of their own frame of reference.

Objectivism is the cornerstone of the culture of positivism in public education. Adulating "facts" and empirically based discourse, positivist rationality provides no basis for acknowledging its own historically contingent character. As such, it represents not only an assault on critical thinking, it also grounds itself in the politics of "what is." As Gouldner points out, "It is the tacit affirmation that 'what is,' the status quo, is basically sound."[62] Assuming that problems are basically technocratic in nature, it elevates methodology to the status of a truth and sets aside questions about moral purposes as matters of individual opinion. Buried beneath this "end of ideology" thesis is a form of positivist pedagogy that tacitly supports deeply conservative views about human nature, society, knowledge, and social action.

Objectivism suggests more than a false expression of neutrality. In essence, it tacitly represents a denial of ethical values. Its commitment to rigorous techniques, mathematical expression and lawlike regularities supports not only *one* form of scientific inquiry but social formations that are inherently repressive and elitist as well. Its elimination of "ideology" works in the service of the ideology of social engineers. By denying the relevance of certain norms in guiding and shaping how we ought to live with each other, it tacitly supports principles of hierarchy and control. Built into its objective quest for certainty is not simply the elimination of intellectual and valuative conflict, but the suppression of free will, intentionality, and collective struggle. Clearly, such interests can move beyond the culture of positivism only to the degree that they are able to make a distinction between emancipatory political practice and technological administrative control.

Unfortunately, "methodology madness" is rampant in public school pedagogy and has resulted in a form of curricula design and implementation that *substitutes* technological control for democratic processes and goals. For instance, Fenwick W. English, a former superintendent of schools and curriculum designer, provides a model for curriculum design in which technique and schooling become synonymous. Echoing the principles of the scientific management movement of the 1920s, English states that there are three primary developments in curriculum design. These are worth quoting in full:

> The first is to establish the mission of the school system in terms that are assessable and replicable. The second is to effectively and efficiently configure the resources of the system to accomplish the mission. The third is to use feedback obtained to make adjustments in order to keep the mission within agreed-upon costs.[63]

In perspectives such as this, unfortunately pervasive in the curriculum field, manipulation takes the place of learning, and any attempt at intersubjective understanding is substituted for a science of educational technology in which "choices exist only when they make the systems more rational, efficient, and controllable."[64] In a critical sense, the Achilles heel of the culture of positivism in public school pedagogy is its refusal to acknowledge its own ideology as well as the relationship between knowledge and social control. The claim to objectivism and certainty are themselves ideological and can be most clearly revealed in the prevailing view of school knowledge and classroom social relationships.

The way knowledge is viewed and used in public school classrooms, particularly at the elementary through secondary levels, rests on a number of assumptions that reveal its positivist ideological underpinnings. In other words, the way classroom teachers view knowledge, the way knowledge is mediated through specific classroom methodologies, and the way students are taught to view knowledge, structure classroom experiences in a way that is consistent with the principles of positivism.

In this view, knowledge is objective, "bounded and 'out there.'"[65] Classroom knowledge is often treated as an external body of information, the production of which appears to be independent of human beings. From this perspective, objective knowledge is viewed as independent of time and place; it becomes universalized, ahistorical knowledge. Moreover, it is expressed in a language that is basically technical and allegedly value free. This language is instrumental and defines knowledge in terms that are empirically verifiable and suited to finding the best possible means for goals that go unquestioned.[66] Knowledge, then, becomes not only countable and measurable, it also becomes impersonal. Teaching in this pedagogical paradigm is usually discipline based and treats subject matter in a compartmentalized and atomized fashion.[67]

Another important point concerning knowledge in this view is that it takes on the appearance of being context free. That is, knowledge is divorced from the political and cultural traditions that give it meaning. And in this sense, it can be viewed as technical knowledge, the knowledge of instrumentality.[68] Stanley Aronowitz points out that this form of empiricist reasoning is one in which "reality is dissolved into object-hood,"[69] and results in students being so overwhelmed by the world of "facts" that they have "enormous difficulty making the jump to concepts which controvert appearances."[70]

By resigning itself to the registering of "facts," the positivist view of knowledge not only represents a false mode of reasoning that under-mines reflective thinking, it does this and more. It is also a form of legiti-mation that obscures the relationship between "valued" knowledge and the constellation of economic, political, and social interests that such knowledge supports. This is clearly revealed in a number of important studies that have analyzed how knowledge is presented in elementary and secondary social studies textbooks.[71]

For example, Jean Anyon found in her analysis of the content of ele-mentary social studies textbooks that the "knowledge which 'counts' as social studies knowledge will tend to be that knowledge which provides formal justification for, and legitimation of, prevailing institutional arrangements, and forms of conduct and beliefs."[72] In addition to point-ing out that social studies textbooks provide a systematic exposure to se-lected aspects of the dominant culture, she found that material in the texts about dominant institutional arrangements was presented in a way that eschewed social conflict, social injustice, and institutional vio-lence. Instead, social harmony and social consensus were the pivotal concepts that described American society. Quoting Fox and Hess, she points out that in a study of 58 elementary social studies textbooks used in eight states, the United States political system was described in one-dimensional consensual terms. "People in the textbooks are pictured as easily getting together, discussing their differences and rationally arriv-ing at decisions. . . . (Moreover), everyone accepts the decisions."[73] These textbooks present a problematic assumption as an unquestioned truth: conflict and dissent among different social groups is presented as inherently bad. Not only is American society abstracted from the dic-tates of class and power in the consensus view of history, but students are viewed as value receiving and value transmitting persons.[74] There is no room in consensus history for intellectual, moral, and political con-flict. Such a view would have to treat people as *value creating* agents. While it is true that some of the newer elementary and secondary texts discuss controversial issues more often, "social conflict" is still avoided.[75]

Popkewitz has argued cogently that many of the social studies cur-riculum projects that came out of the discipline-based curriculum movements of the sixties did more to impede critical inquiry than to promote it. Based on fundamentally flawed assumptions about theory, values, knowledge, and instructional techniques in social studies curricular design and implementation, these projects "ignored the multiplicity of perspectives found in any one discipline."[76] With the social nature of conflict and skepticism removed from these projects, ideas appear as inert and ahistorical, reified categories whose underlying ideology is only matched by the tunnel vision they produce.

Human intentionality and problem solving in these texts are either ignored or stripped of any viable, critical edge. For instance, in one set of texts pioneered under the inquiry method, comparative analysis exercises are undercut by the use of socially constructed biases built into definitional terms that distort the subjects to be compared. In analyzing the political systems of the United States and the Soviet Union, the United States is labeled as a "democratic system" and the Soviet Union as a "totalitarian state."[77] Needless to say, the uncriticized and simplistic dichotomy revealed in categories such as these represent nothing other than an updated version of the vulgar "democracy" vs. "communism" dichotomy that characterized so much of the old social studies of the 1950s and early 1960s. While the labels have changed, the underlying typifications have not. What is new is not necessarily better. The "alleged" innovative discipline-centered social studies curriculum of the last fifteen years has based its reputation on its claim to promote critical inquiry. Instead, this approach appears to have created "new forms of mystification which make the social world seem mechanistic and predeterministic."[78]

A more critical view of knowledge would define it as a social construction linked to human intentionality and behavior. But if this view of knowledge is to be translated into a meaningful pedagogical principle, the concept of knowledge as a social construct will have to be linked to the notion of power. On one level this means that classroom knowledge can be used in the interest of either emancipation or domination. It can be critically used and analyzed in order to break through mystifications and modes of false reasoning.[79] Or it can be used unreflectively to legitimize specific sociopolitical interests by appearing to be value free and beyond criticism. If the interface between knowledge, power, and ideology is to be understood, knowledge will have to be defined not only as a set of meanings generated by human actors, but also as a communicative act embedded in specific forms of social relationships. The principles that govern the selection, organization, and control of classroom knowledge have important consequences for the type of classroom encounter in which such knowledge will be distributed.

The point is that the notion of "objectified" knowledge as it operates in the classroom obscures the interplay of meaning and intentionality as the foundation for all forms of knowledge. Absent from this perspective is a critical awareness of the varying theoretical perspectives, assumptions, and methodologies which underlie the construction and distribution of knowledge.[80] Unfortunately, the notion of "objectified" knowledge represents more than a conceptual problem; it also plays a decisive role in shaping classroom experiences. Thus, one is apt to find classroom situations in which "objective" information is "impartially" relayed to "able" students willing to "learn" it. Within this pedagogical framework, what is deemed "legitimate" public school knowledge is often matched by models of socialization that reproduce authoritarian modes of communication. Regardless of how a pedagogy is defined, whether in traditional or progressive terms, if it fails to encourage self-reflection and communicative interaction, it ends up providing students with the illusion rather than the substance of choice; moreover, it ends up promoting manipulation and denying critical reflection.[81] Alternative forms of pedagogy, such as those developed by Paulo Freire, not only emphasize the interpretive dimensions of knowing, they also highlight the insight that any progressive notion of learning must be accompanied by pedagogical relationships marked by dialogue, questioning, and communication.[82] This view of knowledge stresses structuring classroom encounters that *synthesize and demonstrate* the relationship between meaning, critical thinking, and democratized classroom encounters.

The role that teachers play in the schooling process is not a mechanistic one. To the degree that they are aware of the hidden assumptions that underlie the nature of the knowledge they use and the pedagogical practices they implement, classroom teachers will be able to minimize the worst dimensions of the culture of positivism. More specifically, under certain circumstances teachers can work to strip away the unexamined reality that hides behind the objectivism and fetishism of "facts" in positivist pedagogy. In doing so, the fixed essences, the invariant structures, and the commonsense knowledge that provide the foundation for much of existing public school pedagogy can be shown for what they are: social constructs that serve to mystify rather than illuminate reality.

But at the present time, it appears that the vast majority of public school teachers have yet to step beyond the taken-for-granted assumptions that shape their view of pedagogy and structure their educational experiences. Mass culture, teaching training institutions, and the power of the state all play a powerful role in pressuring teachers to give unquestioning support to the basic assumptions of the wider dominant culture. Maxine Greene captures part of this dynamic when she writes:

> It is not that teachers consciously mystify or deliberately concoct the positive images that deflect critical thought. It is not even that they themselves are necessarily sanguine about the health of the society. Often submerged

in the bureaucracies for which they work, they simply accede to what is taken-for-granted. Identifying themselves as spokespersons for or representatives of the system in its local manifestations, they avoid interrogation and critique. They transmit, often tacitly, benign or neutral versions of the social reality. They may, deliberately or not, adopt these to accommodate to what they perceive to be the class origins or the capacities of their students, but, whether they are moving those young people towards assembly lines or administrative offices, they are likely to present the world around as given, probably unchangeable and predefined.[83]

For many students, the categories that shape their learning experience and mediate their relationship between the school and the larger society have little to do with the value of critical thinking and social commitment. In this case, the objectification of knowledge is paralleled by the objectification of the students themselves. There is little in the positivist pedagogical model that encourages students to generate their own meanings, to capitalize on their own cultural capital, or to participate in evaluating their own classroom experiences. The principles of order, control, and certainty in positivist pedagogy appear inherently opposed to such an approach.

In the objectified forms of communication that characterize positivist public school pedagogy, it is difficult for students to perceive the socially constructed basis of classroom knowledge. The arbitrary division between objective and subjective knowledge tends to remain undetected by students and teachers alike. The results are not inconsequential. Thus, though the routines and practices of classroom teachers and the perceptions and behavior of their students are sedimented in varying layers of meaning, questions concerning how these layers of meaning are mediated and in whose interest they function are given little attention in the learning and research paradigms that dominate public school pedagogy at the present time. The behavioral and management approaches to such pedagogy, particularly at the level of middle and secondary education, reduce learning to a set of practices that neither define nor respond critically to the basic normative categories that shape day to day classroom methods and evaluation procedures. As C. A. Bowers writes, ". . . the classroom can become a precarious place indeed, particularly when neither the teacher nor student is fully aware of the hidden cultural messages being communicated and reinforced."[84]

The objectification of meaning results in the objectification of thought itself, a posture that the culture of positivism reproduces and celebrates in both the wider society and in public schools. In the public schools prevailing research procedures in the curriculum field capitalize upon as well as reproduce the most basic assumptions of the positivist paradigm. For instance, methodological elegance in educational research appears to rate higher esteem than its purpose of truth value. The consequences are not lost on schools. As one critic points out:

> Educational research has social and political ramifications which are as important as the tests of reliability. First, people tacitly accept institutional assumptions, some of which are defined by school professionals themselves. Achievement, intelligence and "use of time" are accepted as useful variables for stating problems about schools and these categories provide the basis for research. Inquiry enables researchers to see how school categories relate, but it does not test assumptions or implications underlying the school categories. For example, there is no question about the nature of the tasks at which children spend their time. Research conclusions are conceived within parameters provided by school administrators. Second, researchers accept social myths as moral prescriptions. Social class, social occupation (engineer or machinist) or divorce are accepted as information which should be used in decision making. These assumptions maintain a moral quality and criteria which may justify social inequality. Third, the research orientation tacitly directs people to consider school failure as caused by those who happen to come to its classes. Social and educational assumptions are unscrutinized.[85]

It does not seem unreasonable to conclude at this point that critical thinking as a mode of reasoning appears to be in eclipse in both the wider society and the sphere of public school education. Aronowitz has written that critical thought has lost its contemplative character and "has been debased to the level of technical intelligence, subordinate to meeting operational problems."[86] What does this have to do with the suppression of historical consciousness? This becomes more clear when we analyze the relationship between critical thinking, historical consciousness, and the notion of emancipation.

If we think of emancipation as praxis, as both an understanding as well as a form of action designed to overthrow structures of domination, we can begin to illuminate the interplay between historical consciousness, critical thinking, and emancipatory behavior. At the level of understanding, critical thinking represents the ability to step beyond commonsense assumptions and to be able to evaluate them in terms of their genesis, development, and purpose. In short, critical thinking cannot be viewed simply as a form of progressive reasoning; it must be seen as a fundamental, political act. In this perspective, critical thinking becomes a mode of reasoning that, as Merleau-Ponty points out, represents the realization that "I am able," meaning that one can use individual capacities and collective possibilities "to go beyond the created structures in order to create others."[87] Critical thinking as a political act means that human beings must emerge from their own "submersion and acquire the ability to invervene in reality as it is unveiled."[88] Not only does this indicate that they must act with others to intervene in the shaping of history, it also means that they must "escape" from their own history, i.e., that which society has made of them. As Sartre writes, "you become what you are in the context of what others have made of you."[89] This is a crucial point which links praxis and historical consciousness. For we must turn to history in order to understand the traditions that have shaped our individual biographies and intersubjective relationships with other human beings. This critical attentiveness to one's own history represents an important element in examining the socially constructed sources underlying one's formative processes. To become aware of the processes of historical self-formation indicates an important beginning in breaking through the taken-for-granted assumptions that legitimize existing institutional arrangements.[90] Therefore, critical thinking demands a form of hermeneutic understanding that is historically grounded. Similarly, it must be stressed that the capacity for a historically grounded critique is inseparable from those conditions that foster collective communication and critical dialogue. In this case, such conditions take as a starting point the need to delegitimize the culture of positivism and the socio-economic structure it supports.

IV

Schools play a crucial, though far from mechanistic, role in reproducing the culture of positivism. While schools function so as to mediate the social, political, and economic tensions of the wider society, they do so in a complex and contradictory fashion. This is an essential point. Schools operate in accordance, either implicitly or explicitly, with their established roles in society. But they do so in terms not entirely determined by the larger society. Diverse institutional restraints, different school cultures, varied regional and community forces, different social formations and a host of other factors lend varying degrees of autonomy and complexity to the school setting. All of these factors must be analyzed and taken into account if the mechanisms of domination and social control in day to day school life are to be understood.[91]

Moreover, the assumptions and methods that characterize schooling are themselves representations of the historical process. But the mechanisms of social control that characterize school life are not simply the factual manifestations of the culture of positivism. They also represent a historical condition that has functioned to transform human needs as well as buttress dominant social and political institutions. Put another way, the prevailing mode of technocratic rationality that permeates both the schools and the larger society has not just been tacked on to existing social order. It has developed historically over the last century and with particular intensity in the last fifty years; consequently, it deeply saturates our collective experiences, practices, and routines. Thus, to overcome the culture of positivism means that social studies educators will have to do more than exchange one set of principles of social organization for another. They will have to construct alternative social formations and world views that affect both the consciousness as well as the deep vital structure of needs in their students.[92]

Unfortunately, classroom teachers and curriculum developers, in general, have been unaware of the historical nature of their own fields. This is not meant to suggest that they should be blamed for either the present failings in public education or the suppression of historical consciousness and critical thinking in the schools. It simply means that the pervasiveness of the culture of positivism and its attendant commonsense assumptions exert a powerful mode of influence on the process of schooling. Moreover, this analysis does not suggest that there is little that teachers can do to change the nature of schooling and the present structure of society. Teachers at all levels of schooling represent a potentially powerful force for social change. But one thing should be clear, the present crisis in history, in essence, is not an academic problem but a political problem. It is a problem that speaks to a form of technological domination that goes far beyond the schools and permeates every sphere of our social existence. There is a lesson to be learned here. What classroom teachers can and must do is work in their respective roles to develop pedagogical theories and methods that link self-reflection and understanding with a commitment to change the nature of the larger society. There are a number of strategies that teachers at all levels of schooling can use in their classrooms. In general terms, they can question the commonsense assumptions that shape their own lives as well as those assumptions that influence and legitimize existing forms of public school classroom knowledge, teaching styles, and evaluation. In adopting such a critical stance while concomitantly reconstructing new educational theories and practices, classroom teachers can help to raise the political consciousness of themselves, their fellow teachers and their students.[93]

In more specific terms, social studies teachers can treat as problematic those socially constructed assumptions that underlie the concerns of curriculum, classroom social relationships, and classroom evaluation. They can make these issues problematic by raising fundamental questions such as: (1) What counts as social studies knowledge? (2) How is this knowledge produced and legitimized? (3) Whose interests does this knowledge serve? (4) Who has access to this knowledge? (5) How is this knowledge distributed and reproduced in the classroom? (6) What kinds of classroom social relationships serve to parallel and reproduce the social relations of production in the wider society? (7) How do the prevailing methods of evaluation serve to legitimize existing forms of knowledge? (8) What are the contradictions that exist between the ideology embodied in existing forms of social studies knowledge and the objective social reality?

Similarly, questions such as these, which focus on the production, distribution, and evaluation of classroom knowledge and social relationships, should be related to the principles and practices that characterize institutional arrangements in the larger society. Moreover, these questions should be analyzed before social studies teachers structure their classroom experiences. In other words, these are important subsequent questions that should provide the foundation for educational theory and practice. It is important to recognize that these questions can become an important force in helping teachers identify, understand, and generate those pivotal social processes needed to encourage students to become active participants in the search for knowledge and meaning, a search designed to foster rather than suppress critical thinking and social action.

While it is true that such action will not in and of itself change the nature of existing society, it will set the foundation for producing generations of students who might. As indicated, an important step in that direction can begin by linking the process of classroom pedagogy to wider structural processes. To do so will enable educators to develop a better understanding of the political nature of schooling and the role they might play in shaping it. The relationship between the wider culture of positivism and the process of schooling is, in essence, a relationship between ideology and social control. The dynamic at work in this relationship is complex and diverse. To begin to understand that dynamic is to understand that history is not dead, it is waiting to be seized. Marcuse has stated elegantly what it means to "remember history."

> All reification is forgetting. . . . Forgetting past suffering and past joy alienates life under a repressive reality principle. In contrast, remembrance is frustrated: joy is overshadowed by pain. Inexorably so? The horizon of history is still open. If the remembrance of things past would become a motive power in the struggle for changing the world, the struggle would be waged for a revolution hitherto suppressed in the previous historical revolutions.[94]

Notes

1. John O'Neil, "Merleau-Ponty's Criticism of Marxist Scientism," *Canadian Journal of Political and Social Theory* 2, 1 (Winter 1978): 45.

2. Michael W. Apple, "The Hidden Curriculum and the Nature of Conflict," *Interchange* 2, 4 (1971): 22–70. C. A. Bowers, "Curriculum and Our Technocracy

Culture: The Problem of Reform," *Teachers College Record* 78, 1 (September 1976): 53–67. Thomas S. Popkewitz, "The Latent Values of the Discipline Centered Curriculum," *Theory and Research in Social Education* V, 1 (April 1977): 41–61. Henry A. Giroux and Anthony N. Penna, "Social Education in the Classroom: The Dynamics of the Hidden Curriculum," *Theory and Research in Education* VII, 1 (Spring 1979): 21–42. Henry A. Giroux, "Toward a New Sociology of Curriculum," *Educational Leadership* (in press).

3. Michael F. D. Young, ed., *Knowledge and Control* (London: Collier-Macmillan, 1976).

4. Samuel Bowles and Herbert Gintis, *Schooling in Capitalist America* (New York: Basic Books, 1976). Pierre Bourdieu and Jean-Claude Passeron, *Reproduction in Education, Society, and Culture* (London: Sage Publications, 1977).

5. Rachel Sharp, "The Sociology of the Curriculum: A Marxist Critique of the Work of Basil Bernstein, Pierre Bourdieu, and Michael Young," unpublished manuscript 1978. Mandan Sarup, *Marxism and Education* (London: Routledge and Kegan Paul, 1978).

6. David Donald quoted in Christopher Lasch. *The Culture of Narcissism* (New York: W. W. Norton, 1978), p. xiv.

7. Herbert Marcuse, *One Dimensional Man* (Boston: Beacon Press, 1964), p. 208.

8. Ibid., p. 98.

9. Russell Jacoby, *Social Amnesia* (Boston: Beacon Press, 1975), p. 4.

10. Antonio Gramsci, *Selections from Prison Notebooks*, translation Quinton Hoare and Goeffrey Smith (New York: International Publishers, 1971).

11. Louis Althusser, *Lenin and Philosophy* (New York: Monthly Review Press, 1971), pp. 127–186.

12. Michael W. Apple, "The New Sociology of Education: Analyzing Cultural and Economic Reproduction," *Harvard Educational Review* 48, 4 (November 1978): 495–503. Basil Bernstein, *Class, Codes and Control*, Vol. 3, 2nd ed. (London and Boston: Routledge and Kegan Paul, 1977).

13. Apple, "The New Sociology of Education," p. 496.

14. Paul Willis, *Learning to Labour: How Working Class Kids Get Working Class Jobs* (Westmead, England: Saxon House, 1977).

15. Theodore W. Adorno, *Prisms* (London: Nevill Spearman, 1967).

16. Hans Magnus Enzenberger, *The Consciousness Industry* (New York: Seabury Press, 1974). Trent Schroyer, *The Critique of Domination* (Boston: Beacon Press, 1973). David Noble, *America by Design* (New York: Knopf, 1977). Christopher Lasch, *Haven in a Heartless World* (New York: Basic Books, 1978).

17. Stuart Ewen, *Captains of Consciousness* (New York: McGraw-Hill, 1976), p. 202.

18. Harry Braverman, *Labor and Monopoly Capital* (New York: Monthly Review Press, 1974). Ewen, *Captains of Consciousness*, p. 195.

19. Herbert Marcuse, "Remarks on a Redefinition of Culture," *Daedalus* (Winter 1965): 190–207.

20. Thomas McCarthy, *The Critical Theory of Jurgen Habermas* (Cambridge: The MIT Press, 1978), p. 37.

21. Ibid., p. 11.

22. Mihailo Markovic, *From Affluence to Praxis* (Ann Arbor: University of Michigan Press, 1974). Richard Bernstein, *The Restructuring of Social and Political Theory* (Philadelphia: University of Pennsylvania Press, 1976).

23. Fred R. Dallmayr and Thomas McCarthy, ed., *Understanding and Social Inquiry* (Notre Dame: University of Notre Dame Press, 1977), p. 285.

24. Theodore Abel, "The Operation Called Verstehen," *The American Journal of Sociology* 54: 211–218.

25. Brian Fay, *Social Theory and Political Practice* (London: George Allen and Unwin Ltd., 1975), p. 39.

26. Jurgen Habermas, *Knowledge and Human Interest* (Boston: Beacon Press, 1971), p. 304.

27. Gertrud Lenzer, *August Comte and Positivism* (New York: Harper and Row, 1975), p. xxxix.

28. Hannah Arendt, *The Human Condition* (Chicago: University of Chicago Press, 1958).

29. Herbert Marcuse, "On Science and Phenomenology," in *The Essential Frankfurt Reader,* ed. Andrew Arato and Eike Gebhardt (New York: Urizen Books, 1978), pp. 466–476.

30. Richard Bernstein, *The Restructuring of Social and Political Theory,* p. 5.

31. Karl-Otto Apel, "The A Priori of Communication and the Foundation of the Humanities," in *Understanding and Social Inquiry,* ed. Fred R. Dallmayr and Thomas McCarthy (Notre Dame: University of Notre Dame Press, 1977), p. 293.

32. Jurgen Habermas, *Toward a Rational Society,* translated by Jeremy Shapiro (Boston: Beacon Press, 1970), pp. 81–122.

33. Elliot G. Mishler, "Meaning in Context: Is There Any Other Kind?" *Harvard Educational Review* 49, 1 (February 1979): 1–19.

34. Howard Zinn, *The Politics of History* (Boston: Beacon Press, 1970), pp. 10–11.

35. Raymond Williams, *Marxism and Literature* (New York: Oxford University Press, 1977).

36. Alvin W. Gouldner, *The Dialectic of Ideology and Technology* (New York: Seabury Press, 1976), p. 50.

37. Max Horkheimer, *Eclipse of Reason* (New York: Seabury Press, 1974), p. 178.

38. Fay, *Social Theory and Political Practice,* p. 27.

39. Edmund Husserl, *Phenomenology and the Crisis of Philosophy* (New York: Harper, 1966).

40. Schroyer, *The Critique of Domination,* p. 213.

41. Horkheimer, *Eclipse of Reason,* p. 73.

42. Habermas, *Toward A Rational Society,* p. 113.

43. Marcuse, *One Dimensional Man,* p. 99.

44. Marcuse, *One Dimensional Man.* Jacoby, *Social Amnesia.*

45. Nicos Poulantzas, *Political Power and Social Classes,* translated by Timothy O'Hagen (London: New Left Books, 1973).

46. Richard S. Kirkendall, "The Status of History in the Schools," *The Journal of American History* (September 1975): 557–558.

47. Kirkendall, "The Status of History in the Schools," p. 465.

48. Warren L. Hickman, "The Erosion of History," *Social Education* 43, 1 (January 1977): 22.

49. Richard Bernstein, *The Restructuring of Social and Political Theory*. Mishler, "Meaning in Context."

50. Michael Quinn Patton, *Alternative Evaluation Research Design*, North Dakota Study Group on Evaluation Monograph (Grand Forks: University of North Dakota Press, 1975), p. 41.

51. William Pinar, "The Reconceptualization of Curriculum Studies," *Journal of Curriculum Studies* 10, 3 (July–September 1978): 205–214.

52. James McDonald, "Curriculum and Human Interests," in *Curriculum Theorizing*, ed. William F. Pinar (Berkeley: McCutchan, 1975), p. 289.

53. Thomas S. Popkewitz, "Educational Research: Values and Visions of a Social Order," *Theory and Research in Social Education* VI, IV (December 1978): 28.

54. Thomas S. Kuhn, *The Structure of Scientific Revolutions* (Chicago: University of Chicago Press, 1970), p. 80.

55. Alfred Schutz and Thomas Luckmann, *The Structure of the Life-World* (Evanston, Illinois: Northwestern University Press, 1973).

56. Marcuse, *One Dimensional Man*, p. 172. Trent Schroyer, "Toward a Critical Theory of Advanced Industrial Society," in *Recent Sociology No. 2*, ed. Hans Peter Dreitzel (New York: Macmillan Co., 1970), pp. 210–234.

57. William F. Pinar. "Notes on the Curriculum Field 1978," *Educational Researcher* (September 1978): 5–12.

58. T. W. Adorno, H. Albert, R. Dahrendorf, J. Habermas, H. Pilot, and K. R. Popper, *The Positivist Dispute in German Sociology* (New York: Harper and Row, 1976), p. 135.

59. W. James Popham, "Probing the Validity of Arguments Against Behavioral Goals," in *Behavioral Objectives and Instruction*, ed. Robert J. Kibler, et al. (Boston: Allyn and Bacon, 1970), p. 116.

60. George Bauchamp, "A Hard Look at Curriculum," *Educational Leadership* (February 1978): 409.

61. Richard Bernstein, *The Restructuring of Social and Political Theory*, p. 112.

62. Alvin W. Gouldner, *The Dialectic of Ideology and Technology* (New York: Seabury Press, 1976), p. 50.

63. Fenwick W. English, "Management Practice as a Key to Curriculum Leadership," *Educational Leadership* (March 1979): 408–409.

64. Popkewitz, "Educational Research," p. 32.

65. Peter Woods, *The Divided School* (London and Boston: Routledge and Kegan Paul, 1979), p. 137.

66. John Friedman, "The Epistemology of Social Practice: A Critique of Objective Knowledge," *Theory and Society* 6, 1 (July 1978): 75–92.

67. An interesting lament on this subject can be found in Frank R. Harrison, "The Humanistic Lesson of Solzhenitzen and Proposition 13," *Chronicle of Higher Education* (July 24, 1978): 32.

68. Michael W. Apple, "The Production of Knowledge and the Production of Deviance Schools." Speech given at Sociology of Knowledge Conference in Birmingham, England. January 2–4, 1979.

69. Stanley Aronowitz, *False Promises* (New York: McGraw-Hill, 1973), p. 270.

70. Ibid., p. 270.

71. Thomas E. Fox and Robert D. Hess, "An Analysis of Social Conflict in Social Studies Textbooks," Final Report, Project No. 1–1–116, United States Department of Health, Education, and Welfare, 1972. Popkewitz, "Discipline Centered Curriculum." Jean Anyon, "Elementary Social Studies Textbooks and Legitimating Knowledge," *Theory and Research in Social Education* 6, 3: 40–55.

72. Anyon, "Elementary Social Studies Textbooks," p. 40.

73. Ibid., p. 43.

74. Alvin W. Gouldner, *The Coming Crisis in Western Sociology* (New York: Basic Books, 1970), p. 193.

75. Anyon, "Elementary Social Studies Textbooks," p. 44.

76. Popkewitz, "Educational Research," p. 44.

77. Edwin Fenton, ed., *Holt Social Studies Curriculum* (New York: Holt, Rinehart and Winston, 1967, 1968).

78. Popkewitz, "Discipline Centered Curriculum," p. 58.

79. Maxine Greene, *Landscapes of Learning* (New York: Teachers College Press, 1978).

80. Ratton, *Alternative Evaluation,* p. 22.

81. Rachel Sharp and Anthony Green, *Education and Social Control* (London: Routledge and Kegan Paul, 1975).

82. Paulo Freire, *Pedagogy of the Oppressed* (New York: Seabury Press, 1973).

83. Greene, *Landscapes of Learning,* p. 56.

84. Bowers, "Curriculum and Our Technocracy Culture."

85. Popkewitz, "Educational Research," pp. 27–28. Also see J. Karabel and H. Halsey, eds., "Educational Research: A Review and an Interpretation," in *Power and Ideology* (New York: Oxford University Press, 1977), pp. 1–88. Ulf P. Lundgren and Stern Pettersson, eds., *Code, Context and Curriculum Processes* (Stockholm, Sweden: Stockholm Institute of Education, 1979), pp. 5–29.

86. Aronowitz, *False Promises,* p. 278.

87. M. Merleau-Ponty, *The Structure of Behavior* (Boston: Beacon Press, 1967), p. 175.

88. Freire, *Pedagogy of the Oppressed,* pp. 100–101. Henry A. Giroux, "Beyond the Limits of Radical Educational Reform," *Journal of Curriculum Theorizing* 2, 1 (1980), pp. 20–46.

89. Jean-Paul Sartre, *Sartre by Himself,* translated by Michael Seaver (New York: Urizen Books, 1977), p. 54.

90. Henry A. Giroux and Anthony N. Penna, "Social Education in the Classroom," *Theory and Research in Social Education* 7 (Spring 1979): 21–42.

91. Willis, *Learning to Labour.* Williams, *Marxism and Literature.* Other penetrating critiques of the correspondence theory as a truncated view of "manipulation" theory can be found in Richard Lichtman, "Marx's Theory of Ideology," *Socialist Revolution* 23 (April 1975): 45–76. Also see Daniel Ben-Horin, "Television Without Tears: An Outline of a Socialist Approach to Popular Television," *Socialist Review* 35 (September–October 1977): 7–35.

92. Agnes Heller, *Theory of Need in Marx* (London: Allen and Busby, 1974).

93. Henry A. Giroux, "Writing and Critical Thinking in the Social Studies," *Curriculum Inquiry* 8, 4 (1978): 291–310. Richard J. Bates, "The New Sociology of Education: Directions for Theory and Research." *New Zealand Journal of Educational Studies* 13, 1 (May 1978): 3–22.

94. Herbert Marcuse, *The Aesthetic Dimension* (Boston: Beacon Press, 1978), p. 73.

2 Culture and Rationality in Frankfurt School Thought: Ideological Foundations for a Theory of Social Education

History and Background

The Institute for Social Research (The Institut Fur Sozialforschung) was officially created in Frankfurt, Germany, in February 1923 and was the original home of the Frankfurt School. Established by a wealthy grain merchant named Felix Weil, the Institute eventually came under the directorship of Max Horkheimer in 1930. Under Horkheimer's directorship most of the members who later became famous joined the Institute. These included Erich Fromm, Herbert Marcuse, and Theodor Adorno. As Martin Jay (1973) points out in his now famous history of the Frankfurt School,

> If it can be said that in the early years of its history the Institut concerned itself primarily with an analysis of bourgeois society's socio-economic substructure, in the years after 1930 its prime interests lay in its cultural superstructure. (p. 21)

The changing of the Institute's theoretical focus was soon followed by a geographical shift in its location. Threatened by the Nazis because of the avowedly Marxist orientation of the Institute's work and because most of its members were Jews, the Institute was forced to relocate for a short time in Geneva in 1933. It was moved to New York City in 1934, where it was housed in one of Columbia University's buildings. Emigration to New York was followed by a stay in Los Angeles, California, in 1941; and, by 1953, the Institute was reestablished in Frankfurt, Germany.[1]

The strengths and weaknesses of the Frankfurt School project become intelligible only if seen as part of the social and historical context in which it developed. In essence, the questions it pursued, along with the forms of social inquiry it supported, represent both a particular moment in the development of Western Marxism as well as a critique of it. React-ing to the rise of Fascism and Naziism on the one hand, and the failure of orthodox Marxism on the other, the Frankfurt School had to refashion and rethink the meaning of domination and emancipation. The rise of Stalinism, the failure of the European or Western working class to con-test capitalist hegemony in a revolutionary manner, and the power of capitalism to reconstitute and reinforce its economic and ideological control forced the Frankfurt School to reject the orthodox reading of Marx and Engels, particularly as it had developed through the conven-tional wisdom of the Second and Third Internationals. It is particularly in the rejection of certain doctrinal Marxist assumptions, developed under the historical shadow of totalitarianism and the rise of the con-sumer society in the West that Horkheimer, Adorno, and Marcuse at-tempted to construct a more sufficient basis for social theory and politi-cal action. Certainly such a basis was not to be found in standard Marxist assumptions such as: a) the notion of historical inevitability, b) the primacy of the mode of production in the shaping of history, and c) the notion that class struggle as well as the mechanisms of domination take place primarily within the confines of the labor process. For the Frankfurt School, orthodox Marxism assumed too much while simulta-neously ignoring the benefits of self-criticism. It had failed to develop a theory of consciousness and by doing so expelled the human subject from its own theoretical calculus. Thus, it is not surprising that the focus of the Frankfurt School's research downplayed the area of political econ-omy and focused instead of the issue how subjectivity was constituted, as well as on the issue of how the spheres of culture and everyday life represented a new terrain of domination. It is against this historical and theoretical landscape that we can begin to abstract categories and modes of analysis that speak to the nature of schooling as it presently exists, and the possibilities it contains for developing into a force for so-cial change.

Rationality, Theory, and the Critique of Instrumental Reason

Fundamental to an understanding of the Frankfurt School's view of the-ory and their critique of instrumental reason is their analysis of the her-itage of Enlightenment rationality. Echoing Nietzsche's (1957) warning about humanity's unbounded faith in reason, Adorno and Horkheimer (1972) voiced a trenchant critique of modernity's unswerving faith in the promise of Enlightenment rationality to rescue the world from the chains of superstition, ignorance, and suffering. The problematic nature of such a promise marks the opening lines of *Dialectic of Enlightenment* (1972):

In the most general sense of progressive thought the Enlightenment has always aimed at liberating men from fear and establishing their sovereignty. Yet the fully enlightened earth radiates disaster triumphant. (p. 3)

The faith in scientific rationality and the principles of practical judgment did not constitute a legacy that developed exclusively in the 17th and 18th centuries when people of reason united on a vast intellectual front in order to master the world through an appeal to the claims of reasoned thought. According to the Frankfurt School, the legacy of scientific rationality represented one of the central themes of Western thought and extended as far back as Plato (Horkheimer, 1974 pp. 6–7). Habermas (1973), a later member of the Frankfurt School, argues that the progressive notion of reason reaches its highest point and most complex expression in the work of Karl Marx, after which it is reduced from an all encompassing concept of rationality to a particularized instrument in the service of industrialized society. According to Habermas (1973),

On the level of the historical self reflection of a science with critical intent, Marx for the last time identifies reason with a commitment to rationality in its thrust against dogmatism. In the second half of the 19th century, during the course of the reduction of science to a productive force in industrial society, positivism, historicism, and pragmatism, each in turn, isolate one part of this all encompassing concept of rationality. The hitherto undisputed attempts of the great theories, to reflect on the complex of life as a whole is henceforth itself discredited as dogma . . . the spontaneity of hope, the art of taking a position, the experience of relevance or indifference, and above all, the response to suffering and oppression, the desire for adult autonomy, the will to emancipation, and the happiness of discovering one's identity—all these are dismissed for all time from the obligating interest of reason. (pp. 262–263)

Marx may have employed reason in the name of critique and emancipation, but it was still a notion of reason that was limited to an over-emphasis on the labor process and the exchange rationality that was both its driving force and ultimate mystification. In contrast to Marx, Adorno, Horkheimer, and Marcuse believed that "the fateful process of rationalization" (Wellmer, 1974, p. 133) had penetrated all aspects of everyday life, whether it be the mass media, the school or the workplace. The crucial point here is that no social sphere was free from the encroachments of a form of reason in which "all theoretical means of transcending reality became metaphysical nonsense" (Horkheimer, 1974, p. 82).

In the Frankfurt School's view, reason has not been stripped permanently of its positive dimensions. Marcuse, for instance, believed that reason contained a critical element and was still capable of reconstituting history or, as he put it, "reason represents the highest potentiality of man and existence; the two belong together" (Marcuse, 1968, p. 136). But if reason was to preserve its promise of creating a more just society, it would have to demonstrate its power of critique and negativity. According to Adorno (1973), the crisis of reason takes place as society becomes more rationalized because under such historical circumstances it loses its critical faculty in the quest for social harmony, and as such, becomes an instrument of the existing society. As a result, reason as insight and critique turns into its opposite, i.e., irrationality.

For the Frankfurt School the crisis in reason is linked to the crisis in science and the more general crisis of society. Horkheimer (1972) argued that the starting point for understanding "the crisis of science depends on a correct theory of the present social situation" (p. 9). In essence, this speaks to two crucial aspects of Frankfurt School thought. First, it argues that the only solution to the present crisis lies in developing a more fully self-conscious notion of reason, one that embraces both the notion of critique and the element of human will and transformative action. Second, it means entrusting to theory the task of rescuing reason from the logic of technocratic rationality or positivism. It was the Frankfurt School's view that positivism had emerged as the final ideological expression of the Enlightenment. The victory of positivism represented not the high point but the low point of Enlightenment thought. Rather than being the agent of reason, it became its enemy and emerged in the 20th century as a new form of social administration and domination. Friedman (1981) sums up the essence of this position:

> To the Frankfurt School, philosophical and practical positivism constituted the end point of the Enlightenment. The social function of the ideology of Positivism was to deny the critical faculty of reason by allowing it only the ground of utter facility to operate upon. By so doing, they denied reason a critical moment, reason, under the rule of Positivism, stands in awe of the fact. Its function is simply to characterize the fact. Its task ends when it has affirmed and explicated the fact. . . . Under the rule of positivism, reason inevitably stops short of critique. (p. 118)

It is in its critique of positivistic thought that the Frankfurt School makes clear the specific mechanisms of ideological control that permeate the consciousness and practices of advanced capitalistic societies. It is also in its critique of positivism that it develops a notion of theory that has major implications for educational critics. But the route to understanding the latter necessitates that one first analyze the Frankfurt School's critique of positivism, particularly since the logic of positivist thought (though in varied forms) represents the major theoretical impetus that currently shapes educational theory and practice.

The Frankfurt School defined positivism in the broad sense as an amalgam of diverse traditions that included the work of Saint-Simon and Comte, the logical positivism of the Vienna Circle, the early Wittgenstein, and the more recent forms of logical empiricism and pragmatism that dominate the social sciences in the West. While the history of each of these traditions is complex and cluttered with detours and qualifications, each of them has supported the goal of developing forms of social inquiry patterned after the natural sciences and based on the methodological tenets of sense observation and quantification. Marcuse (1964) provides both a general definition of the notion of positivism as well as a starting point for some of the reservations the Frankfurt School expressed regarding its most basic assumptions:

> Since its first usage, probably in the school of Saint-Simon, the term "positivism" has encompassed (1) the validation of cognitive thought by experience of facts; (2) the orientation of cognitive thought to the physical science as a model of certainty and exactness; (3) the belief that progress in knowledge depends on this orientation. Consequently, positivism is a struggle against all metaphysics, transcendentalisms, and idealisms as obscurantist and regressive modes of thought. To the degree to which the given reality is scientifically comprehended and transformed, to the degree to which society becomes industrial and technological, positivism finds in the society the medium for the realization (and validation) of its concepts— harmony between theory and practice, truth and facts. Philosophic thought turns into affirmative thought; the philosophic critique criticizes within the societal framework and stigmatizes non-positive notions as mere speculation, dreams or fantasies. (p. 172)

Positivism, according to Horkheimer (1972), presented a view of knowledge and science that stripped both of their critical possibilities. Knowledge was reduced to the exclusive province of science, and science itself was subsumed within a methodology that limited "scientific activity to the description, classification, and generalization of phenomena, with no care to distinguish the unimportant from the essential" (p. 5). Accompanying this view is the notion that knowledge derives from sense experience and that the ideal it pursues takes place "in the form of a mathematically formulated universe deducible from the smallest possible number of axioms, a system which assures the calculation of the probable occurrence of all events" (Horkheimer, 1972, p. 138).

For the Frankfurt School, positivism did not represent an indictment of science, instead it echoed Nietzche's (1966) insight that "it is not the victory of science that is the distinguishing mark of our nineteenth century, but the victory of the scientific method over science" (p. 814). Science, in this perspective, was separated from the question of ends and ethics, the latter being rendered insignificant because they defied "explication in terms of mathematical structures" (Marcuse, 1964, p. 147). According to the Frankfurt School, the suppression of ethics in positivist rationality precludes the possibility for self critique, or more specifically, the questioning of its own normative structure. Facts become separated from values, objectivity undermines critique, and the notion that essence and appearance may not coincide is lost in the positivist view of the world. The latter point becomes particularly clear in the Vienna Circle pronouncement: "The view that thought is a means of knowing more about the world than may be directly observed . . . seems to us entirely mysterious" (Hahn, 1933, p. 9). For Adorno, the idea of value freedom was perfectly suited to a perspective that was to insist on a universal form of knowledge while it simultaneously refused to inquire into its own socio-ideological development and function in society.

According to the Frankfurt School, the outcome of positivist rationality and its technocratic view of science represented a threat to the notion of subjectivity and critical thinking. By functioning within an operational context free from ethical commitments, positivism wedded itself to the immediate and "celebrated" the world of "facts." The question of essence, or the difference between the world as it is and that which it could be, is reduced to the merely methodological task of collecting and classifying that which is, the world of facts. In this schema, "knowledge relates solely to what is and to its recurrence" (Horkheimer, 1972, p. 208). Questions concerning the genesis, development and normative nature of the conceptual systems that select, organize and define the facts appear to be outside of the concern of positivist rationality.

Since it recognizes no factors behind the "fact," positivism freezes both human beings and history. In the case of the latter, the issue of historical development is left aside since the historical dimension contains truths that cannot be assigned "to a special fact-gathering branch of science" (Adorno, quoted in Gross, 1979, p. 340). Of course, positivism is not impervious to history because it ignores it, i.e., the relationship between history and understanding. On the contrary, its key notions regarding objectivity, theory, and values as well as its modes of inquiry are both a consequence and a force in the shaping of history. In other words, positivism may ignore history but it cannot escape it. What is important to stress is that fundamental categories of socio-historical development are at odds with the positivist emphasis on the immediate, or, more specifically, that which can be expressed, measured, and calculated in precise mathematical formulas. Russell Jacoby (1980) points concisely to this issue in his claim that "the natural reality and natural sciences do not know the fundamental historical categories: consciousness and self consciousness, subjectivity and objectivity, appearance and essence" (p. 30).

By not reflecting on its paradigmatic premises positivist thought ignores the value of historical consciousness and consequently endangers the nature of critical thinking itself. That is, inherent in the very structure of positivist thought, with its emphasis on objectivity and its lack of theoretical grounding regarding the setting of tasks (Horkheimer 1972), are a number of assumptions that appear to preclude its ability to judge the complicated interactions of power, knowledge and values and to reflect critically on the genesis and nature of its own ideological presuppositions. Moreover, situated within a number of false dualisms (facts vs. values, scientific knowledge vs. norms, and description vs. prescription) positivism dissolves the tension between potentiality and actuality in all spheres of social existence. Thus, under the guise of neutrality, scientific knowledge and all theory become rational on the grounds of whether they are efficient, economic or correct. In this case a notion of methodological correctness subsumes and devalues the complex philosophical concept of truth. As Marcuse points out, "the fact that a judgment can be correct and nevertheless without truth has been the crux of formal logic from time immemorial" (quoted in Arato and Gebhardt, 1978, p. 394). For instance, an empirical study that concludes that native workers in a colonized country work at a slower rate than imported workers who perform the same job may provide an answer that is correct, but such an answer tells us little about the notion of domination or the resistance of workers under its sway. That the native workers may slow down their rate as an act of resistance is not considered here. Thus, the notions of intentionality and historical context get dissolved within the confines of a limiting quantifying methodology. For Adorno, Marcuse, and Horkheimer, the fetishism of facts and the belief in value neutrality represented more than an epistemological error; more importantly, such a stance served as a form of ideological hegemony that infused positivist rationality with a political conservatism that make it an ideological prop of the status quo. The latter should not suggest an intentional support for the status quo on the part of the individuals who work within a positivist rationality. Instead, it suggests a particular relationship to the status quo which in some situations is a consciously political one, while in others it is not. In other words, in the latter stance the relationship to the status quo is a conservative one, but it is not self-consciously recognized by those who help to reproduce it.

The Frankfurt School's Notion of Theory

According to the Frankfurt School any understanding about the nature of theory had to begin with a grasp of the relationships that exist in society between the particular and the whole, the specific and the universal.

This position appears in direct contradiction to the empiricist claim that theory is primarily a matter of classifying and arranging facts. In rejecting the absolutizing of facts, the Frankfurt School argued that in the relation between theory and the wider society mediations exist that function to give meaning not only to the constitutive nature of a fact but also to the very nature and substance of theoretical discourse. As Horkheimer (1972) writes:

> The facts of science and science itself are but segments of the life process of society, and in order to understand the significance of facts or of science, generally one must possess the key to the historical situation, the right social theory. (p. 159)

This speaks to another constitutive element of critical theory. If theory is to move beyond the positivist legacy of neutrality, it must develop the capacity of a meta-theory. That is, it must acknowledge the normative interests it represents and be able to reflect critically on both the historical development or genesis of such interests and the limitations they may present within certain historical and social contexts. In other words, "methodological correctness" does not provide a guarantee of truth nor does it raise the fundamental question of why a theory functions in a given way under specific historical conditions to serve some interests and not others. Thus, a notion of self critique is essential to a critical theory.

A third constitutive element for a critical theory takes its cue from Nietzche's dictum that "a great truth wants to be criticized not idolized" (Quoted in Arato and Gebhardt, 1978, p. 383). The Frankfurt School believed that the critical spirit of theory should be represented in its unmasking function. The driving force of such a function was to be found in the Frankfurt School's notions of immanent criticism and dialectical thought. Immanent critique is the assertion of difference, the refusal to collapse appearance and essence, i.e., the willingness to analyze the reality of the social object against its possibilities. As Adorno et al. (1976) wrote:

> Theory . . . must transform the concepts which it brings, as it were, from outside into those which the object has of itself, into what the object, left to itself, seeks to be, and confront it with what it is. It must dissolve the rigidity of the temporally and spatially fired object into a field of tension of the possible and the real: each one in order to exist, is dependent upon the other. In other words, theory is indisputably critical. (p. 69)

Dialectical thought, on the other hand, speaks to both critique and theoretical reconstruction (Giroux, 1980). As a mode of critique it uncovers values that are often negated by the social object under analysis. The notion of dialectics is critical because it reveals "the insufficiencies and imperfections of 'finished' systems of thought . . . it reveals incompleteness where completeness is claimed. It embraces that which is in terms of that which is not, and that which is real in terms of potentialities not yet realized" (Held, 1980, p. 177). As a mode of theoretical reconstruction, dialectical thought points to historical analysis in the critique of conformist logic, and traces out the "inner history" of the latter's categories and the way in which they are mediated within a specific historical context. By looking at the social and political constellations stored in the categories in any theory, Adorno (1973) believed that their history could be traced and thus their existing limitations revealed. As such, dialectical thought reveals the power of human activity and human knowledge as both a product and force in the shaping of social reality, but does so not simply to proclaim that humans give meaning to the world, a position that has always plagued the sociology of knowledge (Adorno, 1967). Instead, as a form of critique, dialectical thought argues that there is a link between knowledge, power, and domination. Thus it is acknowledged that some knowledge is false, and that the ultimate purpose of critique should be critical thinking in the interest of social change. For instance, as I mentioned earlier, one can exercise critical thought and not fall into the ideological trap of relativism in which the notion of critique is negated by the assumption that all ideas should be given equal weight. Marcuse (1960) points to the connection between thought and action in dialectical thought:

> Dialectical thought starts with the experience that the world is unfree; that is to say, man and nature exist in conditions of alienation, exist as 'other than they are.' Any mode of thought which excludes this contradiction from its logic is faulty logic. Thought 'corresponds' to reality only as it transforms reality by comprehending its contradictory structure. Here the principle of dialectic drives thought beyond the limits of philosophy. For to comprehend reality means to comprehend what things really are, and this in turn means rejecting their mere factuality. Rejection is the process of thought as well as of action. . . . Dialectical thought thus becomes negative in itself. Its function is to break down the self-assurance and self-contentment of common sense, to undermine the sinister confidence in the power and language of facts, to demonstrate that unfreedom is so much at the core of things that the development of their internal contradictions leads necessarily to qualitative change: the explosion and catastrophe of the established state of affairs. (p. ix)

According to the Frankfurt School all thought and theory are tied to a specific interest in the development of a society without injustice. Theory, in this case, becomes a transformative activity that views itself as explicitly political and commits itself to the projection of a future that is as yet unfulfilled. Thus, critical theory contains a transcendent element in which critical thought becomes the precondition for human freedom. Rather than proclaiming a positivist notion of neutrality, critical theory openly takes sides in the interest of struggling for a better world. In one of his most famous early essays comparing traditional and critical theory, Horkheimer (1972) spelled out the essential value of theory as a political endeavor:

> It is not just a research hypothesis which shows its value in the ongoing business of men; it is an essential element in the historical effort to create a world which satisfies the needs and powers of men. However extensive the interaction between the critical theory and the special sciences whose progress the theory must respect and on which it has for decades exercised a liberating and stimulating influence, the theory never aims simply at an increase of knowledge as such. Its goal is man's emancipation from slavery. (p. 245)

Finally, there is the question of the relationship between critical theory and empirical studies. In the ongoing debate over theory and empirical work, the same old dualisms appear, though in recycled forms, in which one presupposes the exclusion of the other.[2] One manifestation of this debate is the criticism that the Frankfurt School rejected against many educational critics who have drawn upon the work of the Frankfurt School.[3] Both sets of criticisms appear to have missed the point. Certainly, it is true that for the Frankfurt School the issue of empirical work was a problematic one, but what was called into question was its universalization at the expense of a more comprehensive notion of rationality. In writing about his experience as an American scholar, Adorno (1969) spelled out a view of empirical studies that was representative of the Frankfurt School in general:

> My own position in the controversy between empirical and theoretical sociology . . . I may sum up by saying that empirical investigations are not only legitimate but essential, even in the realm of cultural phenomena. But one must not confer autonomy upon them or regard them as a universal key. Above all they must terminate in theoretical knowledge. Theory is no mere vehicle that becomes superfluous as soon as data are in hand. (p. 353)

By introducing the primacy of theoretical knowledge in the realm of empirical investigations, the Frankfurt School also wanted to highlight the limits of the positivist notion of experience, where research had to confine itself to controlled physical experiences that would be conducted by any researcher. Under such conditions, the research experience is limited to simple observation. As such, generalizable and abstract methodology follows rules that preclude any understanding of the forces that shape both the object of analysis as well as the subject conducting the research. In contrast, a dialectical notion of society and theory would argue that observation cannot take the place of critical reflection and understanding. That is, one begins not with an observation but with a theoretical framework that situates the observation in rules and conventions that give it meaning while simultaneously acknowledging the limitations of such a perspective or framework. A further qualification must be made here. The Frankfurt School's position on the relation between theory and empirical studies helps to illuminate its view of theory and practice. Once again, critical theory insists that theory and practice are interrelated, but it cautions about calling for a specious unity. As Adorno (1973) points out, "the call for the unity of theory and practice has irresistibly degraded theory to the servants's role, removing the very traits it should have brought to that unity. The visa stamp of practice which we demand of all theory became a censor's place. Yet whereas theory succumbed in the vaunted mixture practice became nonconceptual, a piece of the politics it was supposed to lead out of; it became the prey of power" (p. 143). Theory, in this case, should have as its goal emancipatory practice, but at the same time it requires a certain distance from such practice. Theory and practice represent a particular alliance, not a unity in which one dissolves into the other. The nature of such an alliance might be better understood by illuminating the drawbacks inherent in the traditional anti-theoretical stance in American education in which it is argued that concrete experience is the great "teacher."[4]

Experience, whether on the part of the researcher or others, contains in itself no guarantees that it will generate the insights necessary to make it transparent to itself. In other words, while it is indisputable that experience may provide us with knowledge, it is also indisputable that knowledge may distort rather than illuminate the nature of social reality. The point here is that the value of any experience "will depend not on the experience of the subject but on the struggles around the way that experience is interpreted and defined" (Bennet, 1980, p. 126). Moreover, theory cannot be reduced to the mistress of experience, empowered to provide recipes for pedagogical practice. Its real value lies in its ability to establish the possibilities for reflexive thought and practice on the part of those who use it, and in the case of teachers, it becomes invaluable as an instrument of critique and understanding. As a mode of critique and analysis, theory functions as a set of tools inextricably affected by the context in which it is brought to bear, but it is never reducible to that context. It has its own distance and purpose, its own element of practice. The crucial element in both its production and use is not the structure at which it is aimed, but the human agents who use it to give meaning to their lives.

Conclusion

In conclusion, Adorno, Horkheimer and Marcuse provided forms of historical and sociological analyses that pointed to the premise as well as the limitations of the existing dominant rationality as it developed in the 20th century. Such an analysis took as a starting point the conviction that for self conscious human beings to act collectively against the modes of technocratic rationality that permeated the work place and other socio-cultural spheres, their behavior would have to be preceded and mediated by a mode of critical analysis. In other words, the precondition for such action was a form of critical theory. But it is important to stress that in linking critical theory to the goals of social and political emancipation, the Frankfurt School redefined the very notion of rationality. Rationality was no longer merely the exercise of critical thought, as had been its earlier Enlightenment counterpart. Instead, rationality now became the nexus of thought and action in the interest of the liberation of the community or society as a whole. As a higher rationality, it contained a transcendent project in which individual freedom merged with social freedom. Marcuse (1964) articulated the nature of such a rationality in his claim that:

A. it offers the prospect of preserving and improving the productive achievements of civilization;
B. it defines the established totality in its very structure, basic tendencies, and relations;
C. its realization offers a greater chance for the pacification of existence, within the framework of institutions which offer a greater chance for the free development of human needs and faculties. (p. 220)

The Frankfurt School's Analysis of Culture

Central to the Frankfurt School's critique of positivist rationality was its analysis of culture. Rejecting the definition and role of culture found in both traditional sociological accounts and orthodox Marxist theory, Adorno and Horkheimer (1972), in particular, developed a view of culture that assigned it a key place in the development of historical experience and everyday life. On the other hand, the Frankfurt School rejected the mainstream sociological notion that culture existed in an autonomous fashion unrelated to the political and economic life processes of society. In their view, such a perspective neutralized culture and, in doing so, abstracted it from the historical and societal context that gave it meaning. For Adorno (1967) the truth value of such a view was shot through with a contradiction that reduced culture to nothing more than a piece of ideological shorthand since:

> It overlooks what is decisive: the role of ideology in social conflicts. To suppose, if only methodologically, anything like an independent logic of culture is to collaborate in the hypostasis of culture, the ideological *proton pseudos*. The substance of culture . . . resides not in culture alone but in relation to something external, to the material life-process. Culture as Marx observed of juridicial and political systems, cannot be fully 'understood either in terms of itself . . . or in terms of the so-called universal development of the mind.' To ignore this . . . is to make ideology the basic matter and to establish it firmly. (p. 29)

On the other hand, while orthodox Marxist theory established a relationship between culture and the material forces of society, it did so by reducing culture to a mere reflex of the economic realm. In this view, the primacy of economic forces and the logic of scientific laws took precedence over any concern with issues concerning the terrain of everyday life, consciousness, or sexuality (Aronowitz, 1981). For the Frankfurt School, changing socio-economic conditions had made traditional Marxist categories of the 1930s and 1940s untenable. They were no longer adequate for understanding the integration of the working class in the West or the political effects of technocratic rationality in the cultural realm.

Within the Frankfurt School perspective the role of culture in Western society had been modified with the transformation of critical Enlightenment rationality into repressive forms of positivist rationality. As a result of the development of new technical capabilities, greater concentrations of economic power, and more sophisticated modes of administration, the rationality of domination increasingly expanded its influence to spheres outside of the locus of economic production. Under the sign of Taylorism and scientific management instrumental rationality extended its influence from the domination of nature to the domination of human beings. As such, mass cultural institutions such as schools took on a new role in the first half of the 20th century as "both a determinant and fundamental component of social consciousness" (Aronowitz, 1976, p. 20). According to the Frankfurt School, this meant that the cultural realm now constituted a central place in the production and transformation of historical experience. Like Gramsci (1971), Adorno and Horkheimer (1972) argued that domination had assumed a new form. Instead of being exercised primarily through the use of physical force (the army and police), the power of the ruling classes was now reproduced through a form of ideological hegemony; that is, it was established primarily through the rule of consent, and mediated via cultural institutions such as the schools, the family, the mass media, the churches, etc. Briefly put, the colonization of the workplace was not supplemented by the colonization of all other cultural spheres (Aronowitz, 1973; Enzensberger, 1974; and Ewen, 1976).

According to the Frankfurt School, culture—like everything else in capitalist society—had been turned into an object. That is, under the dual rationalities of administration and exchange the elements of critique and opposition, which the Frankfurt School believed inherent in traditional culture, had been lost. Moreover, the objectification of culture did not simply result in the repression of the critical elements in its form and content, such objectification also represented the negation of critical thought itself. In Adorno's (1975) words:

> . . . culture, in the true sense, did not simply accommodate itself to human beings;. . . it always simultaneously raised a protest against the petrified relations under which they lived, thereby honoring them. Insofar as culture becomes wholly assimilated to and integrated into those petrified relations, human beings are once more debased. (p. 13)

As far as the Frankfurt School was concerned the cultural realm has become a new locus of control for that aspect of Enlightenment rationality in which the domination of nature and society proceeded under the guise of technical progress and economic growth. For Adorno and Horkheimer (1972) culture had become another industry, one which not only produced goods but also legitimated the logic of capital and its institutions. The term, "culture industry," was coined by Adorno as a response to the reification of culture and it had two immediate purposes. First, it was coined in order to expose the notion that "culture arises spontaneously from the masses themselves" (Lowenthal, 1979, pp. 388–389). Second, it pointed to the concentration of economic and political determinants that control the cultural sphere in the interest of social and political domination. The term "industry" in the metaphor provided a point of critical analysis. That is, it pointed not only to a concentration of political and economic groups who reproduced and legitimated the dominant belief and value system, it also referred to the mechanisms of rationalization and standardization as they permeated everyday life. Or, as Adorno (1975) put it, "the expression 'industry' is not to be taken literally. It refers to the standardization of the thing itself—such as the Western, familiar to every moviegoer—and to the rationalization of distribution techniques . . . [and] not strictly to the production process" (p. 14).

At the core of the theory of culture advanced by Horkheimer, Adorno, and Marcuse was an attempt to expose, through both a call for and demonstration of critique, how positivist rationality manifested itself in the cultural realm. For instance, they criticized certain cultural products such as art for excluding the principles of resistance and opposition that once informed their relationship to the world while simultaneously helping to expose it (Horkheimer, 1972). Likewise, for Marcuse (1978), "the truth of art lies in its power to break the monopoly of established reality (i.e., of those who established it) to define what is real. In this rupture . . . the fictitious world of art appears as true reality" (p. 9). The Frankfurt School argued that in the one dimensional society art collapses, rather than highlights, the distinction between reality and the possibility of a higher truth or better world. In other words, in the true spirit of positivist harmony, art becomes simply a mirror of the existing reality and in doing so affirms it. Thus, either the memory of a historical truth or the image of a better way of life is rendered impotent in the ultra realism of the Warhol Campbell soup painting or the Stakhanovite paintings of socialist realism.

The dictates of positivist rationality and the attendant mutilation of the power of imagination are also embodied in the techniques and forms that shape the messages and discourse of the culture industry. Whether it be in the glut of interchangeable plots, gags, or stories, or in the rapid pace of a film's development, the logic of standardization reigns supreme. The message is conformity, and the medium for its attainment is amusement, which proudly packages itself as an escape from the necessity of critical thought. Under the sway of the culture industry, style subsumes substance and thought becomes an afterthought banished from the temple of official culture. Marcuse (1972) states this argument as well as anyone in his comment:

> By becoming components of the aesthetic form, words, sounds, shapes, and colors are insulated against their familiar, ordinary use and function;. . . This is the achievement of style, which *is* the poem, the novel, the painting, the composition. The style, embodiment of the aesthetic form, in subjecting reality to another order, subjects it to the laws of beauty. True and false, right and wrong, pain and pleasure, calm and violence become aesthetic categories within the framework of the oeuvre. Thus deprived of their (immediate) reality, they enter a different context in which even the ugly, cruel, sick become parts of the aesthetic harmony governing the whole. (pp. 98–99)[5]

Inherent in the reduction of culture of amusement is a significant message, one which points to the root of the ethos of positivist rationality, i.e., the structural division between work and play. Within the latter division, work is confined to the imperatives of drudgery, boredom and powerlessness for the vast majority while culture becomes the vehicle by which to escape from such toil. The power of the Frankfurt School's analysis lies in its exposure of the ideological fraud that constitutes this division of labor. Rather than being an escape from the mechanized work process, the cultural realm becomes an extension of it. Adorno and Horkheimer (1972) write:

> Amusement under late capitalism is the prolongation of work. It is sought after as an escape from the mechanized work process, and to recruit strength in order to be able to cope with it again. But at the same time mechanization has such power over a man's leisure and happiness and so profoundly determines the manufacture of amusement goods, that his experiences are after images of the work process itself. The ostensible content is merely a faded background; what sinks in is an automatic succession of standardized operations. (p. 137)

The most radical critique of the division of labor among the three theorists under study finds its expression in the work of Herbert Marcuse (1955, 1969). Marcuse (1969) claims that Marxism has not been radical enough in its attempt to develop a new sensibility that would develop as "an instinctual barrier against cruelty, brutality, ugliness" (p. 3). Marcuse's (1955) point is that a new rationality which takes as its goal the erotization of labor "and the development and fulfillment of human needs" (p. 205) would necessitate new relations of production and organizational structures under which work could take place. This should not suggest that Marcuse abandons all forms of authority or that he equates hierarchical relationships with the realm of domination. On the contrary, he argues that work and play can interpenetrate each other without either losing their primary character. As Agger (1979) points out:

> Marcuse is . . . saying that . . . work and play converge without abandoning the 'work' character of work itself. He retains the rational organization of work without abandoning the Marxian goal of creative praxis. As he (Marcuse) notes . . . 'hierarchical relationships are not unfree per se.' That is, it depends upon the kind of hierarchy which informs relationships . . . Marcuse . . . suggests two things: in the first place, he hints at a theory of work which rests upon the merger of work and play components. His views in this regard are captured in his vision of the 'erotization of labor.' In the second place, Marcuse hints at a form of organizational rationality which is nondominating. (p. 194)

According to Marcuse (1964) science and technology have been integrated under the imprint of a dominating rationality that has penetrated the world of communicative interaction (the public sphere) as well as the world of work. It is worth mentioning that Habermas (1970), in contrast, argues that science and technology within the sphere of work are necessarily limited to technical considerations, and that the latter organization of work represents the price an advanced industrial order must pay for its material comfort. This position has been challenged by a number of theorists including Aronowitz (1980) who astutely argues that Habermas separates "communications and normative judgments from the labor process" (p. 80), and in doing so "had ceded to technological consciousness the entire sphere of rational purposive action [work]" (pp. 81–82). In opposition to Habermas, Marcuse (1964) argues that radical change means more than simply the creation of conditions that foster critical thinking and communicative competence. Such change also entails the transformation of the labor process itself and the fusion of science and technology under the guise of a rationality that stresses cooperation and self-management in the interest of a democratic community and social freedom.

While there are significant differences among Adorno, Horkheimer, and Marcuse regarding their indictment of positivist rationality and their respective notions about what constitutes an aesthetic or radical sensibility, their views converge on the existing repressiveness underlying positivist rationality and the need for the development of a collective critical consciousness and sensibility that would embrace a discourse of opposition and non-identity as a precondition of human freedom. Thus, for them, criticism represented an indispensible element in the struggle for emancipation, and it is precisely in their call for criticism and a new sensibility that one finds an analysis of the nature of domination that contains invaluable insights for a theory of social education. The analysis, in this case, includes the Frankfurt School's theory of depth psychology to which I will now briefly turn.

The Frankfurt School's Analysis of Depth Psychology

As I have pointed out previously, the Frankfurt School faced a major contradiction in attempting to develop a critical tradition within Marxist theory. On the one hand, the historical legacy since Marx had witnessed increased material production and the continued conquest of nature in both the advanced industrial countries of the West and the countries of the socialist bloc as well. In both camps, it appeared that the objective conditions that promoted alienation, despite economic growth, had deepened. For example, in the West the production of goods and the ensuing commodity fetishism made a mockery of the concept of the good life, reducing it to the issue of purchasing power. In the socialist bloc, the centralization of political power led to political repression instead of political and economic freedom as had been promised. Yet in both cases the consciousness of the masses failed to keep pace with such conditions.

For the Frankfurt School it became clear that a theory of consciousness and depth psychology was needed to explain the subjective dimension of liberation and domination. Marx had provided the political and economic grammar of domination, but he relegated the psychic dimension to a secondary status and believed that the latter would follow any significant changes in the economic realm. Thus, it was left to the Frankfurt School, especially Marcuse (1955, 1964, 1969, 1970), to analyze the formal structure of consciousness in order to discover how a dehumanized society could continue to maintain its control over its inhabitants, and similarly, how it was possible that human beings could participate willingly at the level of everyday life in the reproduction of their own dehumanization and exploitation. For answers, the Frankfurt School turned to a critical study of Freud.

If a general theory of culture had been fashioned from the tools of sociological and historical analyses, it remained to merge Marx with Freud in order to complete the task. But the notion of depth psychology as a social and political category did not make its first appearance in the work of the Frankfurt School; its historical, political and theoretical roots were first established in the early works of Wilhelm Reich (1949, 1970, 1969, 1970, 1971). Reich's work is important because it exercised a strong influence on figures such as Erich Fromm, who was one of the first members of the Frankfurt School to display a serious interest in Freud's work. Moreover, the work of Reich and Fromm influenced in both a positive and negative manner the way in which Adorno, Horkheimer, and Marcuse developed their own perspectives on Freudian psychology.

Historical Background to Depth Psychology

Wilhelm Reich (1949, 1970) began with the assumption that the rise of authoritarianism in Europe in the 1920s and the willingness of sections of the working class to participate in such movements could not be explained by the breakdown of social relations into merely economic and political categories. While the latter were clearly important in any discussion of domination, such categories did not address the question of how domination was internalized by the oppressed. Put another way, such categories could not provide an answer to the question of how it was possible that the oppressed could participate actively in their own oppression.

In attempting to answer the above questions, Reich's early work provided both a critique of orthodox Marxism and an elaboration of the role that Freudian thought might play in deepening and extending a critical Marxist perspective. For Reich, as well as for the Frankfurt School, "crude" Marxism had eliminated the notion of subjectivity and as such had blundered both theoretically and politically. That is, theoretically European Marxism in the early 1920s had failed to develop a much needed political psychology because of its indifference to the issues of subjectivity and the politics of everyday life. On the other hand, it blundered politically because by abandoning a concern for issues such as human motivation, the nature of human desire, and the importance of human needs as fundamental components of a theory of political change it had "surrendered" to Hitler and Fascism the opportunity to mobilize both working class and middle class groups by engaging their emotions and appealing through propagandistic techniques to important psychic needs, i.e., solidarity, community, nationalism, self-identity, etc. Reich (1971) is worth quoting on this issue:

> One element in the fundamental cause of the failure of socialism—only an element, but an important one, no longer to be ignored, no longer to be regarded as secondary—is the absence of an effective doctrine of political psychology. . . . This shortcoming of ours has become the greatest advantage of the class enemy, the mightiest weapon of fascism. While we presented the masses with superb historical analyses and economic treatises on the contradictions of imperialism, Hitler stirred the deepest roots of their emotional being. As Marx would have put it, we left the praxis of the subjective factor to the idealists; we acted like mechanistic, economistic materialists. (p. 19)

For Reich, the obstacles to political change could, in part, be overcome by delineating "the exact place of psychoanalysis within Marxism" (Jacoby, 1975, p. 90). In Reich's (1972) terms, this meant uncovering the way in which concrete mediations, whether they be in the form of discourse, social relations, or the productions of the mass media, functioned so as to produce the internalization of values and ideologies that inhibited the development of individual and collective social consciousness. Central to Reich's (1970, 1971) early focus on explaining the role of psychoanalysis within a Marxist perspective was his emphasis on character structure, the role of the family as an oppressive agency of socialization, and the importance of sexual repression as a basis for authoritarianism.

In brief, Reich (1949) argued that the patriarchal family under capitalist social relations "creates those character forms which it needs for its preservation" (p. xxii). In this case, Reich believed that the family was a microcosm of the dominant society and that through its perpetuation of sexual repression it created personality structures receptive to authoritarian ideologies and movements. As Reich (1970) puts it:

> Authoritarian society's fight against the sexuality of children and adolescents, and the consequent struggle in one's own ego, takes place within the framework of the authoritarian family, which has thus far proven to be the best institution to carry out this fight successfully . . . it is the authoritarian family that represents the foremost and most essential source of reproduction of every kind of reactionary thinking; it is a factory where reactionary ideology and reactionary structures are produced. Hence, the 'safeguarding of the family,' i.e., of the authoritarian and large family, is the first cultural precept of every reactionary policy. (pp. 56, 60)

While members of the Frankfurt School saw both the role of the family and the importance of sexual repression in generating fascism in more expansive and dialectical terms, they were strongly influenced by Reich's formulations on the role and nature of depth psychology in providing the basis for a more critical Marxism.

Erich Fromm. As one of the first members of the Frankfurt School to display a sustained interest in Freud's work, Erich Fromm occupies an important place in the attempt to locate psychoanalysis within a Marxist framework. Like Reich, Fromm was interested in Freud's attempt to reveal those linkages between the individual and society that illuminated the dynamics of psychological repression and social domination. As such, Fromm's (1970) early work on the patriarchical family as well as his modifications of Freud's ahistorical view of the unconscious exercised a significant influence on Adorno, Horkheimer, and Marcuse. Equally important is the negative influence that Fromm had on latter theorists. As Fromm (1941, 1947) later rejected many of his early formulations regarding Freud's work, particularly as he shifted his focus from a psychology of the unconscious to one of the conscious, from sexuality to morality, and from repression to personality development (Jacoby, 1975), the Frankfurt School began to fashion their own diverse versions of Freudian theory in reaction to Fromm's revisionist reading of psychoanalysis.

Adorno, Horkheimer, and Marcuse on Depth Psychology

For the Frankfurt School, Freud's metapsychology provided an important theoretical foundation for revealing the interplay between the individual and society. More specifically, the value of Freudian psychology in this case rested with its illumination of the antagonistic character of social reality. As a theoretician of contradictions, Freud provided a radical insight into the way in which society reproduced its powers both in and over the individual. As Jacoby (1975) puts it:

> Psychoanalysis shows its strength; it demystifies the claims to liberated values, sensitivities, emotions, by tracing them to a repressed psychic social, and biological dimension . . . it keeps to the pulse of the psychic underground. As such it is more capable of grasping the intensifying social unreason that the conformist psychologies repress and forget: the barbarism of civilization itself, the barely suppressed misery of the living, the madness that haunts society. (p. 18)

The Frankfurt School theorists believed that it was only in an understanding of the dialectic between the individual and society that the depth and extent of domination as it existed both within and outside of the individual could be open to modification and transformation. Thus, for Adorno, Horkheimer, and Marcuse, Freud's emphasis on the constant struggles between the individual's desire for instinctual gratification and the dynamics of social repression provided an indispensible clue to understanding the nature of society and the dynamics of psychic domination and liberation. Adorno (1967) points to this in the following comments:

> The only totality the student of society can presume to know is the antagonistic whole, and if he is to attain to totality at all, then only in contradiction. . . . The jarring elements that make up the individual, his 'properties,' are invariably moments of the social totality. He is, in the strict sense a monad, representing the whole and its contradictions, without however, being at any time conscious of the whole. (pp. 74–77)

In order to explore the depth of the conflict between the individual and society, the Frankfurt School accepted with some major modifications most of Freud's most radical assumptions. More specifically, Freud's theoretical schema contained three important elements for developing a depth psychology. First, Freud provided a formal psychological structure for the Frankfurt School theorists to work with. That is, the Freudian outline of the structure of the psyche with its underlying struggle between eros (the life instinct), the death instinct, and the outside world represented a key conception in the depth psychology developed by the Frankfurt School.

Secondly, Freud's studies on psychopathology, particularly his sensitivity to humanity's capacity for self-destructiveness and his focus on the loss of ego-stability and the decline of the influence of the family in contemporary society, added significantly to the Frankfurt School analyses of mass society and the rise of the authoritarian personality. For the Frankfurt School, the growing concentration of power in capitalist society along with the pervasive intervention of the state in the affairs of everyday life had altered the dialectical role of the traditional family as both a positive *and* negative site for identify formation. That is, the family traditionally had provided, on the one hand, a sphere of warmth and protection for its members, while, on the other hand, it also functioned as a repository for social and sexual repression. But under the development of advanced industrial capitalism, the latter dual function of the family was gradually giving way to functioning exclusively as a site for social and cultural reproduction.

Finally, by focusing on Freud's theory of instincts and metapsychology, the Frankfurt School devised a theoretical framework for unraveling and exposing the objective and psychological obstacles to social change. This issue is important because it provides significant insights into how depth psychology might be useful for developing a more comprehensive theory of social education. Since there were some major differences between Adorno and Horkheimer, on the one side, and Marcuse on the other regarding Freud's theory of instincts as well as his view of the relationship between the individual and society, I will treat their respective contributions separately.

Adorno and Horkheimer on Depth Psychology

Adorno (1968) was quick to point out that while Freud's denunciation of "man's unfreedom" over-identified with a particular historical period and thus "petrified into an anthropological constant" (p. 81), it did not seriously distract from his greatness as a theoretician of contradictions. That is, in spite of the limitations in Freudian theory, Adorno and Horkheimer firmly believed that psychoanalysis provided a strong theoretical bulwark against those psychological and social theories that exalted the idea of the "integrated personality" and the "wonders" of social harmony. True to Adorno's (1968) view that "every image of man is ideology except the negative one" (p. 84), Freud's work appeared to transcend its own shortcomings because at one level it personified the spirit of negation. Adorno (1967, 1968) clearly exalted the negative and critical features of psychoanalysis and saw them as major theoretical weapons to be used against every form of identity theory. The goals of identity theory and revisionist psychology were both political and ideological in nature, and it was precisely through the use of Freud's metapsychology that they could be exposed as such. As Adorno (1968) put it:

> The goal of the 'well integrated personality' is objectionable because it expects the individual to establish an equilibrium between conflicting forces which does not obtain in existing society. Nor should it, because these forces are not of equal moral merit. People are taught to forget the objective conflicts which necessarily repeat themselves in every individual instead of being helped to grapple with them. (p. 83)

While it was clear to the Frankfurt School that psychoanalysis could not solve the problems of repression and authoritarianism, they believed that it did provide important insights into how "people become accomplices to their own subjugation" (Benjamin, 1977, p. 22). Yet, beneath the analyses put forth on psychoanalysis by Adorno (1967, 1968, 1972, 1973) and Horkheimer (1972) there lurked a disturbing paradox. While both theorists went to great lengths to explain the dynamics of authoritarianism and psychological domination, they said very little about those formal aspects of consciousness that might provide a basis for resistance and rebellion. That is, while Freudian psychology in their view registered a powerful criticism of existing society in exposing its antagonistic character, Horkheimer and Adorno failed to locate in either individuals or social classes the psychological or political grounds for recognizing such contradictions and acting to transform them. Consequently, Adorno and Horkheimer provided a view of Freudian psychology that consigned Freud to the ambiguous status of being a radical as well as a prophet of gloom.

Marcuse's Search for Freud

If Adorno and Horkheimer viewed Freud as a revolutionary pessimist, Marcuse (1955) read him as a revolutionary utopian. That is, though Marcuse (1955) accepts most of Freud's most controversial assumptions, his interpretation of the latter are both unique and provocative. In one sense, Marcuse's (1955, 1968, 1970) analysis contained an original dialectical twist in that it pointed to a utopian integration of Marx and Freud. While Marcuse (1955) accepted Freud's view of the antagonistic relations between the individual and society as a fundamental insight, he nevertheless altered some of Freud's basic categories and in doing so situated Freud's pessimism within a historical context that revealed its strengths as well as limitations. In doing so, Marcuse was able to illuminate the importance of Freud's metapsychology as a basis for social change. This becomes particularly clear if we examine how Marcuse

(1955, 1968, 1970) reworked Freud's basic claims regarding the life and death instincts, the struggle between the individual and society, the relationship between scarcity and social repression, and, finally, the issues of freedom and human emancipation.

Marcuse (1955, 1964) begins with the basic assumption that inherent in Freud's theory of the unconscious and theory of the instincts the theoretical elements for a more comprehensive view of the nature of individual and social domination could be found. Marcuse (1955) points to this possibility when he writes:

> The struggle against freedom reproduces itself in the psyche of man, as the self repression of the repressed individual, and his self repression in turn sustains his masters and their institutions. It is in the mental dynamic which Freud unfolds as the dynamic of civilization. . . . Freud's metapsychology is an ever renewed attempt to uncover, to question, the terrible necessity of the inner connection between civilization and barbarism, progress and suffering, freedom and unhappiness—a connection which reveals itself ultimately as that between Eros and Thanatos. (pp. 16–17)

For Marcuse (1955, 1970) Freudian psychology posited, as a result of its analysis of the relationship between civilization and instinctual repression, the theoretical basis for understanding the distinction between socially necessary authority and authoritarianism. That is, in the interplay between the need for social labor and the equally important need for sublimation of sexual energy, the dynamic connection between domination and freedom, on the one hand, and authority and authoritarianism, on the other, starts to become discernible. Freud presented the conflict between the individual's instinctual need for pleasure and the society's demand for repression as an insoluble problem rooted in a transhistorical struggle; as such, he pointed to the continuing repressive transformation of eros in society along with the growing propensity for self destruction. Marcuse (1970) believed that the "Freudian conception of the relationship between civilization and the dynamics of the instincts [was] in need of a decisive correction" (p. 20). That is, whereas Freud (1949) saw the increased necessity for social and instinctual repression, Marcuse (1955, 1970) argued that any understanding of social repression had to be situated within a specific historical context and judged as to whether such systems of domination exceeded their bounds. To ignore such a distinction was to forfeit the possibility of analyzing the difference between the exercise of legitimate authority and illegitimate forms of domination. For Marcuse (1955), Freud had failed to capture in his analysis the historical dynamic of organized domination and thus he gave it the status and dignity of a biological development that was universal rather than historically contingent.

While Marcuse (1955) accepts the Freudian notion that the central conflict in society is between the reality principle and the pleasure principle, he rejects the position that the latter had to adjust to the former. In other words, Freud (1949) believed that "the price of civilization is paid for in forfeiting happiness through heightening of the sense of guilt" (p. 114). This is important because at the core of Freud's notion that humanity was forever condemned to diverting pleasure and sexual energy into alienating labor was an appeal to a transhistorical "truth": that scarcity was inevitable in society and that labor was inherently alienating. In opposition to Freud, Marcuse (1955) argued that the reality principle referred to a particular form of historical existence when scarcity legitimately dictated instinctual repression. But in the contemporary period, such conditions had been superceded and as such abundance, and not scarcity, characterized or informed the reality principle governing the advanced industrial countries of the West.

In order to add a more fully historical dimension to Freud's analysis, Marcuse (1955) introduced the notions of performance principle and surplus repression. By arguing that scarcity was not a universal aspect of the human condition, Marcuse (1955, 1970) claimed that the moment had arrived within the industrial West when it was no longer necessary to submit men and women to the demands of alienating labor. The existing reality principle, which Marcuse (1955) labeled as the performance principle, had outstripped its historical function, i.e., the sublimation of eros in the interest of socially necessary labor. The performance principle, with its emphasis on technocratic reason and exchange rationality, was, in Marcuse's (1955) terms, both historically contingent and socially repressive. As a relatively new mode of domination it tied people to values, ideas and social practices that blocked their possibilities for gratification and happiness as ends in themselves.

In short, Marcuse (1955) believed that inherent in Marx's view of societal abundance and Freud's theory of instincts was the basis for a new performance principle, one that was governed by the principles of socially necessary labor as well as by those aspects of the pleasure principle that integrated work, play, and sexuality. This leads us to Marcuse's second important notion, i.e., the concept of surplus repression. The excessiveness of the existing nature of domination could be measured through what Marcuse (1955) labeled as surplus repression. Making a distinction between socially useful repression and surplus repression, Marcuse (1955) claims that:

> Within the total structure of the repressed personality, surplus repression is that portion which is the result of specific societal conditions sustained in the specific act of domination. The extent of this surplus-repression provides the standard of measurement: the smaller it is, the less repressive is

the stage of civilization. The distinction is equivalent to that between the biological and the historical sources of human suffering. (pp. 87–88)

According to Marcuse (1955, 1970), it is within this dialectical interplay of the personality structure and historically conditioned repression that the nexus exists for uncovering the historical and contemporary nature of domination. Domination in this sense is *twice* historical: first, it is rooted in the historically developed socio-economic conditions of a given society; second, it is rooted in the sedimented history or personality structure of individuals. In speaking of domination as a psychological as well as political phenomenon, Marcuse (1955, 1970) did not give a blank check to wholesale gratification. On the contrary, he agreed with Freud that some forms of repression were generally necessary; what he objected to was the unnecessary repression that was embodied in the ethos and social practices that characterized social institutions such as the school, workplace, and family.

For Marcuse (1969) the most penetrating marks of social repression are generated in the inner history of individuals, in the "needs, satisfactions, and values which reproduce the servitude of human existence" (p. 6). As such needs are mediated and reinforced through the patterns and social routines of everyday life, and the "false" needs that perpetuate toil, misery, and aggressiveness become anchored in the personality structure as second nature. That is, the historical character of such needs is "forgotten" and they become reduced to patterns of habit.

In the end, Marcuse (1955) grounds even Freud's important notion of death instinct (the autonomous drive that increasingly leads to self destruction) in a radical problematic. That is, by claiming that the primary drive of humanity is pleasure, Marcuse (1955) redefines the death instinct by arguing that it is mediated not by the need for self destruction, although that is a form it may take, but by the need to resolve tension. Rooted in such a perspective, the death instinct is not only redefined, it is also politicized in that Marcuse (1955) argues that in a non-repressive society it would be subordinated to the demands of eros. As such, Marcuse (1955, 1969) ends up supporting the Frankfurt School's notion of negative thinking, but with an important qualification. He insists on its value as a mode of critique, but he equally insists that it is grounded in socio-economic conditions that can be transformed. Thus, it is the promise of a better future rather than despair over the existing nature of society that informs both Marcuse's work, and its possibilities as a mode of critique for social educators.

The relevance of Marcuse's analysis for educational theory becomes obvious in the more recent work of Pierre Bourdieu (1977a, 1977b). Bourdieu argues that the school and other social institutions legitimate and reinforce through specific sets of practices and discourses class based systems of behavior and dispositions that function to reproduce the existing dominant society. As such, Bourdieu extends Marcuse's insights by pointing to a notion of learning in which a child internalizes the cultural messages of the school not only via the latter's official discourse (symbolic mastery), but also through the messages embodied in the 'insignificant' practices of daily classroom life. Bourdieu (1977b) is worth quoting at length on this issue:

> [Schools] . . . set such a store on seemingly most insignificant details of dress, bearing, physical and verbal manners. . . . The principles embodied in this way are placed beyond the grasp of consciousness, and hence cannot be touched by voluntary, deliberate transformation, cannot even be made explicit. . . . The whole trick of pedagogic reason lies precisely in the way it extorts the essential while seeming to demand the insignificant: in obtaining respect for forms and forms of respect which constitute the most visible and at the same time the best hidden manifestations to the established order. (pp. 94–95)

Unlike Bourdieu, Marcuse believes that historically conditioned needs that function in the interest of domination can be changed. That is, Marcuse (1955) argues any viable form of political action must begin with a notion of political education in which a new language, qualitatively different social relations, and a new set of values would have to operate with the purpose of creating a new environment "in which the nonaggressive, erotic, receptive faculties of man, in harmony with the consciousness of freedom, strive for the pacification of man and nature" (Marcuse, 1969, p. 31). Thus, the notion of depth psychology developed by the Frankfurt School not only provides new insights into how subjectivities are formed or how ideology functions as lived experience, it also provides theoretical tools to establish the conditions for new needs, new systems of values, and new social practices that take seriously the imperatives of a critical pedagogy.

Conclusion

While it is impossible to elaborate in any detail what the implications of the work of the Frankfurt School might be for theories of social education, I can point briefly to some general considerations. I believe it is clear that the thought of the Frankfurt School provides a major challenge and stimulus to educational theorists who are critical of theories of social education that are tied to functionalist paradigms based on assumptions drawn from a positivist rationality. For instance, against the positivist spirit that infuses existing educational theory and practice, whether it takes the form of the Tyler model or various systems approaches, the Frankfurt School offers an historical analysis as well as a penetrating philosophical framework that indict the wider culture of positivism, while at the same time providing insights into how the latter becomes incorporated within the ethos and practices of schools. Though there is a growing body of educational literature that is critical of positivist rationality in schools, it lacks the sophistication found in the work of the Frankfurt School. Moreover, even some of the better histories of curriculum theory and social education have failed to analyze the positivist underpinnings of curriculum development within a wider historical context, one that demonstrates the relationship between the dominant culture of positivism and the mechanisms of schooling (Giroux, 1981a and Wexler, 1996). Similarly, the importance of historical consciousness as a fundamental component of critical thinking in the Frankfurt School paradigm creates a valuable epistemological terrain upon which to develop modes of critique that illuminate the interaction of the social and the personal, on the one hand, and history and private experience on the other. Through this form of analysis, dialectical thought replaces positivist forms of social inquiry. That is, the logic of predictability, verifiability, transferability, and operationalism is replaced by a dialectical mode of thinking that stresses the historical, relational and normative dimensions of social inquiry and school knowledge.

In addition, the Frankfurt School's theory of culture offers new concepts and categories for analyzing the role that schools play as agents of social and cultural reproduction. By illuminating the relationship between power and culture, the Frankfurt School provides a perspective on the way in which dominant ideologies are constituted and mediated via specific cultural formations. The concept of culture in this sense exists in a particular relationship to the material base of society; and the explanatory power of such a relationship is to be found in making problematic the specific content of a culture, its relationship to dominant and subordinate social groups, the socio-historical genesis of the ethos and practices of legitimating cultures and their role in constituting relations of domination and resistance. For example, by pointing to schools as cultural sites that embody conflicting political values and practices, it becomes possible to investigate how schools can be studied as an expression of the wider organization of society, particularly with respect to the class and gender based nature of the content, methods and modes of educational research that characterize school life. Marcuse's (1964) study of language, Adorno's (1976) analysis of the sociology of music, and Horkheimer's (1972, 1974) investigations into the normative grounding of theory provide a number of theoretical constructs through which to investigate the socially constructed nature of school experience and to weigh the truth claims inherent in such experiences against the reality of the existing society.

The treatment of culture as a political entity in the work of the Frankfurt School also points to a mode of analysis by which educators can develop theories of social education that give a central role to the history or cultural capital that students from different groups bring with them to the school. It is no small matter to argue that students need to affirm their own histories through the use of a language, set of practices, and subject matter that dignifies the cultural constructs and experiences that make up the tissue and texture of their daily lives. Once the affirmative nature of such a pedagogy is established, it becomes possible for students, especially those students who have been traditionally voiceless in schools, to learn the skills, knowledge, and modes of inquiry that will allow them to analyze critically what role the existing society has played in both shaping and thwarting their aspirations and goals. Moreover, it is important that such students come to grips with what this society has made of them, how it has incorporated them both materially and ideologically, and what it is they need to affirm and reject in their own histories in order to begin the process of struggling for a self-managed existence.

Unlike models of a functionalist orientation, whether they be drawn from a conservative or radical orientation, the Frankfurt School's theory of culture also stresses the importance of consciousness and subjectivity in the process of learning and self-formation. While it is true that Adorno, Marcuse, and Horkheimer placed a heavy weight on the notion of domination in their analysis, and the integration of the masses into the existing society, I believe that such an emphasis was meant to highlight the forces of social and political domination at a time when it was difficult to understand or even recognize the nature of such domination. Such an analysis was not meant to downplay the importance of human intervention or the possibilities for social change; in fact, the notion of hope and the possibility of transcendence were embodied in the Frankfurt School's notion of critique. That is, inherent in the latter view was the idea that a better world was possible, that people could speak, act, and think in terms that spoke to a qualitatively better life. Thus, the notion of critique and the development of an active critical consciousness were pointed to and focused on as the preconditions for cultural and political mobilization.

Finally, it is clear that almost all theories of social education are too cognitive. They lack a depth psychology, as well as an appreciation of a sensibility that points to the importance of the sensual and imaginative as central dimensions of the schooling experience. The Frankfurt School's notion of depth psychology, especially Marcuse's work, opens up new terrain for developing a critical pedagogy. In other words, it speaks to the need to fashion new categories of analyses that will enable educators to become more knowledgeable regarding how teachers, students, and other educational workers become part of the system of social and cultural reproduction, particularly as it works through the messages and values that are constituted via the social practices of the hidden curriculum (Giroux, 1981c). By acknowledging the need for a critical social psychology, educators can begin to identify how ideologies get constituted and they can then identify and reconstruct social practices and processes that break rather than continue existing forms of social and psychological domination.

The task of translating the work of the Frankfurt School into terms that inform and enrich educational theory and practice will be difficult, especially since any attempt to use such work will have to begin with the understanding that it contains shortcomings and that in addition such work cannot be imposed in grid-like fashion onto a theory of social education. For instance, the Frankfurt School theorists did not develop a comprehensive theoretical approach for dealing with the patterns of conflict and contradictions that existed in various cultural spheres; moreover, they never developed adequately the notion of dual consciousness. That is, the contradictory modes of thinking that characterize the way most people view the world were not explored adequately nor were such modes of thinking analyzed carefully enough with respect to the value they might have for developing counter-hegemonic struggles. As such, the notion of resistance was underplayed by the Frankfurt School.

Any attempt to read the work of Adorno, Marcuse, and Horkheimer, then, must be done critically and then it must be applied selectively within the specificity of the context in which it will be used. It should also be stressed that beyond the complexity and shortcomings inherent in such work, there are the structural and political constraints that may prevent teachers and others from incorporating it into their educational experiences. To use such work presupposes the development of a mode of radical pedagogy that might encounter enormous resistance and even endanger one's job. These constraints cannot be taken lightly, even though such risks are involved in all struggles that attempt to strive for a better society and world. Thus, the conditions under which this work is to be used have to be given serious thought or one may fall into the trap of either expecting too much too soon from such work or one may attempt to abstract it from the context in which it is to be used and be unable to deal with the way in which such a context might resist or alter the nature of such a theoretical approach. If one is to avoid the pitfalls of either a false utopianism or an equally false despair, the theoretical insights gleaned from the work of the Frankfurt School must be mediated by the ideological and material conditions that give meaning to specific school settings and classroom sites. Finally, it is important to note that while schools are not the sole sites for implementing social change, they do offer an important terrain on which to provide future generations with new ways for thinking about the building of a more just society. The work of the Frankfurt School provides a major contribution to educators who want to play a role in helping students think and struggle in the interest of a better world.

Notes

1. It is important to note that Erich Fromm and Herbert Marcuse remained in the United States. In fact, this geographic separation, in part, may have contributed to the diverging perspectives that separated Marcuse from Adorno and Horkheimer from 1955 onwards.

2. See Arato and Gebhardt (1979), "A Critique of Methodology" for an excellent analysis of this issue, especially pages 371–406.

3. See, for instance, the debate between Tanner and Tanner (1979) and Pinar (1980) over this issue.

4. For an example of the issues involved in this debate, see my response to Linda McNeil (1981) in Giroux (1981d).

5. The implication that Marcuse's insight has for educational criticism, particularly analyses of the ideologies implicit in textbook design is an important one. Francis Fitzgerald (1979) illustrates its use in analyzing some recent social studies textbooks: "The use of all this art and high-quality design contains some irony. The nineteenth-century photographs of child laborers or urban slum apartments are so beautiful that they transcend their subjects. To look at them, or at the Victor Gatto painting of the Triangle Shirtwaist Factory fire, is not to see misery or ugliness but an art object. In the modern chapters, the contrast between junkyards or polluted rivers look as enticing as *Gourmet's* photographs of food. The book that is perhaps most stark in its description of modern problems illustrates the horrors of nuclear testing with a pretty Ben Shahn picture of the Bikini explosion, and the potential for global ecological disaster with a color photograph of the planet swirling its mantel of white clouds" (pp. 15–16).

References

Adorno, Theodor W. *Prisms,* translated by Samuel and Shierry Weber (London: Neville Spearman Limited, 1967).

_____. "Sociology and Psychology," Part I, *New Left Review* No. 46 (1967), pp. 67–80.

_____. "Sociology and Psychology," Part II, *New Left Review* No. 47 (1968), pp. 79–97.

_____. "Freudian Theory and the Pattern of Fascist Propaganda," in Geza Ro-heim (ed.), *Psychoanalysis and the Social Sciences;* Vol. III (N.Y.: International Universities Press, 1951), pp. 279–300.

_____. "Scientific Experiments of a European Scholar in America," in Donald Fleming and Bernard Bailyn, (eds), *The Intellectual Migration* (Cambridge, MA.: Harvard University Press, 1969).

_____ and Max Horkheimer, *Dialectic of Enlightenment,* translated by John Cumming (New York: The Seabury Press, 1973).

_____. *Negative Dialectics* (New York: The Seabury Press, 1973).

_____. *Minima Moralia* (London: New Left Books, 1974).

_____. "The Culture Industry Reconsidered," *New German Critique,* 6 (Fall 1975), 12–19.

_____. *Introduction to the Sociology of Music* (New York: Seabury Press, 1976).

_____. "On the Logic of the Social Sciences," in Theodor Adorno, et al. *The Positivist Dispute in German Sociology* (London: Hienman, 1976).

_____. "On Culture and Administration," *Telos* 37 (Fall 1978), 83–111.

Agger, Ben. "Work and Authority in Marcuse and Habermas," *Human Studies* 2:3 (July 1978), 191–207.

Anyon, Jean. "Social Class and the Hidden Curriculum of Work," *Journal of Education* 162:1 (Winter 1980): 67–92.

Apple, Michael, Subkoviak, Michael J. and Henry Lufler, Jr. eds., *Educational Evaluation: Analysis and Responsibility* (Berkeley, Ca.: McCutchan Publishing, 1974).

Apple, Michael. *Ideology and Curriculum* (Boston: Routledge and Kegan Paul, 1979).

Apple, Michael and Nancy King. "What Do Schools Teach," in Richard H. Weller, ed., *Humanistic Education* (Berkeley, Ca., McCutchan Publishing, 1977.)

Arato, Andrew and Eike Gebhardt, eds., *The Essential Frankfurt School Reader* (New York: Urizen Books, 1978.)

Aronowitz, Stanley. *False Promises* (New York: McGraw-Hill, 1973).

_____. "Enzenberger on Mass Culture: A Review Essay," *The Minnesota Review* 7 (Fall 1976), 91–99.

_____. "Science and Ideology," *Current Perspectives in Social Theory* (1980), 75–101.

_____. *The Crisis in Historical Materialism: Class, Politics and Culture in Marxist Theory* (New York: Praeger, 1981.)

Benjamin, Jessica. "The End of Internalization: Adorno's Social Psychology," *Telos* No. 32 (Summer 1977), pp. 42–64.

Bennet, Tony, "The Not-So-Good, the Bad, and the Ugly," *Screen Education* 36 (Autumn 1980), 119–130.

Bourdieu, Pierre, and Jean-Claude Passeron. *Reproduction in Education, Society and Culture* (Beverly Hills: Sage, 1977) (a)

Bourdieu, Pierre. *Outline of Theory and Practice* (Cambridge, England: Cambridge University Press, 1979) (b)

Bowles, Samuel, and Herb Gintis. *Schooling in Capitalist America: Educational Reform and the Contradictions of Economic Life* (New York: Basic Books, 1976.)

Bredo, Eric, and Walter Feinberg, "Meaning, Power and Pedagogy," *Journal of Curriculum Studies* 11:4 (1974), 315–332.

Breines, Paul, "Toward an Uncertain Marxism," *Radical History Review* 22 (Winter 1979–1980), 103–115.

Brosio, Richard A. *The Frankfurt School* (Muncie, Indiana: Ball State, 1980).

Brown, Bruce. *Marx, Freud and the Critique of Every Day Life* (N.Y.: Monthly Review Press, 1973.)

Brown, S. C., ed., *Philosophical Disputes in the Social Sciences* (Sussex, United Kingdom: Harvester Press, 1979.)

Buck-Morss, Susan. *The Origin of Negative Dialectics* (New York: The Free Press, 1977).

Cherryholmes, Cleo, "Social Knowledge and Citizenship Education: Two Views of Truth and Criticism," *Curriculum Inquiry* 10:2 (Summer 1980), 115–151.

Connterton, Paul, ed., *Critical Sociology* (London: Penguin Books, 1976.)

Enzenberger, Hans Magnus. *The Consciousness Industry* (New York: Seabury Press, 1974.)

Ewen, Stuart. *Captains of Consciousness: Advertising and the Social Roots of the Consumer Culture* (New York: McGraw-Hill, 1976.)

Feinberg, Walter. *Reason and Rhetoric* (New York: John Wiley, 1975.)

_____. "Educational Studies and the Disciplines of Educational Understanding," *Educational Studies* 10:4 (Winter 1980), 375–391.

Fitzgerald, Frances. *American Revisited* (Boston: Little, Brown, 1979).

Freire, Paulo. *Pedagogy of the Oppressed* (New York: Seabury Press, 1973.)

Freud, Sigmund. *Civilization and its Discontents* (London: Hogarth Press, 1949.)

_____. *Group Psychology and the Analysis of Ego* (N.Y.: Bonni-Liveright, 1922.)

Friedman, George. *The Political Philosophy of the Frankfurt School* (Ithaca: Cornell University Press, 1981.)

Fromm, Erich. *Escape from Freedom* (N.Y.: Farrar & Rinehart, 1941.)

_____. *Man for Himself* (N.Y.: Rinehart, 1947.)

_____. *Beyond the Chains of Illusion: My Encounter with Marx and Freud* (N.Y.: Simon & Schuster, 1962.)

_____. *The Crisis of Psychoanalysis* (N.Y.: Holt, Rinehart & Winston, 1970.)

_____. "The Human Implications of Instinctive 'Radicalism'" *Dissent:*4 (Autumn 1955), 342–349.

Furhman, Ellsworth, "The Normative Structure in Critical Theory," *Human Studies* 2:3 (July 1979), 209–227.

Giroux, Henry A. *Ideology, Culture, and the Process of Schooling* (Philadelphia: Temple University Press, 1981) (a).

_____. "Hegemony, Resistance and the Paradox of Educational Reform," in H.A. Giroux, Anthony N. Penna, and William Pinar, eds., *Curriculum and Instruction: Alternatives in Education* (Berkeley: McCutchan Publishing, 1981) (b).

_____. "Schooling and the Myth of Objectivity: Stalking the Hidden Curriculum," McGill *Journal of Education* 17 (1981) (c), 282–304.

_____. "Pedagogy, Pessimism, and the Politics of Conformity: Response to Linda McNeil," *Curriculum Inquiry* 17 (1981) (d), 282–304.

_____ and Anthony N. Penna, "Social Education in the Classroom: The Dynamics of the Hidden Curriculum," *Theory and Research in Social Education* 7 (Spring 1979), 21–42.

Gleason, Denis, and Geoff Whitty. *Developments in Social Studies Teaching* (London: Open Books, 1976.)

Gramsci, Antonio. *Selections from Prison Notebooks,* edited and translated by Quinten Hoare and Geoffrey Smith (New York: International Publishers, 1971.)

Greene, Maxine. *Landscapes of Learning* (New York: Teachers College Press, 1978.)

Greer, Colin. *The Great School Legend* (New York: Basic Books, 1972.)

Gross, Harvey, "Adorno in Los Angeles: The Intellectual Emigration," *Humanities in Society,* 2:4 (Fall 1979), 339–351.

Habermas, Jurgen. *Knowledge and Human Interest* (Boston: Beacon Press, 1971) (a)

_____. *Toward a Rational Society* (Boston: Beacon Press, 1971) (b)

_____. *Theory and Practice* (Boston: Beacon Press, 1973.)

_____. *Communication and the Evolution of Society,* translated by Thomas McCarthy (Boston: Beacon Press, 1979.)

Hahn, Hans, "Logik Mathematic und Naturerkennen," *Einheitswissenschaft* in Otto Neurath, et. al., eds., (Vienna, 1933).

Held, David. *Introduction to Critical Theory: Horkheimer to Habermas* (Berkeley, Ca.: University of California Press, 1980.)

Horkheimer, Max. *Critical Theory* (New York: The Seabury Press, 1972.)

_____. "The Authoritarian State," translated by the People's Translation Service, *Telos* 15 (Spring 1973), 3–20.

_____. *Eclipse of Reason* (New York: The Seabury Press, 1974.)

_____. *Dawn and Decline,* translated by Michael Shaw (New York: The Seabury Press, 1978.)

Jacoby, Russell. *Social Amnesia* (Boston: Beacon Press, 1975.)

_____. "What is Conformist Marxism," *Telos* 45 (Fall 1980), 19–42.

_____. "The Politics of Narcissism." *Humanities in Society,* Vol. 3, No. 2 (1980), pp. 189–198.

Jay, Martin. *The Dialectical Imagination: A History of the Frankfurt School and the Institute of Social Research, 1923–1950* (Boston: Little, Brown, 1973.)

Karier, Clarence. *The Shaping of the American Educational State: 1900 to the Present* (New York: Free Press, 1975.)

King, Richard. *The Party of Eros: Radical Social Thought and the Realm of Freedom* (N.Y.: Dell Publishing Company, 1972.)

Kozik, Karol. *Dialectics of the Concrete* (Boston: D. Reidel Publishing Co., 1976.)

Katz, Michael. *The Irony of Early School Reform* (Boston: Beacon Press, 1969.)

Lowenthal, Leo, "Theodor W. Adorno: An Intellectual Memoir," *Humanities in Society* 2:4 (Fall 1979), 387–399.

Lukacs, George. *History and Class Consciousness* (Cambridge, Ma.: MIT Press, 1968.)

Macdonald, James B., and Esther Zaret, eds., *Schools in Search of Meaning* (Washington, D.C.: Association for Supervision and Curriculum Development, 1975.)

MacDonald, Madeleine M. *The Curriculum and Cultural Reproduction* (Milton Keynes, England: Open University Press, 1977.)

Marcuse, Herbert. *Eros and Civilization* (Boston: Beacon Press, 1955.)

_____. *Reason and Revolution* (Boston: Beacon Press, 1960)

_____. *One Dimensional Man* (Boston: Beacon Press, 1964.)

_____. *Negotiations: Essays in Critical Theory* (Boston: Beacon Press, 1968.)

_____. *An Essay on Liberation* (Boston: Beacon Press, 1968.)

_____. *Five Lectures*, translated by Jeremy Shapiro and Sheirry Weber (Boston: Beacon Press, 1970).

_____. *Counterrevolution and Revolt* (Boston: Beacon Press, 1972.)

_____. *Studies in Critical Philosophy*, translated by Joris DeBros (Boston: Beacon Press, 1973.)

_____. *The Aesthetic Dimension: Toward a Critique of Marxist Aesthetics* (Boston: Beacon Press, 1978.)

Marx, Karl, *The Economic & Philosophical Manuscripts of 1844*, translated by Martin Milligan (New York: International Publishers, 1947.)

McNeil, Linda, "Response to Henry A. Giroux's Critical Theory and Rationality in Citizenship Education," *Curriculum Inquiry* 17 (1981.)

Nietzche, Friedrich. *The Use and Abuse of History*, translated by A. Collins (Indianapolis: Bobbs-Merrill, 1957.)

_____. "Aus dem Nachlass der Achtzigerjahre," in Karl Schleckta (ed.) *Werke*, Volume III (Munchen: Hanser, 1966.)

Pinar, William F. ed., *Heightened Consciousness and Curriculum Theory* (Berkeley, Ca.: McCutchan Publishing, 1974.)

_____ ed., *Curriculum Theorizing: The Reconceptualists* (Berkeley, Ca.: McCutchan, 1975.)

_____. "A Reply to My Critics," *Curriculum Inquiry* 10:2 (Summer 1980), 199–205.

_____. "The Abstract and Concrete in Curriculum Theorizing," in Henry A. Giroux, Anthony N. Penna, and William F. Pinar (eds.), *op. cit.*, 1981.

Popkewitz, Thomas S. "Paradigms in Educational Science: Different Meanings and Purpose in Theory," *Journal of Education* 162:1 (Winter 1980), 28–46.

Reich, Wilhelm. *Sex-Pol. Essays, 1929–1934*, edited by Lee Banandall (New York: Vintage Books, 1972.)

_____. *The Mass Psychology of Fascism*, translated by Vincent Carfango (New York: Farrar, Straus, and Giroux, 1970.)

_____. *Character Analysis*, 3rd ed. (New York: Farrar, Straus, and Giroux, 1949.)

_____. "What is Class Consciousness?" translated by Anna Bostock, *Liberation* (October 1971), pp. 15 51.

Robinson, Paul. *The Freudian Left* (New York: Harper Colophon Books, 1969.)

Schneider, Michael. *Neurosis and Civilization: A Marxist/Freudian Synthesis* (N.Y.: Seabury Press, 1975.)

Simon, Roger, and Don Dippo, "Dramatic Analysis: Interpretative Inquiry for the Transformation of Social Settings," *Journal of Curriculum Theorizing* 2:1 (1980), 109–134.

Tanner, Daniel, and Laurel Tanner, "Emancipation From Research: The Reconceptualist Prescription," *Educational Researcher* 8:6 (1979), 8–12.

Wellmer, Albrecht. *Critical Theory of Society*, translated by John Cumming (New York: The Seabury Press, 1974.)

Wesley, Edgar, and Stanley P. Wronski, *Teaching Secondary Social Studies in a World Society*, 33rd ed. (Lexington, Mass.: Heath, 1973.)

Wexler, Philip. *The Sociology of Education: Beyond Equality* (Indianapolis: Bobbs-Merrill Publishing, 1976.)

_____. "Structure, Text, and Subject: A Sociology of School Knowledge," Unpublished paper, n.d.

_____. *A Critical Social Psychology*, 2nd ed. (New York: Peter Lang, 1996.)

Whitty, Geoff, and Michael Young, eds., *Society, State and Schooling* (Sussex, England: Falmer Press, 1977.)

Willis, Paul. *Learning to Labour: How Working Class Kids Get Working Class Jobs* (Westmead, England: Saxon House, 1977.)

Zaretsky, Eli. *Capitalism, The Family and Personal Life* (N.Y.: Harper-Colophon Books, 1976.)

3 | *Ideology and Agency in the Process of Schooling*

EDUCATIONAL THEORY AND PRACTICE stand at an impasse. Despite the important outpouring of work in the last decade on such topics as the hidden curriculum, class and gender reproduction, ideology and culture, and theories of the state and schooling, educational theorizing remains trapped in a dualism that separates issues of human agency from structural analyses. Both traditional and radical perspectives on schooling are caught in a theoretical straitjacket that either suppresses the significance of human agency and subjectivity, or ignores those structural determinants that lie outside of the immediate experiences of teachers, administrators, students, and other human actors. The absence of a full consideration of the dialectic between consciousness and structure in the work of radical educational theorists is at the root of their failure to develop a more critical theory of schooling. This becomes particularly clear in those modes of discourse that presuppose that schools are *merely* agencies of social and cultural reproduction. In these all too familiar accounts, power and agency are attributes almost exclusively of the dominant classes and the institutions they control. Even where resistance, agency, and mediation appear in accounts of the "excluded majorities" in the schools, such constructs are situated within the context of a paralyzing pessimism that often consigns them to the logic of defeat and domination rather than to the imperatives of struggle and emancipation (Giroux, 1981).

Central to the development of a radical pedagogy is a reformulation of this dualism between agency and structure, a reformulation that can make possible a critical interrogation of how human beings come together within historically specific social sites such as schools in order to both make and reproduce the conditions of their existence. Essential to this project is a fundamental concern with the question of how we can make schooling meaningful in order to make it critical, and how we can make it critical in order to make it emancipatory. I will argue in this essay that the precondition for the development of a critical theory of schooling is a reworking of the notion of ideology; it is through a fuller understanding of ideology that a theory can be developed which takes seriously the issues of agency, struggle, and critique. It is to an exploration of this issue that I will now turn.

Ideology and Educational Theory and Practice

The relationship between ideology and schooling is problematic. In part, this results from the powerful influence that technocratic rationality has exercised historically on the development of educational theory and practice. Within this tradition, the fact that schools are both ideological *and* instructional sites has been ignored. Wedded to the celebration of facts and the management of the "visible," positivist rationality excludes from its perspective those categories and questions that point to the terrain of ideology. Fixated on the logic of immediacy, such theorists found refuge in the world of appearances and thus refused to interrogate the internal logic of the curriculum in order to reveal its hidden meanings, structured silences, or unintended truths. Notions such as "essence," false consciousness, and immanent critique were safely tucked away in favor of the discourse of administration, management, and efficiency. Consequently, there has been little room within the logic of dominant educational theory and practice to deconstruct the established meanings and received practices that characterize the day-to-day workings of schools.

From a radically different perspective, Marxism has had a long and extensive tradition in which ideology has played a significant role as a critical concept in the ongoing critique of capitalism and its institutions. However, within that tradition the meaning and applicability of the notion of ideology has remained elusive and equivocal (Sumner, 1979; Larrain, 1979). The result has been that Marxist thought, with few exceptions, has failed to develop a systematic treatment of the concept; consequently, the concept of ideology as a heuristic and critical theoretical tool has not played a role consistent with its potential in radical theory and practice.

The Marxist tradition is not informed by a unitary concept of ideology; one finds instead a plethora of interpretations and analyses of the meaning and value of the concept. Among these wide ranging interpretations there are hints and fleeting images of what the theoretical terrain of ideology might look like; needless to say, if the relation between schooling and ideology is to be understood, the most important of these theoretical insights need to be identified and integrated into a more comprehensive theoretical framework. Thus it is important to interrogate the dominant Marxist versions of ideology in order to see what is missing from them. This in turn demands a brief critical analysis of some of the assumptions that underlie the often contradictory and complex treatment of ideology in current Marxist social theory.

I think it is accurate and fitting to begin by arguing that ideology in the most traditional and orthodox Marxist sense has been primarily concerned with relations of domination rather than with the relations of struggle and resistance. One consequence has been a host of interpretations that define ideology in largely pejorative terms: as false consciousness (Marx, 1972), as nonscientific beliefs (Althusser, 1969), or as a set of beliefs that function so as to legitimize domination (Habermas, 1975). In these interpretations, ideology has operated at such a high level of abstraction that it provides few clues as to how subjectivities are constituted in schools; by denying the complex and contradictory nature of human consciousness and behavior, these accounts suppress the possibilities of mediation and resistance. Ideology has also been treated by a smaller number of Marxist theorists in the positive sense as a set of beliefs and modes of discourse constructed to satisfy the needs and interests of specific groups. For example, Lenin (1971) viewed ideology as a positive force to the degree that it provided the working class with the attitudes and skills necessary for self-determination. Similarly, Gouldner (1976) has made one of the most compelling attempts to rescue ideology from its pejorative status by arguing that all ideologies contain the possibility for developing a critical view of the world. However, in addition to the question of whether ideology is to be viewed in a positive or pejorative light there is a related question as to whether ideology should be viewed primarily in objective or subjective terms. For instance, both Althusser (1969, 1971) and Volosinov (1973) view ideology as having a materiality rooted, respectively, either in practices produced in Ideological State Apparatuses such as schools, or in the materiality of language, representations, and "signs." For both Althusser and Volosinov, ideologies address and constitute the human subject. But the human subject is the missing referent here, as are relations of struggle waged outside the "text," among real human beings who bleed, cry, despair, and think. On the other hand, the subjective and psychological character of ideology can be found in the work of critical theorists such as Marcuse (1964), or in the work of culturalists such as Williams (1977) and Thompson (1966). In these perspectives, either ideology is situated within the psychic structure of the oppressed or it is the central, active force constituted through shared experiences and common interests.

In the Marxist tradition, then, there is a central tension between a view of ideology as an all-encompassing mode of domination and a view of ideology as an active force in the construction of human agency and critique. Similarly, there is a tension between the notion of ideology as a material force and ideology as a mode of meaning. Each of these positions is by itself theoretically flawed, and each alone is only partially useful in providing a critical theory of ideology for radical educators. In order to constitute a theory of ideology as the basis for a critical theory of schooling, it will be necessary to situate it within a theoretical perspective that takes seriously the notion of human agency, struggle, and critique.

Ideology: Definition, Locations, and Features

Any definition of ideology has to wrestle not only with the question of what it is but also with the question of what it is not. I want to begin with the latter point. One view of ideology in particular that must be abandoned before the concept can be rescued from its own history is the Althusserian notion that ideology exists in material apparatuses and has a material existence. As Johnson (1979a) points out, Althusser's argument transforms a "genuine insight" into a "reckless hyperbole" (p. 59). To argue that ideologies are located in concrete social practices and have specific effects on such practices is an important insight, but to stretch the meaning of ideology to make it synonymous with the material world so generalizes the concept as to render it meaningless as an analytical tool. Moreover, this definition of ideology falsely collapses the distinction between ideological struggle and material struggle. That is, it confuses struggles over meanings, discourse, and representation with struggles over the concrete appropriation and control of capital, territory, and other such resources. Of course, both forms of struggle are related, but they cannot be collapsed into each other. For example, schools are cultural apparatuses involved in the production and transmission of ideologies. It is one thing to talk about the school as a site where conflicting ideologies are fought over, a site where a conflict is waged over relations of meaning; it is another thing altogether to view schools as political and economic institutions—material embodiments of lived experience and historically sedimented antagonistic relations—that need to be seized and controlled by subordinate groups so they can be used in the interests of such groups.

The distinction between ideology and the materiality of culture is an important one; it cannot be reduced to a simple dualism of ideas counterposed to material reality. The relation is more complex than this. On the one hand, ideology can be viewed as a set of representations produced and inscribed in human consciousness and behavior, in discourse, and in lived experiences. On the other hand, ideology is concretized in various "texts," material practices, and material forms. Hence, the character of ideology is mental, but its effects are both psychological and behavioral; they are not only felt in human action but are also inscribed in material culture. Thus, ideology as a construct includes a notion of mediation that does not limit it to an ideal form (Aronowitz, 1981). I want to argue that ideology has an active quality, the character of which is defined by those processes "by which meaning is produced, challenged, reproduced and transformed" (Barrett, 1980, p. 97). Within this perspective, ideology refers to the production, consumption, and representation of ideas and behavior, all of which can either distort or illuminate the nature of reality. As a set of meanings and ideas, ideologies can be either coherent or contradictory; they can function within the spheres of both consciousness and unconsciousness; and, finally, they can exist at the level of critical discourse as well as within the sphere of taken-for-granted lived experience and practical behavior (Bourdieu, 1977; Bourdieu & Passeron, 1977; Giddens, 1979; Marcuse, 1955). The complexity of the concept is captured in the notion that while ideology is an active process involving the production, consumption, and representation of meaning and behavior, it cannot be reduced to either consciousness or a system of practices on the one hand, or to either a mode of intelligibility or a mode of mystification on the other. Its character is dialectical, and its theoretical strength stems both from the way it shuns reductionism, and from the way it bridges the seemingly contradictory moments mentioned above.

But a number of qualifications must be made if the definition of ideology developed thus far is to be prevented from collapsing into the kind of sociology of knowledge that, as Adorno (1967) remarks, suffers from the weakness of calling "everything into question and criticizing nothing" (p. 37). While the characteristic feature of ideology is its location in the category of meaning and thought production, its critical potential only becomes fully clear when it is linked to the concepts of struggle and critique. When linked to the notion of struggle, ideology illuminates the important relationships among power, meaning, and interest. This suggests at one level the important insight provided by Marx in his claim that ideologies constitute the medium of struggle among classes at the level of ideas (Marx 1969b), as well as the correlary insight provided by Gramsci's (1971) comment that ideologies "organize masses, and create the terrain on which men move, acquire consciousness of their position, struggle, etc." (p. 377).

Both Marx and Gramsci suggest that any theory of ideology has to include a theory of power, one that takes as its central concern social antagonisms and class struggle. The linkage of ideology and struggle points to the inseparability of knowledge and power; it emphasizes that ideology refers not only to specific forms of discourses and the social relations they structure but also to the interests they further (Gouldner,

1976). Thus, when Marx (1969a) linked ideology to the sectional interests of dominant groups in society he pointed to a form of ideology critique whose function is, in part, to uncover class-specific mystification and to point to concrete struggles aimed at the overcoming of class domination.

This form of ideology critique indicates the need to penetrate beyond the discourse and consciousness of human actors to the conditions and foundation of their day-to-day experiences. Critique in this sense functions to uncover falsifications and to identify the conditions and practices that generate them. Ideology critique in this instance centers around a critical analysis of the subjective and objective forces of domination, and at the same time reveals the transformative potential of alternative modes of discourse and social relations rooted in emancipatory interests. It is also important to argue that ideology critique involves more than critically analyzing modes of knowledge and social practices in order to determine whose interests they serve. It is important to recognize that in addition to its functional role in the construction and maintenance of the power of dominant social formations, ideology operates as a relatively autonomous set of ideas and practices, whose logic cannot be reduced merely to class interests. Again, its meaning and specificity cannot be exhausted by defining its functional relation to class interests and struggle. In this case, ideology critique not only focuses on whether a specific ideology functions so as to serve or resist class or other forms of domination; on the contrary, it also identifies the contents of the ideologies in question and judges the "truth or falsity of the contents themselves" (Adorno, 1973, p. 131). That is, if the notions of ideology and ideology critique are really to serve emancipatory class interests, ultimately they cannot be separated from the question of truth claims. It is important to maintain this understanding of the transformative and active quality of ideology when we consider the link between ideology and human agency. As both the medium and the outcome of lived experience, ideology functions not only to limit human action but also to enable it. That is, ideology both promotes human agency and at the same time exercises force over individuals and groups through the "weight" it assumes in dominant discourses, selected forms of socio-historical knowledge, specific social relations, and concrete material practices. Ideology is something we all participate in, and yet we rarely understand either the historical constraints that produce and limit the nature of that participation, or what the possibilities are for going beyond existing parameters of action in order to think and act in terms that speak to a qualitatively better existence. The nature of ideology and its usefulness as a critical construct for radical pedagogy can be further illuminated by focusing on its location and functions within what I choose to call its operational field. In the most general sense, ideology operates at the level of lived experience, at the level of representations embedded in various cultural artifacts, and at the level of messages signified in material practices produced within certain historical, existential, and class traditions. I want to examine briefly the relations between ideology and each of these respective locations while concentrating primarily on how ideology functions at the level of lived experience. In doing so, I will further delineate a notion of ideology critique and its relevance to radical pedagogy.

Ideology, Human Experience, and Schooling

Central to understanding how ideology functions in the interest of social reproduction is the issue of how ideology works on and through individuals to secure their consent to the basic ethos and practices of the dominant society. Equally important for an understanding of how ideology functions in the interest of social transformation is the issue of how ideology creates the terrain for reflection and transformative action. I do not believe that the concept of ideology can be located either in the sphere of consciousness, as in traditional Marxism, or exclusively within the realm of the unconscious, as Althusser (1969, 1971) and his followers argue. Following Gramsci (1971), I want to argue that human behavior is rooted in a complex nexus of structured needs, common sense, and critical consciousness, and that ideology is located in all of these aspects of human behavior and thought so as to produce multiple subjectivities and perceptions of the world and everyday life. The interface of ideology and individual experience can be located within three specific areas: the sphere of the unconscious and the structure of needs; the realm of common sense; and the sphere of critical consciousness. Needless to say, these areas cannot be neatly defined nor do they exist in isolation. But by using them we can move from an analysis focusing on whether consciousness is true or false, to the more fundamental issue of what consciousness is and how it is constituted. Moreover, the argument that ideology exists as part of the unconscious, common sense, and critical consciousness points to an ideological universe in which contradictions exist both in and outside of the individual. This is similar to Williams's (1977) argument that the ideological field in any given society includes contradictions within and between what he calls emerging, residual, and dominant ideologies. Meaning as it is produced and received within this complex of ideologies and material forces is clearly not reducible to the individual but has to be understood in its articulation with ideological and material forces as they circulate and constitute the wider society. In other words, ideology has to be conceived as both the source and effect of social and institutional practices as they operate within a society that is characterized primarily by relations of domination, a society in which men and women are basically unfree in both objective and subjective terms. This becomes clearer if we examine the relations between ideology and these three spheres of meaning and behavior separately.

Ideology and the Unconscious

Traditional Marxism limited the parameters of ideology almost exclusively to the realm of consciousness and the notion of domination. Lost from these approaches was any attempt to analyze the effects of ideology on the body and the structure of personality. In other words, there were very few attempts to examine how ideology produced effects at not only the level of knowledge but also at the level of needs and desires. Locked within a theoretical straitjacket that defined ideology as "merely" oppressive, orthodox Marxism failed to explore either how people acted against their own interests, thereby sharing in their own oppression, or what compelled them to stand up and resist oppression in the face of intolerable odds. Foucault (1980) raises this point poignantly in his comment: "What enables people . . . to resist the Gulag . . . what can give [them] the courage to stand up and die in order to utter a word or a poem?" (p. 136).

Within the last few decades, Marcuse (1955), Althusser (1969), and others have attempted to reconstruct the meaning of ideology and to demarcate its location and effects so as to include the sphere of the unconsciousness and the structure of needs. Althusser's (1969, 1971) insistence that ideology is grounded unconsciously represents a major contribution in redefining the meaning and workings of the concept. It points to the limits of consciousness in explaining the nature of domination while simultaneously pointing to the power of the material practices and social relations through which people live their experiences and generate meanings. But although Althusser provides a service in linking ideology to the unconscious, he is still trapped within a notion of domination that leaves little room for resistance, or, for that matter, for a dialectical notion of ideology.

The work of the Frankfurt School, especially Marcuse's (1955) analysis of how ideology becomes sedimented as second nature in the structure of needs represents a much more productive starting point for investigating the link between ideology and its unconscious grounding. Marcuse claims that domination is rooted historically not only in the socioeconomic conditions of society, but also in the sedimented history or structure of needs that constitute each person's disposition and personality. For Marcuse, ideology as repression is a historical construct rooted in the reified relations of everyday life, relations characterized by "the submission of social reality to forms of calculability and control" (Feenberg, 1981, pp. 62–63). Lukacs (1968) points to the social character of repressive ideology in his notion of reification, in which concrete relations between human beings are made to appear as objectified relations between things. Adorno (1967–1968) and Marcuse (1955) capture the subjective dynamic of reification in the concept of second nature. For them ideology as reification implies a mode of unconsciousness in which the historically contingent nature of social relations under capitalism has been "forgotten" and takes on the appearance of mythic permanence and unchanging reality. Ideology as second nature is history congealed into habit, rooted in the very structure of needs. Thus, ideology not only shapes consciousness but also reaches into the depths of personality and reinforces through the patterns and routines of everyday life needs that limit "the free self activity of social individuals and . . . their qualitatively many sided system of needs" (Heller, 1974, p. 104).

Unlike Althusser (1971) and Bourdieu (1977), who cast the connection between ideology and the unconscious in modes of ironclad domination from which there appears no escape, Marcuse (1955) and Heller (1974) treat the linkage dialectically and posit its emancipatory as well as dominating possibilities. For instance, both theorists argue that since needs are historically conditioned they can be changed. Moreover, the unconscious grounding of ideology is rooted not only in needs that are repressive but also in needs that are emancipatory in nature, i.e., needs based on meaningful social relations, community, freedom, creative work, and a fully developed aesthetic sensibility. This emphasis on the contradictory nature of needs reveals the tensions within the personality structure as well as the corresponding tensions in the larger society. Inherent in these contradictory tensions is the possibility of the full and many-sided development of "radical" needs and the elimination of the conditions that repress them. Thus, ideology as located in the unconscious is both a moment of self-creation and a force for domination.

A number of important questions emerge from this analysis, two of which will be explored below. First, what elements of ideology critique can be developed from the analysis provided by the Frankfurt School theorists and Heller? Second, what is the relevance of this type of ideology critique for a theory of schooling?

The critique of ideology as grounded in the unconscious provides the basis for an analysis of those aspects of everyday life that structure human relations in order to reveal their historical genesis and the interests they embody. What appears as "natural" must be demystified and revealed as a historical production both in its content, with its unrealized claims or distorting messages, and in the elements that structure its form. Ideology critique becomes historical in a double sense: on the one hand, it reaches into the history of social relations and reveals the truth or falsity of the underlying logic that structures such relations; on the other hand, it probes into the sedimented history of the personality and attempts to illuminate the sources and influences at work in the very tissue of the need and personality structure. In addition, it points to the importance of identifying, analyzing, and transforming those social practices that sustain the gap between economic and cultural wealth and the reality of human impoverishment. Furthermore, ideology critique within this perspective suggests the importance of educating people to recognize the interest structure that limits human freedom, while simultaneously calling for the abolition of those social practices that are its material embodiment. Heller (1974) is quite correct in arguing that for radical needs to be developed, individuals and groups have to nurture an ongoing self-critical awareness of their existence while at the same time developing qualitatively different social relations to sustain them.

What is crucial to recognize is the role that needs play in structuring our behavior, whether it be in the interest of social and cultural reproduction or in the interest of self-determination. If we are to take human agency seriously, we must acknowledge the degree to which historical and objective societal forces leave their ideological imprint upon the psyche itself. To do so is to set the groundwork for a critical encounter between oneself and the dominant society and to acknowledge what this society has made of us and what it is we no longer want to be. Finally, ideology critique as it is applied to the unconscious grounding of human behavior becomes meaningful only if it is ultimately explored in relation to consciousness and the possibility of a critical monitoring of the relationship between consciousness and the structures and ideologies that make up the dominant society.

The implications of this form of ideology critique for educational theory and practice center primarily around the development of a depth psychology that can unravel the way in which historically specific experiences and traditions get produced, reproduced, and resisted at the level of daily school life. This approach points to two major concerns. First, it points to the need to identify the tacit messages embodied in the day-to-day routines that structure all aspects of the school experience and to uncover the emancipatory or repressive interests they serve. It also suggests developing a mode of critique that comprehends the forces at work that mediate between the structural relations of schooling and their lived effects. Students bring different histories with them to school; these histories are embedded in class-, gender-, and race-specific interests that shape their needs and behavior, often in ways they do not understand and often in ways that work against their own interests. To work with working-class students, for instance, under the purported impetus of a radical pedagogy would mean not only changing their consciousness, but simultaneously developing social relations that sustain and are compatible with the radical needs in which such a consciousness would have to be grounded in order to be meaningful. A case in point would be developing a pedagogy that made working-class sexism an object of analysis and change. It would be essential that such a pedagogy not only interrogate the language, ideas, and relations that are informed by the logic of sexism, but that it be developed within classroom social relations based on nonsexist principles and concerns. Second, this approach to radical pedagogy points to the need for an understanding by teachers of the relation between cultural capital and ideology as a basis for confirming the experiences that students bring with them to the school. Students must first view their own ideologies and cultural capital as meaningful before they can critically probe them. The point here may be obvious. Students cannot learn about ideology simply by being taught how meanings get socially constructed in the media, and other aspects of daily life. Working-class students also have to understand how they participate in ideology through their own experiences and needs. It is their own experiences and needs that have to be made problematic to provide the basis for exploring the interface between their own lives and the constraints and possibilities of the wider society. Thus, a radical pedagogy must take seriously the task of providing the conditions for changing subjectivity as it is constituted in the individual's needs, drives, passions, and intelligence as well as changing the political, economic, and social foundation of the wider society.

In short, an essential aspect of radical pedagogy centers around the need for students to interrogate critically their inner histories and experiences. It is crucial for them to be able to understand how their own experiences are reinforced, contradicted and suppressed as a result of the ideologies mediated in the material and intellectual practices that characterize daily classroom life. Clearly, this form of analysis is not meant to reduce ideology and its effects to the sphere of the unconscious; rather it is to argue for its importance as a major component of educational theory and radical praxis. For it is in the dialectical relations between consciousness and unconsciousness on the one hand and experience and objective reality on the other that the basis for critical thought and action has to be grounded and developed. The prevailing system of needs in capitalist society, or any repressive society, must be understood in terms of its historical genesis and the interests it embodies and serves. For radical educators, this is the first step in breaking with the logic and institutions of domination. This must be followed by a radicalization of consciousness and the reconstruction of social relations that materially reinforce the logic of emancipatory interests.

Ideology and Common Sense

One of the major contributions of Marx was his insight that consciousness has to be explained as part of the historical mode of one's existence. That is, thought and its production cannot be separated from one's world; more specifically, forms of consciousness must be recognized as forms of life that are social and historical in nature. At the same time Marx (1969b) was equally insistent that while consciousness is an essential component of any activity, a critical analysis of society has to look beyond the level of lived beliefs and examine the social relations in which these beliefs are embedded. For Marx (1969a), Gramsci (1971), and other Western Marxists, ideology was not exhausted through its representations in the unconscious. While the latter is an important ideological sphere it is not the only one. To reduce ideology exclusively to the realm of the unconscious is to leave human agents without the benefit of critical or any other consciousness. Gramsci (1971), in particular, provides insight into the location and effects of ideology in the sphere of common sense he called contradictory consciousness. He begins with the important assumption that human consciousness cannot be equated with, or exhausted in, the logic of domination. On the contrary, he views consciousness as a complex combination of good and bad sense, a contradictory realm of ideas and behavior in which elements of accommodation and resistance exist in an unsteady state of tension. More specifically, common sense in the Gramscian view points to a mode of subjectivity characterized by forms of discursive consciousness imbued with authentic insights into social reality as well as distorting beliefs that serve to mystify and legitimate that reality. In addition, common sense effects and manifests itself in nondiscursive behavior marked by the same combination of accommodation and resistance. However, both discursive and nondiscursive common sense function without the benefit of critical interrogation. It is the grounding of common sense in an uncritical mode of mediation, a mode of mediation which is unconscious of its relation to the larger social totality, that is its singular characteristic.

Common sense represents a limited mode of self-consciousness, one that is contradictory in nature and ill-equipped to grasp either the force that constitutes it or its effects on the social totality. However, Gramsci's notion of common sense must be distinguished from views of ideology that exist solely in the unconscious or from notions of false consciousness. Common sense represents a realm of consciousness informed by a complex of contrasting subjectivities. Disorder rather than harmony characterizes common sense; it contains a dialectical interplay of hegemonic and insightful beliefs and practices. While agency does not disappear in this account, it lacks the self-consciousness needed to resolve its contradictions and tensions or extend its partial insights into a coherent critical perspective through which it can engage its own principles. Gramsci (1971) points to this issue in his comment on contradictory consciousness:

> The active man-in-the-mass has a practical activity, but has no clear theoretical consciousness of his practical activity, which nonetheless involves understanding the world in so far as it transforms it. His theoretical consciousness can indeed be historically in opposition to his activity. One might almost say that he has two theoretical consciousnesses (or one contradictory consciousness): one which is implicit in his activity and which in reality unites him with all his fellow workers in practical transformation of the real world; and one, superficially explicit or verbal which he has inherited from the past and uncritically absorbed. (p. 333)

Underlying Gramsci's discussion of the relationship between ideology and common sense are a number of assumptions and implications that have relevance for educational theory and practice. First, Gramsci rescues the human subject by positing a notion of ideology that does not obliterate the mediating faculties of ordinary people. At the same time he recognizes that while domination pre-exists, its effects and outcomes are open-ended. Thus, contradictory consciousness does not point *primarily* to domination or confusion, but to a sphere of contradictions and tensions that is pregnant with possibilities for radical change. In my view, ideology becomes a critical construct to the degree to which it reveals the truths as well as the concealing function of common sense as outlined by Gramsci. Second, Gramsci's notion of ideology and common sense addresses an important dialectical relation between discourse and practical activity. In this view, ideology exists not only on the level of speech and language, but also as lived experience, as practical conduct in everyday life. What Gramsci argues for is a mode of analysis that uncovers the contradictory moments in discourse so that they not only can be used to reveal their own underlying interests but also can be restructured into a form of critical consciousness that can "make coherent the problems raised by the masses in their practical activity" (Karabel, 1976, p. 169). In this way, common sense becomes subjected to a critical interrogation via its own thought processes and practical activity as these constitute and reproduce the conduct of everyday life. In pedagogical terms, this suggests taking the typifications of educational discourse and their attendant social relations and stripping them of their objective or so-called natural character. Instead of being treated as a given, they must be viewed within historical and social relations that are produced and socially constructed. This leads to a final insight about common sense, one that is drawn directly from the work of such Frankfurt School members as Adorno, Horkheimer, and Marcuse.

For the Frankfurt School, the notion of common sense could only be understood by analyzing its dialectical relation to the wider social totality. Inherent in the form and substance of common sense was the logic of commodity structure: that is, common sense was constituted by taken-for-granted categories and practical activity divorced from the agents and conditions that produced them. Social practices and categories appeared objectified, as unquestioned givens cut off from the socio-historical processes and interests through which they had evolved. Within this perspective, ideology critique functioned both to unmask the messages revealed in common sense and to interrogate the truth claims and the societal functions of the interests that structure common sense. There is an important dimension of ideology critique in this formulation, one that is indispensable for a radical pedagogy. Radical practice begins, in this case, with a break from the positivist emphasis on immediacy, an immediacy which, as Schmidt (1981) comments, "daily deludes individuals with a nature-like invariance of their life relationships" (p. 104). Ideology critique assumes an added dimension in this case. In other words, it posits the need for a historical consciousness, one that begins with an analysis of the reifications of daily life and takes the rigidified, congealed relations that reduce teachers and students to "bearers" of history as the basis for probing into history and discovering the conditions that generated such conditions in the first place. Historical consciousness as a moment of ideology critique and radical pedagogy, within this perspective, functions "so as to perceive the past in a way that [makes] the present visible as a revolutionary moment" (Buck-Morss, 1981, p. 61). This leads us to the relationship between ideology and reflective consciousness, the most potentially radical of the three spheres in which ideology is located.

Ideology and Critical Consciousness

The notion that ideology has as one of its important features a critical "moment" that situates it in the realm of critical thinking presents a direct challenge to those theories of ideology which either reduce ideology to false consciousness or disparage it by contrasting it to what is termed science. I want to argue here that ideology can act as a critical moment in the production of meaning by illuminating the rules, assumptions, and interests that structure not only the thinking process but also the material such processes take as an object of analysis. The ideological dimension that underlies all critical reflection is that it lays bare the historically and socially sedimented values at work in the construction of knowledge, social relations, and material practices. In other words, it grounds the production of knowledge, including science, in a normative framework linked to specific interests. As Aronowitz (1980) makes clear, those who argue for the science/ideology division reproduce the very notion of ideology they critique, i.e., ideology as mystification. He writes, "The concept of the science/ideology antinomy is itself ideological because it fails to comprehend that all knowledge is a product of social relations" (p. 97).

To locate a theory of ideology in the sphere of critical consciousness highlights the normative basis of all knowledge and points to the active nature of human agents in its construction. The underlying grammar of ideology finds its highest expression in the ability of human beings to think dialectically. To view both the object of analysis and the processes involved in such analysis as part of a complex mode of producing meaning represents not simply the active side of ideology but its most critical dimension. Thus, ideology implies a process whereby meaning is produced, represented, and consumed. The critical aspect of that process represents a reflexive understanding of the interests embodied in the process itself and how these interests might be transformed, challenged, or sustained so as to promote rather than repress the dynamics of critical thought and action. Ideology in this sense suggests that all aspects of everyday life that have a semiotic value are open to reflection and critique just as it points to the need for a critical attentiveness to all aspects of self-expression.

Through ideology critique, critical thinking is made more than an interpretative tool; it is situated within a radical notion of interest and social transformation. Critical analysis, in this case, becomes the distinct but important precondition for radical praxis, with a twofold purpose. On the one hand, it follows Adorno's (1973) insistence that the task of ideology critique is the explosion of reification, a breaking through of mystifications and a recognition of how certain forms of ideology serve the logic of domination. This means not only analyzing the hidden ideological elements in any object of analysis, whether it be a school curriculum or a set of social relations, and revealing their social function; it also means releasing their unintentional truths, the suppressed utopian elements contained in what they include as well as what they leave out. This involves breaking apart or deconstructing the ideas and structuring principles in a cultural artifact and then placing them in a different framework that allows one to see the limits of specific ideas and formal properties, while simultaneously discovering the new and vital elements in them that could be appropriated for radical purposes. For instance, in looking at most literacy models, a radical educator would have to first identify the ideology that informs their content and methodology. It might then be possible to appropriate certain fundamental aspects of the models but within a theoretical framework in which literacy is treated not merely as a technique but as a constitutive process of constructing meaning and critically interrogating the forces that shape one's lived experiences. This points to the second aspect of ideology critique that I alluded to earlier, that such a critique must be informed by a spirit of relentless negativity, one that promotes the critical independence of the subject as well as the restructuring and transformation of an oppressive social reality. Ideology critique as a form of critical consciousness opposes the knowledge of technocratic rationality, and implies instead a dialectical knowledge that illuminates contradictions and informs the critical judgments needed for individual and social action.

The link between ideology and the notion of truth is not to be found in the peddling of prescriptions or in a deluge of endless recipes; instead, it is located in what Benjamin (1969) has called the distance between the interpreter and the material, on the one hand, and the gap between the present and the possibility of a radically different future on the other. The value of viewing ideology as a complex process in the production and critique of meaning becomes more concrete through an examination of how meaning functions as a constitutive force in the structuring and mediation of representations in school artifacts and in classroom social relations.

Ideology, Representations, and Classroom Material Practices

In order to grasp fully the relationship between agency and structure as part of a radical pedagogy, a theory of ideology must be capable of comprehending the way in which meaning is constructed and materialized within "texts," that is, within cultural forms such as films, books, curriculum packages, fashion styles, and so on. Thus, ideology critique is not limited to the hidden or visible processes in the realm of subjectivity and behavior but is extended to the "study of observable material processes—the manipulation of signs in specific ways and specific contexts" (Bennett, 1981, p. 28). The work of Volosinov (1973), Eco (1976), Coward and Ellis (1977), and Kress and Hodge (1979) has been invaluable in this regard in emphasizing the relative autonomy of the representations that construct the limits and parameters within which meaning is produced, negotiated, and received by individuals. Of course, in this structuralist approach, "signs" constitute consciousness and the notion that signs could be both the medium and the product of consciousness is denied. In other words, ideology as representations of expressed ways of thought, experience, and feeling is not given very much theoretical weight. This is clearly captured in Volosinov's claim that "Individual consciousness is not the architect of the ideological superstructure, but only a tenant lodging in the edifice of ideological signs" (Volosinov, 1973, p. 6). But while it is true that representations and signs address (interpolate) and situate individuals, the human beings they address are more than just a reflex of the texts in question. Human agents always mediate the representations and material practices that constitute their lived experiences through their own histories and their class- and gender-related subjectivities. This is true within the parameters defined by the school, the family, the workplace, or any other social site. What is needed to offset the one-sided theory of ideology provided by many structuralists is a more fully developed theory of mediation and reception (Barrett, 1981). Such an approach would link agency and structure in a theory of ideology so as to treat dialectically the roles of the individual and group as producers of meaning within already existing fields of representations and practices. As Johnson (1979b) suggests, failure to address this question means that we run the risk of getting trapped in modes of structuralist analysis that overlook "the moment of self creation, of the affirmation of belief, or the giving of consent" (p. 234).

The starting point for developing a more dialectical theory of ideology and schooling rests with the acknowledgment that individuals and social classes are both the medium and the outcome of ideological discourses and practices. Meaning is located both in the various dimensions of subjectivity and behavior and in "texts" and classroom practices that structure, limit, and enable human action. The theory of ideological processes that follows draws on the concepts of reproduction, production, and reconstruction, all of which will be delineated within the context of the analysis presented below.

Reproduction as used below refers to texts and social practices whose messages, inscribed within specific historical settings and social contexts, function primarily to legitimate the interests of the dominant social order. I want to argue that these can be characterized as texts and social practices *about* pedagogy (Lundgren, 1983) and refer primarily to categories of meaning constructed so as to legitimize and reproduce interests expressed in dominant ideologies. The acts of conception, and construction, and production that characterize texts *about* pedagogy usually have little to do with the contexts in which such texts are applied, and the principles that structure them almost never lend themselves to methods of inquiry that encourage dialogue or debate. Such texts and practices objectively represent the selection, fixation, and legitimation of dominant traditions. For instance, both the form and the content of such texts tend to treat teachers and students as reified elements in the pedagogical process. Even in the more sophisticated versions of such texts such as the Humanities units Buswell (1980) examined, the logic of powerlessness prevailed, albeit in recycled forms. She writes:

> The texts directed pupils to books and information kept elsewhere which was part of the aim of teaching them to "learn." But a "particular" answer was still required and finding it became a complicated orienteering exercise conducted through the printed word whereby acquiring any content was made more difficult. The emphasis in all the units was on following the precise instructions and replicating what someone else had produced, very little creativity was required. (pp. 302–303)

This reified view of knowledge is a classic example of Freire's (1973) "banking model" of schooling and is found not only in the structuring principles that inform such texts but also in their content as well. Brown (1981) in an extensive examination of recent children's history books attempted to find texts that did the following: (a) recognize human agency, (b) relate past experiences to the present so as to stimulate intellectual curiosity, (c) link material conditions to social relations, (d) present history as more than "dressed up" figures and facts, and, finally, (e) treat history as open-ended and subject to interpretation. What he actually found were books that contained an anti-urban bias, promoted their content in "commercial studio aesthetics," celebrated technology outside the human relations in which it functioned, and collapsed history into great moments, while simultaneously using a language that suppressed conflict.

There is a growing amount of research that points to the increased use of prepackaged curriculum materials that accentuate delivering instruction while at the same time removing conception and critique from the pedagogical act. Apple (1982) argues that such curriculum materials represent a new form of control over both teachers and students, one that indicates a process of deskilling and the emergence of more powerful forms of rationality that embody changing modes of control within the nature of capitalist relations of production. Control in this case is removed from face-to-face contact and is now situated in the impersonal processes and logic of highly rationalized managerial relations. The effects of these prepackaged materials on schooling represent a new dimension in the reproduction of texts and material practices *about* pedagogy. This is evident in Apple's (1982) claim that

Skills that teachers used to need, that were deemed essential to the craft of working with children—such as curriculum deliberation and planning, designing teaching and curricular strategies for specific groups and individuals based on intimate knowledge of these people—are no longer as necessary. With the large-scale influx of prepackaged material, planning is separated from execution. The planning is done at the level of production of both the rules for use of the material and the material itself. The execution is carried out by the teacher. In the process, what were previously considered valuable skills slowly atrophy because they are less often required. (p. 146)

Each of these examples provides a mode of ideology critique that reveals how reproductive ideologies work. Buswell illustrates how specific principles structure the text and classroom social relations so as to legitimate modes of learning that promote passivity and rule following rather than critical engagement on the part of teachers and students. Brown (1981) both points to the structural silences in a text, those ideas and values that are left out and thus rendered illegitimate, and at the same time analyzes the social function of the existing text. Apple, on the other hand, shows how the principles that structure the production and use of curriculum materials are rooted in specific interests that reinforce a division of labor that separates conception from execution at the level of teaching itself. In all of these cases texts *about* pedagogy function so as to suppress human agency while at the same time legitimating the power and control of the dominant classes. However, what is missing from these analyses and what is needed to complement them is a historical critique that moves beyond simply registering the ideologies embedded in the form and content of curriculum materials and practices. It is imperative to link such ideological representations to historically constituted social relations as they appear in schools. For example, Barrett (1980) illuminates this issue when she argues that female models are more persuasive to male customers than male models in similar roles are to female customers because the female stereotype bears the weight of social relations that have a long history. Clearly, the only way to understand such stereotypes is to situate them in the social relations that have constituted them historically.

But as important as this mode of ideology critique is, it has failed to develop a *theory of production*. That is, it has failed to analyze how reproductive ideologies as they exist in texts and social practices get mediated. It is particularly important to acknowledge that texts are always mediated in some fashion by human subjects. Meanings are always produced by human agents when they confront and engage cultural forms such as curriculum texts, films, and so forth. As Arnot and Whitty (1982) and Jameson (1979) have stressed, educational meanings and practices are "read" by teachers and students through interpretative and selective principles that bear the weight of pre-existing situations and constituted ideologies. The relation between inscribed messages and lived effects is a tenuous one indeed and cannot be viewed through a reductionist logic that collapses one into the other. The way in which a teacher or student engages a text or specific social relation is, in fact, a "function of his or her place in society" (Barrett, 1980, p. 87). This form of ideology critique must locate the various ideological discourses and multiple subjectivities that construct and constitute meaning for students from different class-, gender-, and race-specific backgrounds (Therborn, 1981). This demands being attentive to the cultural capital that characterizes different student experiences and to the ways in which students actually produce meanings via their historical, positional, family, and class backgrounds. By penetrating these ideologies and cultural forms it becomes possible for teachers to unravel the mediations that give meaning to school experience and to understand how they might function in the interest of accommodation, resistance, or active change.

This leads to my final point regarding the relations among ideology, texts, and social practices. The principle of *reconstruction* shifts the theoretical terrain from the issues of reproduction and mediation to a concern for critical appropriation and transformation. This suggests a mode of ideology critique in which the interests that underlie texts, representations, and social practices would be not only identified but also deconstructed and refashioned with the aim of developing social relations and modes of knowledge that serve radical needs. The task of reconstruction is not simply to analyze knowledge and social relations for either their dominating ideologies or their subversive unintentional truths, but to appropriate their material elements, skills, and critical knowledge in order to restructure them as part of the production of new ideologies and collective experiences. Thus, knowledge production is linked to transformative activities and is situated within a problematic that takes as its ultimate aim the development of forms of radical praxis both within and outside of schools. Brenkman (1979) captures a critical aspect of this issue in his call for the development of a Marxist cultural hermeneutics:

> Its project is twofold. Interpretations which read cultural texts in relation to their historical situations and effects must conserve or subvert meanings according to their validity not for an already constituted tradition but for a community in process. And, secondly, interpretation must be connected to the project of reclaiming language practices that unfold the horizon of this community. Such a hermeneutics becomes valid only as it serves to construct oppositional cultural experiences, an oppositional public sphere. It has a political task. The dominant tendency of our cultural institutions and

practices—from the organization of the learning process in the schools and the academic modes of knowledge which support them to the mass mediated forms of communication which pre-empt speaking itself—is to undermine the very possibility for human beings to interpret the discourses that found their identities, shape their interactions and regulate their activities. Only a process of interpretation which counters this tendency, actively and practically, can preserve the possibilities of a historical consciousness founded on collective experience. (p. 109)

A reconstructive perspective would promote the conditions necessary for the development of what Lundgren (1983) calls texts *for* pedagogy. These would be curriculum materials and school practices appropriated and/or produced by the teachers and educators who use them. Such texts refer to both a process and a product. As a process, such texts embody and demonstrate principles that link conception and execution while simultaneously promoting a critical attentiveness to forms of knowledge and social practices informed by principles that promote enlightenment and understanding. Such texts would be attentive to procedures that locate knowledge in specific historical contexts and would attempt to uncover the human interests in which it is grounded. As products, such texts become the medium for a critical pedagogy aimed at providing students with the knowledge, skills, and critical sensibility they need to be able to think dialectically. That is, students need to be able to grasp the ways in which the concrete world opposes the possibilities inherent in its own conditions; they need to be able to reach into history so as to transform historical into critical thought; and finally, they need to be able to penetrate critically the categories of common sense and begin to move beyond a world constituted through such categories. In short, whereas texts *about* pedagogy, along with the social relations engendered by them, are rooted in the logic of authoritarianism and control, texts *for* pedagogy contain interests that may promote modes of schooling based on the critical dimensions of an emancipatory ideology.

Ideology is a crucial construct for understanding how meaning is produced, transformed, and consumed by individuals and social groups. As a tool of critical analysis, it digs beneath the phenomenal forms of classroom knowledge and social practices and helps to locate the structuring principles and ideas that mediate between the dominant society and the everyday experiences of teachers and students. As a political construct, it makes meaning problematic and poses the question as to why human beings have unequal access to the intellectual and material resources that constitute the conditions for the production, consumption, and distribution of meaning. Similarly, it raises the question of why certain ideologies come to prevail at certain times and whose interests they serve. Hence, ideology "speaks" to the notion of power by accentuating the complex ways in which relations of meaning are produced and fought over.

Note

This essay is abstracted from Henry Giroux, *Theory and Resistance in Education: A Pedagogy for the Opposition* (South Hadley, Mass.: Bergin & Garvey, 1983).

References

Adorno, T. The actuality of philosophy. *Telos*, 1967, *31*, 120–133.

Adorno, T. Sociology and psychology, I & II. *New Left Review*, 1967–1968, Nos. 46 & 47, 67–68; 79–96.

Adorno, T. *Negative dialectics*. New York: The Seabury Press, 1973.

Apple, M. *Education and power*. Boston: Routledge and Kegan Paul, 1982.

Althusser, L. *For Marx*. New York: Vintage Books, 1969.

Althusser, L. Ideology and the ideological state apparatuses. In L. Althusser (Ed.), *Lenin and philosophy and other essays*. New York: Monthly Review Press, 1971.

Arnot, M., & Whitty, G. From reproduction to transformation: Recent radical perspectives on the curriculum from the USA. *British Journal of Sociology of Education*, 1982, *3*, 93–103.

Aronowitz, S. Science and ideology. *Current Perspectives in Social Theory*, 1980, *1*, 75–101.

Aronowitz, S. *Crisis in historical materialism: Class politics and culture in Marxist theory*. New York: J. F. Bergin Publishers, 1981.

Barrett, M. *Women's oppression today*. London: Verso Press, 1980.

Barrett, M. Materialist aesthetics. *New Left Review*, 1981, No. 126, 86–93.

Benjamin, W. *Illuminations*. New York: Schocken Books, 1969.

Bennett, T. *Popular culture: History and theory*. London: Open University Press, 1981.

Bourdieu, P. *Outline of theory and practice*. Cambridge: Cambridge University Press, 1977.

Bourdieu, P., & Passeron, J. C. *Reproduction in education, society, and culture*. London and Beverly Hills: Sage Publications, 1977.

Brenkman, J. Mass media: From collective experience to the culture of privatization. *Social Text*, 1979, *1*, 94–109.

Brown, J. Into the minds of babes: A journey through recent children's books. *Radical History*, 1981, *25*, 127–145.

Buck-Morss, S. Walter Benjamin—Revolutionary writer, I. *New Left Review*, 1981, No. 128, 50–75.

Buswell, C. Pedagogic change and social change. *British Journal of Sociology of Education*, 1980, *1*, 3, 293–306.

Coward, R., & Ellis, J. *Language and materialism*. London: Routledge and Kegan Paul, 1977.

Eco, U. *A theory of semiotics*. Bloomington, Indiana: Indiana University Press, 1976.

Feenberg, A. *Lukacs, Marx and the sources of critical theory*. Totowa, N.J.: Rowman and Littlefield, 1981.

Foucault, M. *Power/knowledge: Selected interviews and other writings* (C. Gordon, Ed.). New York: Pantheon Books, 1980.

Freire, P. *Pedagogy of the oppressed*. New York: The Seabury Press, 1973.

Giddens, A. *Central problems in social theory*. Berkeley: University of California Press, 1979.

Giroux, H. *Ideology, culture and the process of schooling*. Philadelphia: Temple University Press, 1981.

Gouldner, A. *The dialectic of ideology and technology: The origins, grammar, and future of ideology*. New York: The Seabury Press, 1976.

Gramsci, A. [*Selections from prison notebooks*] (Q. Hoare & G. Smith, Eds. and trans.). New York: International Publishers, 1971.

Habermas, J. *Legitimation crisis*. Boston: Beacon Press, 1975.

Heller, A. *The theory of need in Marx*. London: Allison and Busby, 1974.

Jameson, F. Reification and utopia in mass culture. *Social Text*, 1979, *1*, 130–148.

Johnson, R. Histories of culture/theories of ideology: Notes on an impasse. In M. Barrett et al. (Eds.), *Ideology and cultural production*. New York: St. Martin's Press, 1979. (a)

Johnson, R. Three problematics: Elements of a theory of working class culture. In J. Clarke et al. (Eds.), *Studies in history and theory*. London: Hutchinson, 1979. (b)

Karabel, J. Revolutionary contradictions: Antonio Gramsci and the problem of intellectuals. *Politics and Society*, 1976, *6*, 123–172.

Kress, G., & Hodge, R. *Language as ideology*. London: Routledge and Kegan Paul, 1979.

Larrain, J. *The concept of ideology*. London: Hutchinson, 1979.

Lenin, V. I. *What is to be done?* New York: International Publishers, 1971.

Lukacs, G. *History and class consciousness*. Cambridge, Mass.: M.I.T. Press, 1968.

Lundgren, U. *Between the scholared and the school*. Geelong, Australia: Deakin University Press, 1983.

Marcuse, H. *Eros and civilization*. Boston: Beacon Press, 1955.

Marcuse, H. *One dimensional man*. Boston: Beacon Press, 1964.

Marx, K. *The eighteenth Brumaire of Louis Bonaparte*. New York: International Publishers, 1969. (a)

Marx, K. *Preface to the critique of political economy*. New York: International Publishers, 1969. (b)

Marx, K. *The German ideology*. New York: International Publishers, 1972.

Schmidt, A. [*History and structure*] (J. Herf, trans.). Cambridge, Mass: M.I.T. Press, 1981.

Sumner, C. *Reading ideologies*. London: Academic Press, 1979.

Therborn, G. *The ideology of power and the power of ideology*. London: New Left Books, 1981.

Thompson, E. P. *The making of the English working class.* New York: Vintage Press, 1966.
Volosinov, V. V. *Marxism and the philosophy of language.* New York: Seminar Press, 1973.
Williams, R. *Marxism and literature.* London: Oxford University Press, 1977.

4 Authority, Intellectuals, and the Politics of Practical Learning

WE LIVE AT A TIME WHEN DEMOCRACY is in retreat. Nowhere is this more obvious than in the current debate surrounding the relationship between schooling and authority. As is the case with most public issues in the age of Reagan, the new conservatives have seized the initiative and argued that the current crisis in public education is due to the loss of authority. In this discourse, the call for a reconstituted authority along conservative lines is coupled with the charge that the crisis in schooling is in part due to a crisis in the wider culture, which is presented as a "spiritual-moral" crisis. The problem is clearly articulated by Diane Ravitch, who argues that this pervasive "loss of authority" stems from confused ideas, irresolute standards, and cultural relativism.[1] As a form of legitimation, this view of authority appeals to an established cultural tradition, whose practices and values appear beyond criticism. Authority, in this case, represents an idealized version of the American Dream reminiscent of nineteenth-century dominant culture in which the tradition becomes synonymous with hard work, industrial discipline, and cheerful obedience. It is a short leap between this view of the past and the new conservative vision of schools as crucibles in which to forge industrial soldiers fueled by the imperatives of excellence, competition, and down-home character. In effect, for the new conservatives, learning approximates a practice mediated by strong teacher authority and a student willingness to learn the basics, adjust to the imperatives of the social and economic order, and exhibit what Edward A. Wynne calls the traditional moral aims of "promptness, truthfulness, courtesy, and obedience."[2]

What is most striking about the new conservative discourse on schooling is its refusal to link the issue of authority to the rhetoric of freedom and democracy. In other words, what is missing from this perspective as well as from more critical perspectives is any attempt to reinvent a view of self-constituted authority that expresses a democratic conception of collective life, one that is embodied in an ethic of solidarity, social transformation, and an imaginative vision of citizenship.[3] I believe that the established view of authority tells us very little about what is wrong with schools. But it does point to the absolute necessity for critical educators to fashion an alternative and emancipatory view of authority as a central element in a critical theory of schooling. Agnes Heller states the problem well when she argues that "it is not the rejection of all authorities that is at issue here, but the quality of authority and the procedure in which authority is established, observed and tested."[4] Heller's remarks suggest a dual problem that critical educators will have to face. First, they will need a reconstructed language of critique in order to challenge the current conservative offensive in education. Second, they will need to construct a language of possibility that provides the theoretical scaffolding for a politics of practical learning. In both cases, the starting point for such a challenge centers around the imperative to develop a dialectical view of authority and its relationship to public education. Such a view of authority must both serve as a referent for critique and provide a programmatic vision for pedagogical and social change.

Nyberg and Farber point to the importance of making the concept of authority a central concern for educators by suggesting that "this question of how one shall stand in relation to authority is the foundation of educated citizenship: Its importance cannot be overemphasized."[5] I want to develop this position by arguing that if all educators have either an implicit or an explicit vision of who people should be and how they should act within the context of a human community, then the basis of authority through which they structure classroom life is ultimately rooted in questions of ethics and power. Central to my concern is developing a view of authority that defines schools as part of an ongoing movement and struggle for democracy, and teachers as intellectuals who both introduce students to and legitimate a particular way of life. In both instances, I want to fashion a view of authority that legitimates schools as democratic, counterpublic spheres and teachers as transformative intellectuals who work toward a realization regarding their views of community, social justice, empowerment, and transformation. In short, I want to broaden the definition of authority to include educational practices that link democracy, teaching, and practical learning. The substantive nature of this task takes as its starting point the ethical intent of initiating students into a discourse and a set of pedagogical practices that advances the role of democracy within the schools while simultaneously addressing those instances of suffering and inequality that structure the daily lives of millions of people both in the United States and in other parts of the world.

In developing my argument, I will focus on four considerations. First, I will review briefly some major traditional views surrounding the relationship between authority and schooling. This will be followed by a rationale for giving the concept of authority a central role in educational theory and practice. Here I will argue for an emancipatory view of authority, one that provides the ontological grounding for a critical form of teacher work and practice. Next I will present the broad theoretical outlines of a transformative pedagogy that is consistent with an emancipatory view of authority; finally, I will argue that the notion of authority has to be considered within a wider set of economic, political, and social practices in order for teachers to step out of their academic boundaries and enter into alliances with other progressive groups. It is crucial that this emancipatory view of authority become a part of an ongoing social movement whose purpose is to analyze and sustain the struggle for critical forms of education and democracy.

The Discourses of Authority and Schooling

The concept of authority can best be understood as a historical construction shaped by diverse traditions that contain their own values and views of the world. In other words, the concept of authority like any other social category of importance has no universal meaning just waiting to be discovered. As a subject of intense battles and conflicts among competing theoretical perspectives, its meaning has often shifted depending on the theoretical context in which it has been employed. Given these shifting meanings and associations, it becomes necessary in any attempt to redefine the centrality of authority for a critical pedagogy to interrogate the way in which the concept has been treated by preceding ideological traditions. Ideally, such an analysis should take into account the status of the truth claims that particular views of authority reflect as well as the institutional mechanisms that legitimate and sustain their particular version of reality. Only then does it become possible to analyze authority within such diverse ideological traditions for the purpose of revealing both the interests they embody and the cluster of power relations they support. While it is impossible within this article to provide a detailed analysis of the various ways in which authority has been developed within competing educational traditions, I want to highlight some of the more important theoretical considerations inherent in conservative, liberal, and radical analyses. For it is against this general set of criticisms that an argument for the primacy of authority in educational discourse can be situated.

In the new conservative discourse, authority is given a positive meaning and is often related to issues that resonate with popular experience. As an ideal that often embodies reactionary interests, this position legitimates a view of culture, pedagogy, and politics that focuses on traditional values and norms. Authority in this view presents a rich mix of resonant themes in which the notions of family, nation, duty, self-reliance, and standards often add up to a warmed-over dish of Parsonian consensus and cultural reproduction. In educational terms, school knowledge is reduced to an unproblematic selection from the dominant traditions of "Western" culture. Rather than viewing culture as a terrain of competing knowledge and practice, conservatives frame "culture" within the axis of historical certainty and present it as a storehouse of treasured goods constituted as canon and ready to be passed "down" to deserving students.[6] Not surprisingly, pedagogy in this instance is often reduced to the process of transmitting a given body of knowledge with student learning squarely situated in "mastering" the "basics" and appropriate standards of behavior.

If the new conservatives view authority as a positive and inherently traditional set of values and practices, leftist educators almost without exception have taken the opposite position. In this view, authority is frequently associated with an unprincipled authoritarianism while freedom is something that is defined as an escape from authority in general. Authority within this perspective is generally seen as synonymous with the logic of domination. This position has been endlessly repeated in radical critiques in which schools are often portrayed as factories, prisons, or warehouses for the oppressed. While there is a strong element of truth in the notion that schools contribute to the reproduction of the status quo, with all of its characteristic inequalities, it is nevertheless inaccurate to argue that schools are merely agencies of domination and reproduction. Missing from this discourse is any understanding of how authority might be used in the interests of an emancipatory pedagogy. The agony of this position is that it has prevented radical educators from appropriating a view of authority that provides the basis for a programmatic discourse within schools. One consequence of this position is that the Left is bereft of a view of authority that allows for the development of a theoretical strategy through which popular forces might wage a political struggle within schools in order to accumulate power and to shape school policy in their own interests. The irony of this position is that the Left's politics of skepticism translates into an anti-utopian, overburdened discourse that undermines the possibility of any type of programmatic political action.[7]

Liberal theorists in education have provided the most dialectical view of the relationship between authority and education. This tradition is exemplified by Kenneth D. Benne, who has not only argued for a dialectical view of authority, but has also attempted to display its relevance for a critical pedagogy. Benne first defines authority as "a function of concrete human situations in which a person or group, fulfilling some purpose, project, or need, requires guidance or direction from a source outside himself or itself. . . . Any such operating relationship—a triadic relationship between subject(s), bearer(s), and field(s)—is an authority relationship."[8] He elaborates on this general definition by insisting that the basis for specific forms of authority can be respectively found in separate appeals to the logic of rules, the knowledgeability of expertise, and the ethics of democratic community. Benne then makes a strong case for grounding educational authority in the ethical practices of a community that takes democracy seriously. He simultaneously points out the strengths and weaknesses of forms of authority based on either rules or expertise, and rightly argues that the highest forms of authority are rooted in the morality of democratic community. Benne's article is important not only because it provides a working definition of authority but also because it points to ways in which the latter can be useful in developing a more humane and critical pedagogy. At the same time, it illustrates some weaknesses endemic to liberal theory that need to be overcome if the concept of authority is to be reconstructed in the interests of an emancipatory pedagogy.

First, while Benne makes an appeal to the ethics and imperatives of a democratic community, he exhibits an inadequate understanding of how power is asymmetrically distributed within and between different communities. Because of his failure to explore this issue, he is unable to illuminate how the material and ideological grounding of domination works against the notion of authentic community through forms of authority that actively produce and sustain relations of oppression and suffering. In other words, Benne posits a formal dialectical theory of authority that, in the final instance, remains removed from the lived social practices of students. As a consequence, we get no sense of how authority functions as a specific practice within schools shaped by the historical realities of social class, race, gender, and other powerful socioeconomic forces that sometimes prevent authentic forms of authority from emerging within public education. Simply put, Benne's analysis reproduces the shortcomings of liberal theory in general; that is, he unduly emphasizes the positive aspects of authority and in doing so ends up ignoring those "messy webs" of social relations that embody forms of struggle and contestation. By refusing to acknowledge relations of domination and resistance, Benne presents a view of authority that appears abstract and disconnected from the struggles that define schools in their particular historical locations and specificity. We are left with a notion of authority trapped in the reified realm of abstract formalities.

Second, Benne provides us with little understanding of how educational authority can be linked to the collective struggles of teachers both within and outside of schools. His attempt to link authority to the notion of community neither informs us as to how teachers should organize in the interests of such a community, nor provides any referents for indicating what particular kinds of community and forms of subjectivity are worth fighting for.

In the end what most conservative, radical, and liberal educational discourses manage to establish are either reactionary or incomplete approaches to developing a dialectical view of authority and schooling. Conservatives celebrate authority, linking it to popular expressions of everyday life, but in doing so they express and support reactionary and undemocratic interests. On the other hand, radical educators tend to equate authority with forms of domination or the loss of freedom and consequently fail to develop a conceptual category for constructing a programmatic language of hope and struggle. To their credit, they do manage to provide a language of critique that investigates in concrete terms how school authority promotes specific forms of oppression. Liberals, in general, provide the most dialectical view of authority but fail to apply it in a concrete way so as to interrogate the dynamics of domination and freedom as they are expressed within the asymmetrical relations of power and privilege that characterize various aspects of school life.

It is at this point that I want to move to a more programmatic discourse on authority. In doing so, I want to appropriate the most progressive elements in a theory of authority from the political traditions I have discussed above. At the same time, I want to construct a rationale and new problematic for making an emancipatory view of authority a central category in the development of a critical theory of schooling.

Authority and Schooling: A Rationale

It is important for educators to develop a dialectical view of authority for a number of reasons. First, the issue of authority serves as both the referent and the ideal for public schooling. That is, as a form of legitimation and practice necessary to the ongoing ideological and material production and renewal of society, the concept of authority provokes educators to take a critically pragmatic stance regarding the purpose and function that schooling is to play in any given society. As a form of legitimation, authority is inextricably related to a particular vision of what schools should be as part of a wider community and society. In other words, authority makes both visible and problematic the presuppositions that give meaning to the officially sanctioned discourses and values that legitimate what Foucault has called particular "material, historical conditions of possibility [along with] their governing systems of order, appropriation, and exclusion."[9]

Second, the concept of authority raises issues about the ethical and political basis of schooling. That is, it calls into serious question the role that school administrators and teachers play as intellectuals in both elaborating and implementing their particular views of rationality; in other words, such a concept defines what *school* authority means as a particular set of ideas and practice within a historically defined context. In short, the category of authority reinserts into the language of schooling the primacy of the political. It does so by highlighting the social and political function that educators serve in elaborating and enforcing a particular view of school authority.

Third, the concept of authority provides the theoretical leverage to analyze the relationship between domination and power by both raising and analyzing the difference between the shared meanings that teachers elaborate in order to justify their view of authority and the effects of their actions at the level of actualized pedagogical practice. In this case, authority provides both the referent and the critique against which to analyze the difference between the legitimating claims for a particular form of authority and the way such a claim is actually expressed in daily classroom life.

Educational theorists such as Nyberg and Farber, Tozer, and others have rightly argued that the relationship between authority and democracy needs to be made clear if schools are to play a fundamental role in advancing the discourse of freedom and critical citizenship.[10] In what follows, I want to advance and expand the logic of this argument within the parameters of the rationale I presented above, but in doing so, I am going to move from a rather general interrogation of the value of authority to a more specific and committed plea. In other words, I will argue that the concept of authority is fundamental for developing a radical theory of schooling and for contributing to what I call the education of teachers as transformative intellectuals and the development of schools as democratic public spheres.

If the concept of authority is to provide a legitimating basis for rethinking the purpose and meaning of public education and radical pedagogy, it must be rooted in a view of community life in which the moral quality of everyday existence is linked to the essence of democracy.[11] Authority in this view becomes a mediating referent for the ideal of democracy and its expression as a set of educational practices designed to empower students to be critical and active citizens. That is, the purpose of schooling now becomes fashioned around two central questions: What kind of society do educators want to live in and what kind of teachers and pedagogy can be both informed and legitimated by a view of authority that takes democracy and citizenship seriously? Such a view of authority points to a theory of democracy that includes the principles of representative democracy, workers' democracy, and civil and human rights. It is, in Benjamin Barber's terms, a view of authority rooted in "strong democracy," and is characterized by a citizenry capable of genuine public thinking, political judgment, and social action.[12] Such a view of authority endorses a concept of the citizen not as a simple bearer of abstract rights, privileges, and immunities but rather as a member of any one of a diverse number of public spheres that provide a sense of communal vision and civic courage. Sheldon Wolin is worth quoting at length on this issue:

> A political being is not to be defined as . . . an abstract, disconnected bearer of rights, privileges, and immunities, but as a person whose existence is located in a particular place and draws its sustenance from a circumscribed set of relationships: family, friends, church, neighborhood, workplace, community, town, city. These relationships are the sources from which political beings draw power—symbolic, material, and psychological—and that enable them to act together. For true political power involves not only acting so as to effect decisive changes; it also means the capacity to receive power, to be acted upon, to change, and be changed. From a democratic perspective, power is not simply force that is generated; it is experience, sensibility, wisdom, even melancholy, distilled from the diverse relations and circles we move within.[13]

The notion of authority is important, in Wolin's case, because it connects the purpose of schooling to the imperatives of a critical democracy and provides a basis from which to argue for schools as democratic public spheres. That is, schools can now be understood and constructed within a model of authority that legitimates them as places where students learn and collectively struggle for the economic, political, and social preconditions that make individual freedom and social empowerment possible. Within this emancipatory model of authority, a discourse can be fashioned in which educators can struggle against the exercise of authority often used by conservatives to link the purpose of schooling to a truncated view of patriotism and patriarchy that functions as a veil for a suffocating chauvinism. In its emancipatory model, authority exists as a terrain of struggle and as such reveals the dialectical nature of its interests and possibilities; moreover, it provides the basis for viewing schools as democratic public spheres within an ongoing wider movement and struggle for democracy. For radical educators and others working in oppositional social movements, the dominant meaning of authority must be redefined to include the concepts of freedom, equality, and democracy.[14] Furthermore, the more specific concept of emancipatory authority needs to be seen as the central category around which to construct a rationale for defining teachers as transformative intellectuals and teacher work as a form of intellectual practice related to the issues, problems, concerns, and experiences of everyday life.

It is important here to stress the dual nature of the emancipatory model of authority I have been presenting. On the one hand, this model provides the basis for linking the purpose of schooling to the imperatives of a critical democracy, a position I have already discussed. On the other hand, it establishes theoretical support for analyzing teaching as a form of intellectual practice; moreover, it provides the ontological grounding for teachers who are willing to assume the role of transformative intellectuals.

The concept of emancipatory authority suggests that teachers are bearers of critical knowledge, rules, and values through which they consciously articulate and problematize their relationship to each other, to students, to subject matter, and to the wider community. Such a view of authority challenges the dominant view of teachers as technicians or public servants, whose role is primarily to implement rather than conceptualize pedagogical practice. The category of emancipatory authority dignifies teacher work by viewing it as a form of intellectual practice. Within this discourse, teacher work is viewed as a form of intellectual labor that interrelates conception and practice, thinking and doing, and producing and implementing as integrated activities that give teaching its dialectical meaning. The concept of teacher as intellectual carries with it the imperative to judge, critique, and reject those approaches to authority that reinforce a technical and social division of labor that silences and disempowers both teachers and students. In other words, emancipatory authority establishes as a central principle the need for teachers and others to critically engage the ideological and practical conditions that allow them to mediate, legitimate, and function in their capacity as authority-minded intellectuals.

Emancipatory authority also provides the theoretical scaffolding for educators to define themselves not simply as intellectuals, but in a more committed fashion as transformative intellectuals. This means that such educators are not merely concerned with forms of empowerment that promote individual achievement and traditional forms of academic success. Instead, they are also concerned in their teaching with linking empowerment—the ability to think and act critically—to the concept of social transformation. That is, teaching for social transformation means educating students to take risks and to struggle within ongoing relations of power in order to be able to alter the grounds on which life is lived. Acting as a transformative intellectual means helping students acquire critical knowledge about basic societal structures, such as the economy, the state, the work place, and mass culture, so that such institutions can be open to potential transformation. Doug White, the Australian educator, is instructive on this issue:

> In the broadest sense it is education—the bringing of knowledge into social life—which is central to a project which can turn possibilities into actualities. Radical teachers have not made a mistake in being too radical, but in not being radical enough. The task is for teachers, with others, to begin a project in which the forms of social institutions and work are considered and transformed, so that the notion of culture may come to include the development of social structures. The true nature of curriculum . . . is the development of that knowledge, thought and practice which is required by young people to enable them to take part in the production and reproduction of social life and to come to know the character of these processes.[15]

As transformative intellectuals, teachers need to make clear the nature of the appeals to authority they are using to legitimate their pedagogical practices. In other words, radical educators need to make clear the political and moral referents for the authority they assume in teaching particular forms of knowledge, taking a stand against forms of oppression, and treating students as if they ought also to be concerned about the issues of social justice and political action. In my view, the most important referent for this particular view of authority rests in a commitment to a form of solidarity that addresses the many instances of suffering that are a growing and threatening part of everyday life in America and abroad. Solidarity in this instance embodies a particular kind of commitment and practice. As a commitment, it suggests, as Sharon Welch has pointed out, a recognition of and identification with "the perspective of those people and groups who are marginal and exploited."[16] As a form of practice, solidarity represents a break from the bonds of isolated individuality and the need to engage for and with oppressed groups in political struggles that challenge the existing order of society as being institutionally repressive and unjust. This notion of solidarity emerges from an affirmative view of liberation that underscores the necessity of working collectively alongside the oppressed. It is also rooted in an acknowledgement that "truth" is an outcome of particular power struggles that cannot be abstracted from either history or existing networks of social and political control. This position suggests that one's beliefs are always subject to a critical analysis and that the process of learning how to learn is always contingent on the recognition that one's perspective can be superseded. The politics of such a skepticism is firmly rooted in a view of authority that is not dependent merely on the logic of epistemological arguments, but is deeply forged in "a creation of a politics of truth that defines the true as that which liberates and furthers specific processes of liberation."[17]

Transformative intellectuals then need to begin with a recognition of those manifestations of suffering that constitute historical memory as well as the immediate conditions of oppression. The pedagogical rationality at work here is one that defines radical educators as bearers of "dangerous memory," intellectuals who keep alive the memory of human suffering along with the forms of knowledge and struggles in which such suffering was shaped and contested. Dangerous memory has two dimensions: "that of hope and that of suffering . . . it recounts the history of the marginal, the vanquished, and the oppressed,"[18] and in doing so posits the need for a new kind of subjectivity and community in which the conditions that create such suffering can be eliminated. Michel Foucault describes the political project that is central to the meaning of dangerous memory as an affirmation of the insurrection of subjugated knowledges—those forms of historical and popular knowledge that have been suppressed or ignored, and through which it becomes possible to discover the ruptural effects of conflict and struggle. Underlying this view of dangerous memory and subjugated knowledge is a logic that provides the basis on which transformative intellectuals can advance both the language of critique and the language of possibility and hope. Foucault is worth quoting on this issue:

> By subjugated knowledges I mean two things: on the one hand, I am referring to the historical contents that have been buried and disguised . . . blocs of historical knowledge which were present but disguised within the body of functionalist and systematising theory and which criticism . . . draws upon and reveals. . . . On the other hand, I believe that by subjugated knowledges one should understand something else, something which in a sense is altogether different, namely, a whole set of knowledges that have been disqualified as inadequate to their task or insufficiently elaborated: naive knowledges, located low down on the hierarchy, beneath the required level of cognition of scientificity. I also believe that it is through the reemergence of these low-ranking knowledges, these unqualified, even directly disqualified knowledges . . . which involve what I would call a popular knowledge . . . a particular, local, regional knowledge . . . which is opposed by everything around it—that is through the re-appearance of this knowledge, of these local popular knowledges, these disqualified knowledges, that criticism performs its work.[19]

I have spent some time developing the rationale that teachers might use for legitimating a form of authority that both defines and endorses their role as transformative intellectuals. I believe that it is in this combination of critique, the reconstruction of the relationship between knowledge and power, and the commitment to a solidarity with the oppressed that the basis exists for a form of emancipatory authority that can structure the philosophical and political basis for a pedagogy that is both empowering and transformative. Of course, developing a legitimating basis for a form of emancipatory authority does not guarantee that a transformative pedagogy will follow, but it does provide the principles for making such a transformative pedagogy possible. Furthermore, it establishes the criteria for organizing curricula and classroom social relations around goals designed to prepare students to relate, understand, and value the relation between an existentially lived public space and their own practical learning. By public space I mean, as Hannah Arendt did, a concrete set of learning conditions where people come together to speak, to dialogue, to share their stories, and to struggle together within social relations that strengthen rather than weaken the possibility for active citizenship.[20]

School and classroom practices in this sense can be organized around forms of learning in which the knowledge and skills acquired serve to prepare students to later develop and maintain those counterpublic spheres outside of schools that are so vital for developing webs of solidarity in which democracy as a social movement operates as an active force. Maxine Greene, in her usual eloquent manner, speaks to the need for educators to create such public spaces in their own classrooms as a pedagogical precondition for educating students to struggle in an active democracy.

> We need spaces . . . for expression, for freedom . . . a public space . . . where living persons can come together in speech and action, each one free to articulate a distinctive perspective, all of them granted equal worth. It must be a space of dialogue, a space where a web of relationships can be woven, and where a common world can be brought into being and continually renewed. . . . There must be a teachable capacity to bring into being . . . a public composed of persons with many voices and many perspectives, out of whose multiple intelligences may still emerge a durable and worthwhile common world. If educators can renew their hopes and speak out once again, if they can empower more persons in the multiple domains of possibility, we shall not have to fear a lack of productivity, a lack of dignity or standing in the world. We will be in pursuit of the crucial values; we will be creating our own purposes as we move.[21]

Emancipatory Authority and Practical Learning

Central to developing a critical pedagogy consistent with the principles of emancipatory authority is the need for radical educators to reconstruct the relations between knowledge, power, and desire in order to bring together what James Donald refers to as two often separate struggles within schools: the changing of circumstances and the changing of subjectivities.[22] In the first case, the central issue that needs to be explored by educators is identifying the kinds of material and ideological preconditions that need to exist for schools to become effective. This issue covers a wide range of concerns such as active parent involvement in the schools, adequate health care and nutrition for students, high student morale, and adequate financial resources.[23] All of these factors represent resources through which power is exercised and made manifest. Power in this sense refers to the means of getting things done, and as Foucault claims, "consists in guiding the possibility of conduct and putting in order the possible outcome to govern, in this sense, to structure the possible field of action of others."[24]

For teachers, the relationship between authority and power is manifested not only in the degree to which they legitimate and exercise control over students (a central concern of conservatives), but equally important through the capacity they possess to influence the conditions under which they work. I have written on this matter elsewhere and will not pursue it here in any detail,[25] but it is important to stress that unless teachers have both the authority and the power to organize and shape the conditions of their work so that they can teach collectively, produce alternative curricula, and engage in a form of emancipatory politics, any talk of developing and implementing progressive pedagogy ignores the reality of what goes on in the daily lives of teachers and is nonsensical. Simply put, the conditions under which teachers work are currently overtaxing and demeaning, and need to be restructured so as to both dignify the nature of their work and allow them to act in a creative and responsible fashion.

The major issues I will focus on here concern the ways in which teachers can empower their students through what they teach, how they teach, and the means whereby school knowledge can be made worthwhile and interesting at the same time. Central to both concerns is the linking of power to knowledge. This raises the issue regarding the kinds of knowledge educators can provide for students that will empower them not only to understand and engage the world around them, but also to exercise the kind of courage needed to change the wider social reality when necessary.

Radical educators need to begin with a certain amount of clarity regarding the kind of curriculum they want to develop at the different levels of schooling. In my mind this should be a curriculum that gives a central place to the issue of "real" democracy. In developing such a focus, radical educators must rework those aspects of the traditional curriculum in which democratic possibilities exist, but in doing so they must also exercise an incessant critical analysis of those inherent characteristics that reproduce inequitable social relations. At issue here is the need for radical educators to recognize that power relations exist in correlation with forms of school knowledge that both distort the truth and produce it. Such a consideration not only suggests that any attempt at developing a curriculum for democratic empowerment must examine the conditions of knowledge and how such knowledge distorts reality; it also suggests that radical educators reconstitute the very nature of the knowledge/power relationship. In doing so, they need to understand that knowledge does more than distort, it also produces particular forms of life; it has, as Foucault points out, a productive, positive function.[26] It is this productive function of knowledge that must be appropriated with a radical intent. It is important to recognize that while radical educators often refuse, subvert, and, where necessary, critically appropriate dominant forms of knowledge, this does not mean that they should continue working exclusively within the language of critique. On the contrary, the major thrust of a critical pedagogy should center around generating knowledge that presents concrete possibilities for empowering people. To put it more specifically, a critical pedagogy needs a language of possibility, one that provides the pedagogical basis for teaching democracy while simultaneously making schooling more democratic.

In general terms, a critical pedagogy needs to focus on what Colin Fletcher calls themes for democracy and democracy in learning.[27] In the first instance, the curriculum incorporates themes that recognize the urgent problems of adult life. Such knowledge includes not only the basic skills students will need to work and live in the wider society, but also knowledge about the social forms through which human beings live, become conscious, and sustain themselves. This includes knowledge about power and how it works,[28] as well as analyses of those practices such as racism, sexism, and class exploitation that structure and mediate the encounters of everyday life. Of course, the point here is not merely to denounce such stereotypes but rather to expose and deconstruct the processes through which these dominant ideological representations are produced, legitimated, and circulated in society. In many respects, the curriculum should be built on knowledge that starts with the problems and needs of students. It must, however, be so designed that it can provide the basis for a critique of dominant forms of knowledge. Finally, such a curriculum should provide students with a language through which they can analyze their own lived relations and experiences in a manner that is both affirmative and critical. R. W. Connell and his associates in Australia provide a clear analysis of the theoretical elements that characterize this type of curriculum in their formulation of the kinds of knowledge that should be taught to empower working-class children. They write:

> It proposes that working-class kids get access to formal knowledge via learning which begins with their own experience and the circumstances which shape it, but does not stop there. This approach neither accepts the existing organization of academic knowledge nor simply inverts it. It draws on existing school knowledge and on what working-class people already know, and organizes this selection of information around problems such as economic survival and collective action, handling the disruption of households by unemployment, responding to the impact of new technology, managing problems of personal identity and association, understanding how schools work and why.[29]

A curriculum based on an emancipatory notion of authority is one in which the particular forms of life, culture, and interaction that students bring to school are honored in such a way that students can begin to view such knowledge in both a critical and a useful way. All too often students from the working class and other subordinate groups react to dominant school knowledge and ideas as if they were weapons being used against them. On the other hand, curricula developed as part of a radical pedagogy privilege subordinate knowledge forms and reconstruct classroom life as an arena for new forms of sociality. That is, instead of a stress on the individualistic and competitive approaches to learning, students are encouraged to work together on projects, both in terms of their production and in terms of their evaluation. This suggests that students must learn within social forms that allow them to exercise a degree of self-consciousness about their own interactions as class, gendered, racial, and ethnic subjects. In addition to analyzing problems and issues that apply to the immediate contexts of students' lives, a radical pedagogy needs to critically appropriate forms of knowledge that exist outside the immediate experience of students' lives in order to broaden their sense of understanding and possibility. This means that students need to learn and appropriate other codes of experience as well as other discourses in time and place that extend their horizons while constantly pushing them to test what it means to resist oppression, work collectively, and exercise authority from the position of an ever-developing sense of knowledge, expertise, and commitment. It also means providing the pedagogical conditions for raising new wants, needs, and ambitions, and real hope, but always in a context that makes such hope realizable.

Giving students the opportunity to learn by understanding the mediations and social forms that shape their own experiences is important not merely because this provides them with a critical way to understand the familiar terrain of everyday practical life. It is also part of a pedagogical strategy that attempts to both recover and engage the experiences that students exhibit so as to understand how such experiences have been accomplished and legitimated within specific social and historical conditions. I want to stress that the issue of student experience must be seen as central to a critical pedagogy. It is essential that radical educators understand how student experience is both constructed and engaged, because it is through such experiences that students produce accounts of who they are and constitute themselves as particular individuals. Student experience is the stuff of culture, agency, and self-production and must play a definitive role in any emancipatory curriculum. It is therefore imperative that radical educators learn how to understand, legitimate, and interrogate such experience. This means not only understanding the cultural and social forms through which students learn how to define themselves, but also learning how to critically engage such experiences in a way that refuses to disconfirm them or render them illegitimate. Knowledge has first of all to be made meaningful to students before it can be made critical. It never speaks for itself, but rather is constantly mediated through the ideological and cultural experiences that students bring to the classroom. To ignore such experiences is to deny the grounds on which students learn, speak, and imagine. Judith Williamson puts this issue as well as anyone:

> Walter Benjamin has said that the best ideas are no use if they do not make something useful of the person who holds them; on an even simpler level, I would add that the best ideas don't even exist if there isn't anyone to hold them. If we cannot get the "radical curriculum" across, or arouse the necessary interest in the "basic skills," there is no point to them. But in any case, which do we ultimately care more about: our ideas, or the child/student we are trying to teach them to?[30]

Students cannot learn "usefully" unless teachers develop an understanding of the various ways in which subjectivities are constituted through different social domains. At stake here is the need for teachers to understand how experiences produced in the various domains and layers of everyday life give rise to the different "voices" students use to give meaning to their own worlds and, consequently, to their own existence in the larger society. Unless educators address the question of how aspects of the social are experienced, mediated, and produced by students, it will be difficult for radical educators to tap into the drives, emotions, and interests that give subjectivity its own unique "voice" and provide the momentum for learning itself.

Emancipatory Authority, Teachers, and Social Movements

I want to conclude this article by arguing that teachers who want to function as transformative intellectuals who legitimate their role through an emancipatory form of authority will have to do more than gain further control of their working conditions and teach critical pedagogy. They will have to open up every aspect of formal education to active, popular contestation and to other front line-groups and constituencies. This includes community members, parents, support staff, youth-advocacy groups, and others with vital interests in the schools. There are a number of reasons for arguing this position. First, it is impossible to argue for schools as democratic, counterpublic spheres if such institutions narrowly define and exclude various community groups from talking about educational concerns. Second, any notion of educational reform along with its reconstructed view of authority and pedagogy needs to focus on the institutional arrangements that structure and mediate the role of schooling in the wider society. Reforms that limit their focus to specific school problems or the politics of instruction ignore the ways in which public education is shaped, bent, and moved by wider economic, political, and social concerns. Third, radical educators need to make alliances with other progressive social movements in an effort to create public spheres where the discourse of democracy can be debated and where the issues that arise in such a context can be collectively acted on, in a political fashion if necessary.

Teachers must be willing and prepared to make their schools more responsive to the wider community. In doing so, they will have to redefine the role and nature of authority as it is currently constituted around the ideology of professionalism, an ideology that is largely shaped by unions, which often define themselves in opposition to wider school constituencies and community demands. As it stands, teachers tend to legitimate their roles as professionals through appeals to knowledge and expertise that is highly exclusionary and undemocratic. Professionalism as it is presently defined has little to do with democracy as a social movement. By creating active, organic links with the community, teachers can open their schools to the diverse resources offered by the community. In doing so, they can give the schools access to those community traditions, histories, and cultures that are often submerged or discredited within the dominant school culture. It is an unfortunate truism that when communities are ignored by the schools, students find themselves situated in institutions that deny them a voice. As Ann Bastion and her colleagues argue:

School isolation works to deny students a link between what they learn in the classroom and the environment they function in outside the school. The lack of relevance and integration is particularly acute for minority and disadvantaged students, whose social and cultural background is not reflected, or is negatively reflected, in standard curricula based on a white, middle-class mainstream and on elitist structures of achievement. Isolation also denies communities the integrative and empowering capacities of the school as a community institution. Isolation denies schools the energy, resources, and, ultimately, the sympathies of community members.[31]

Community involvement in the schools can help to foster the necessary conditions for a constructive, ongoing debate over the goals, methods, and services that schools actually provide for students in specific localities. Moreover, it is essential that teachers take an active role in organizing with parents and others in their communities in order to remove political power from the hands of those political and economic groups and institutions who exercise an inordinate and sometimes damaging influence on school policy and curriculum.[32]

If radical educators are going to have any significant effect on the unequal economic, political, and social arrangements that plague schools and the wider society, they have no choice but to actively engage in the struggle for democracy with groups *outside* of their classrooms. Martin Carnoy reinforces this point by arguing that democracy has not been created by intellectuals acting within the confines of their classrooms.

> Democracy has been developed by social movements, and those intellectuals and educators who were able to implement democratic reforms in education did so in part through appeals to such movements. If the working people, minorities, and women who have formed the social movements pressing for greater democracy in our society cannot be mobilized behind equality in education, with the increased public spending that this requires, there is absolutely no possibility that equality in education will be implemented.[33]

Teachers need to define themselves as transformative intellectuals who act as radical teachers and educators. Radical teacher as a category defines the pedagogical and political role teachers have within the schools while the notion of radical education speaks to a wider sphere of intervention in which the same concern with authority, knowledge, power, and democracy redefines and broadens the political nature of their pedagogical task, which is to teach, learn, listen, and mobilize in the interest of a more just and equitable social order. By linking schooling to wider social movements, teachers can begin to redefine the nature and importance of pedagogical struggle and in doing so provide the basis to fight for forms of emancipatory authority as a foundation for the establishment of freedom and justice. Nyberg and Farber have performed a theoretical service in raising the importance of authority for educators. The next task is to organize and struggle for the promise emancipatory authority offers to the schools, the community, and the wider society as a whole.

Notes

I want to thank my colleague and friend Peter McLaren for the comments and critical reading of this article. Of course, I am solely responsible for its content.

1. A recent set of writings on this view can be found in Diane Ravitch and Chester E. Finn, Jr., "High Expectations and Disciplined Effort," in *Against Mediocrity,* ed. Robert Fancher and Diane Ravitch (New York: Holmes and Meier, 1984); Diane Ravitch, *The Schools We Deserve* (New York: Basic Books, 1985); and Thomas Sowell, *Education: Assumptions vs. History* (Stanford: Hoover Press, 1986).

2. Edward A. Wynne, "The Great Tradition in Education: Transmitting Moral Values," *Educational Leadership* 43, no. 4 (December 1985): 7; and idem, *Developing Character: Transmitting Knowledge* (Posen, Ill.: ARL Services, 1984).

3. For an exceptional critique of this position, see Barbara Finkelstein, "Education and the Retreat from Democracy in the United States, 1979–198?," *Teachers College Record* 86, no. 2 (Winter 1984): 275–82; and Maxine Greene, "Public Education and the Public Space," *Educational Researcher,* June–July 1982, pp. 4–9.

4. Agnes Heller, "Marx and the Liberation of Humankind," *Philosophy and Society Criticism* 3/4 (1982): 367.

5. See David Nyberg and Paul Farber, "Authority in Education," *Teachers College Record* 88, no. 1 (Fall 1986), pp. 4–14.

6. Critiques of this position can be found in William V. Spanos, "The Apollonial Investment of Modern Humanist Education: The Example of Mathew Arnold, Irving Babbitt, and I. A. Richards," *Cultural Critique* 1 (Fall 1985): 7–22; and Henry A. Giroux et al., "The Need for Cultural Studies: Resisting Intellectuals and Oppositional Public Spheres," *Dalhousie Review* 64, no. 2 (Summer 1984): 472–86.

7. This view of radical educational theory and its various representations is comprehensively analyzed in Stanley Aronowitz and Henry A. Giroux, *Education under Siege* (South Hadley, Mass.: Bergin and Garvey, 1985).

8. Kenneth D. Benne, "Authority in Education," *Harvard Educational Review* 40, no. 3 (August 1970): 392–93.

9. Cited in Colin Gordon, "Afterword," in Michel Foucault, *Power/Knowledge: Selected Interviews and Other Writings, 1972–1977,* ed. Colin Gordon (New York: Pantheon Press, 1980), p. 233.

10. Nyberg and Farber, "Authority in Education"; Steve Tozer, "Dominant Ideology and the Teacher's Authority," *Contemporary Education* 56, no. 3 (Spring 1985): 150–53; idem, "Civism, Democratic Empowerment, and the Social Foun-

dations of Education," in *Philosophy of Education Society, 1985,* ed. David Nyberg (Normal Ill.: Philosophy of Education Society, 1986), pp. 186–200; and George Wood, "Schooling in a Democracy," *Education Theory* 34, no. 3 (Summer 1984): 219–38.

11. John Dewey, *Democracy and Education* (New York: Macmillan, 1916); idem, "Creative Democracy—The Task Before Us," reprinted in *Classic American Philosophers,* ed. Max Fisch (New York: Appleton-Century-Crofts, 1951); and George S. Counts, *Dare the Schools Build a New Social Order* (New York: Day, 1932). See also Richard J. Bernstein, "Dewey, Democracy: The Task Ahead of Us," in *Post-Analytic Philosophy,* ed. John Rajchman and Cornell West (New York: Columbia University Press, 1985).

12. Benjamin Barber, *Strong Democracy: Participating Politics for a New Age* (Berkeley: University of California Press, 1984).

13. Sheldon Wolin, "Revolutionary Action Today," in *Post-Analytic Philosophy,* p. 256.

14. For an important discussion of these concepts, see Richard Lichtman, "Socialist Freedom," in *Socialist Perspectives,* ed. Phyllis Jacobson and Julius Jacobson (New York: Kary-Cohl Publishing, 1983); and Landon E. Beyer and George Wood, "Critical Inquiry and Moral Action in Education," *Educational Theory* 36, no. 1 (Winter 1986): 1–14.

15. Doug White, "Education: Controlling the Participants," *Arena* 72 (1985): 78.

16. Sharon Welch, *Communities of Resistance and Solidarity* (New York: Orbis Press, 1985), p. 31.

17. Ibid.

18. Ibid., p. 36. A critical notion of memory can also be found in the work of the Frankfurt School, especially in the work of Marcuse, Adorno, and Benjamin. For an overview of this issue, see Martin Jay, "Anamnestic Totalization," *Theory and Society* 11 (1982): 1–15.

19. Michel Foucault, "Two Lectures," in *Power/Knowledge,* pp. 82–83.

20. Hannah Arendt, *The Human Condition* (Chicago: University of Chicago Press, 1958).

21. Maxine Greene, "Excellence: Meanings and Multiplicity," *Teachers College Record* 86, no. 2 (Winter 1984): 296.

22. James Donald, "Troublesome Texts: On Subjectivity and Schooling," *British Journal of Sociology of Education* 6, no. 3 (1985): 342; and Roger Simon, "Work Experience as the Production of Subjectivity," in *Pedagogy and Cultural Power,* ed. David Livingstone (South Hadley, Mass.: Bergin and Garvey, 1986).

23. For an excellent analysis of these issues and how progressive educators can deal with them, see Ann Bastion et al., *Choosing Equality: The Case for Democratic Schooling* (New York: New World Foundation, 1985).

24. Michel Foucault, "The Subject of Power," in *Beyond Structuralism and Hermeneutics,* ed. Hubert Dreyfus and Paul Rainbow (Chicago: University of Chicago Press, 1982), p. 221. For an interesting analysis of why power should be a central category in educational discourse, see David Nyberg, *Power over Power* (Ithaca: Cornell University Press, 1981).

25. Aronowitz and Giroux, *Education under Siege.*

26. Foucault, "The Subject of Power."

27. Colin Fletcher, Maxine Caron, and Wyn Williams, *Schools on Trial* (Philadelphia: Open University Press, 1985).

28. Nyberg rightly argues that educators need to develop a theory and pedagogy about power as a central aspect of the curriculum (Nyberg, *Power over Power*).

29. R. W. Connell et al., *Making the Difference* (Sydney, Australia: Allen and Unwin, 1982), p. 199.

30. Judith Williamson, "Is There Anyone Here from a Classroom," *Screen* 26, no. 1 (January–February, 1985): 94; see also Henry A. Giroux, "Radical Pedagogy and the Politics of Student Voice," *Interchange* 17, no. 1 (1986): 48–69.

31. Ann Bastion et al., "Choosing Equality: The Case for Democratic Schooling," *Social Policy* 15, no. 4 (Spring 1985): 47.

32. Timothy Sieber, "The Politics of Middle-Class Success in an Inner-City Public School," *Boston University Journal of Education* 164, no. 1 (Winter 1982): 30–47.

33. Martin Carnoy, "Education, Democracy, and Social Conflict," *Harvard Educational Review* 53, no. 4 (November 1983): 401–02.

PART TWO

Critical Pedagogy in the Classroom

5 Radical Pedagogy and the Politics of Student Voice

WITHIN THE LAST DECADE, PUBLIC schooling in the United States has been criticized quite strongly by both radical and conservative critics. Central to both positions has been a concern with what has been called the reproductive theory of schooling. According to the reproductive thesis, schools are not to be valued in the traditional sense as public spheres engaged in teaching students the knowledge and skills of democracy. On the contrary, schools are to be viewed in more instrumental terms and should be measured against the need to reproduce the values, social practices, and skills needed for the dominant corporate order. Of course, conservative and radical critics have taken opposing positions regarding the significance of schooling as a reproductive public sphere. For conservatives, schools have strayed too far from the logic of capital, and because of this, are now held responsible for the economic recession of the 1970s, the loss of foreign markets to international competitors, and the shortage of trained workers for an increasingly complex technological economy. Conservatives have further argued that schools need to reform their curricula in order to serve the corporate interests of the dominant society more faithfully.[1] Underlying this theoretical shorthand is the demand that schools place a greater emphasis on character formation, basic skills, and corporate needs.

Radical educators, on the other hand, have used the reproductive thesis to criticize the role that schools play in American society. In general terms, they have argued that schools are "reproductive" in that they provide different classes and social groups with forms of knowledge, skills, and culture that not only legitimate the dominant culture but also track students into a labor force differentiated by gender, racial, and class considerations.[2]

Despite their differences, both radicals and conservatives alike have abandoned the Deweyian vision of public schools as democratic spheres, as places where the skills of democracy can be practised, debated, and analyzed. Similarly, both share a disturbing indifference to the ways in which students mediate and express their sense of place, time, and history and their contradictory, uncertain, and incomplete interactions with each other and with the dynamics of schooling. In other words, both radical and conservative ideologies generally fail to engage the politics of voice and representation—the forms of narrative and dialogue—around which students make sense of their lives and schools. While this is an understandable position for conservatives or for those whose logic of instrumentalism and social control is at odds with an emancipatory notion of human agency, it represents a serious theoretical and political failing on the part of radical educators.

This failing is evident in a number of areas. First, radical education theory has abandoned the language of possibility for the language of critique. That is, in viewing schools as primarily reproductive sites, it has not been able to develop a theory of schooling that offers the possibility for counterhegemonic struggle and ideological battle. Within this discourse, schools, teachers, and students have been written off as mere extensions of the logic of capital. Instead of viewing schools as sites of contestation and conflict, radical educators often provide us with a simplified version of domination that seems to suggest that the only political alternative to the current role that schools play in the wider society is to abandon them altogether. Since they view schools as ideologically and politically overburdened by the dominant society, they find unproblematic the moral and political necessity of developing a programmatic discourse for working within them. Thus, the role that teachers, students, parents, and community people might play in waging a political battle in the public schools is rarely explored as a possibility. One consequence is that the primacy of the political in this project turns in on itself and the defeatist logic of capitalist domination is accepted as the basis for a "radical" theory of schooling.

Second, in their failure to develop an educational theory that posits real alternatives within schools, radical educators remain politically powerless to combat the conservative forces which have adroitly exploited and appropriated popular concerns over public education. In other words, the educational Left not only misrepresents the nature of school life and the degree to which schools *do not* merely ape the logic of corporate interests; it also unwittingly reinforces the conservative thrust to fashion schools in their own ideological terms. In short, radical educators have failed to develop a language that engages schools as sites of possibility, that is, as places where students can be educated to take their places in society from a position of empowerment rather than from a position of ideological and economic subordination.

The major problem that I want to inquire into in this essay is one that is central to any legitimate notion of radical pedagogy—that is, how to develop a radical pedagogy that acknowledges the spaces, tensions, and possibilities for struggle within the day-to-day workings of schools. Underlying this problematic is the need to generate a set of categories that not only provides new modes of critical interrogation but also points to alternative strategies and modes of practice around which a radical pedagogy can be realized.

The basis for such a task lies at the outset in redefining the concept of power with respect to everyday experience and the construction of classroom pedagogy and student voice. For radical educators, power has to be understood as a concrete set of practices that produces social forms through which different experiences and modes of subjectivities are constructed. Power, in this sense, includes but goes beyond the call for institutional change or for the distribution of political and economic resources; it also signifies a level of conflict and struggle that plays itself out around the exchange of discourse and the lived experiences that such discourse produces, mediates, and legitimates.

Another major assumption here is that discourse is both a medium and a product of power. In this sense, discourse is intimately connected with those ideological and material forces out of which individuals and groups fashion a "voice." As Bakhtin (1981) puts it:

> Language is not a neutral medium that passes freely and easily into the private property of the speaker's intentions; it is populated—overpopulated— with the intentions of others. Expropriating it, forcing it to submit to one's own intentions and accents, is a difficult and complicated process. (p. 249)

If language is inseparable from lived experience and from how people create a distinctive voice, it is also connected to an intense struggle among different groups over what will count as meaningful and whose cultural capital will prevail in legitimating particular ways of life. Within schools, discourse produces and legitimates configurations of time, space, and narrative, placing particular renderings of ideology, behavior, and the representation of everyday life in a privileged perspective. As a "technology of power," discourse is given concrete expression in the forms of knowledge that constitute the formal curriculum as well as in the structuring of classroom social relations that constitute the hidden curriculum of schooling. Needless to say, these pedagogical practices and forms are "read" in different ways by teachers and students.

The importance of the relationship between power and discourse for a radical pedagogy is that it provides a theoretical grounding for interrogating the issue of how ideology is inscribed in those forms of educational discourse through which school experiences and practices are ordered and constituted. Moreover, it points to the necessity of accounting theoretically for the ways in which language, ideology, history, and experience come together to produce, define, and constrain particular forms of teacher-student practice. The value of this approach is that it refuses to remain trapped in modes of analysis that examine student voice and pedagogical experience from the perspective of the reproductive thesis. That is, power and discourse are now investigated not merely as the single echo of the logic of capital, but as a polyphony of voices mediated within different layers of reality shaped through an interaction of dominant and subordinate forms of power. By recognizing and interrogating the different layers of meaning and struggle that make up the terrain of schooling, radical educators can fashion not only a language of critique but also a language of possibility. The remainder of this essay will engage that task. First I will critically analyze the two major discourses of mainstream educational theory. At the risk of undue simplification, these are characterized as conservative and liberal pedagogical discourses. Then I will attempt to develop a discourse appropriate for a radical pedagogy, one that draws heavily upon the works of Paulo Freire and Mikhail Bakhtin.

Conservative Discourse and Educational Practice

Schooling and Positive Knowledge

Conservative educational discourse often presents a view of culture and knowledge in which both are treated as part of a storehouse of artifacts constituted as canon. While this discourse has a number of characteristic expressions, its most recent theoretical defence can be found in Mortimer J. Adler's *The Paideia Proposal*. Adler calls for the schools to implement a core course of subjects in all 12 years of public schooling. His appeal is to forms of pedagogy that enable students to master skills and specific forms of understanding with respect to predetermined forms of knowledge. In this view, knowledge appears beyond the reach of critical interrogation except at the level of immediate application. In other words, there is no mention of how such knowledge is chosen, whose interests it represents, or why students might be interested in acquiring it. In fact, students in this perspective are characterized as a unitary body removed from the ideological and material forces that construct their subjectivities, interests, and concerns in diverse and multiple ways.

I would argue that the concept of difference in this approach becomes the negative apparition of the "other." This is particularly clear in Adler's case since he dismisses social and cultural differences among students with the simplistic and reductionistic comment that "despite their manifold individual differences the children are all the same in their human nature" (1982, p. 42). In this view, a predetermined and hierarchically arranged body of knowledge is taken as the cultural currency to be dispensed to all children regardless of their diversity and interests. Equally important is the fact that the acquisition of such knowledge becomes the structuring principle around which the school curriculum is organized and particular classroom social relations legitimated. It is worth noting that it is exclusively an appeal to school knowledge that constitutes the measure and worth of what defines the learning experience. That is, the value of both teacher and student experience is premised on the transmission and inculcation of what can be termed "positive knowledge." Consequently, it is in the distribution, management, measurement, and legitimation of such knowledge that this type of pedagogy invests its energies. Phil Cusick (1983) comments in his ethnographic study of three urban secondary schools on the problematic nature of legitimating and organizing school practices around the notion of "positive knowledge":

> By positive knowledge I mean that which is generally accepted as having an empirical or traditional base. . . . The assumption that the acquisition of positive knowledge can be made interesting and appealing in part underlies the laws that compel everyone to attend school, at least until their mid teens. . . . The conventional assumption would have it that the curriculum of a school exists as a body of knowledge, agreed upon by staff and approved by the general community and by district authorities who have some expertise, and that it reflects the best thinking about what young people need to succeed in our society. But I did not find that. (pp. 25, 71)

What Cusick did find was that school knowledge organized in these terms was not compelling enough to interest many of the students he observed. Moreover, educators locked into this perspective responded to student disinterest, violence, and resistance by shifting their concerns—from actually teaching positive knowledge to maintaining order and control, or as they put it, "keeping the lid on." Cusick is worth quoting at length:

> Not only did the administrators spend their time on those matters [administration and control], they also tended to evaluate other elements, such as the performance of teachers, according to their ability to maintain order. They tended to arrange other elements of the school according to how they contributed or failed to contribute to the maintenance of order. The outstanding example of that was the implementation in both urban schools of the five-by-five day, wherein the students were brought in early in the morning, given five periods of instruction with a few minutes in between and a fifteen-minute mid-morning break, and released before one o'clock. There were no free periods, study halls, cafeteria sessions, or assemblies.

No occasions were allowed in which violence could occur. The importance of maintaining order in those public secondary schools could not be underestimated. (p. 108)

Within this form of pedagogical practice, student voice is reduced to the immediacy of its performance, existing as something to be measured, administered, registered, and controlled. Its distinctiveness, its disjunctions, its lived quality are all dissolved under an ideology of control and management. In the name of efficiency, the resources and wealth of student life histories are generally ignored. A major problem with this perspective is that the celebration of positive knowledge does not guarantee that students will have any interest in the pedagogical practices it produces, especially since such knowledge appears to have little connection to the everyday experiences of the students themselves. Teachers who structure classroom experiences out of this discourse generally face enormous problems in the public schools, especially those in urban centres. Boredom and/or disruption appear to be primary products. To some extent, of course, teachers who rely upon classroom practices that exhibit a disrespect for students are themselves victims of labor conditions that virtually make it impossible for them to teach as critical educators. At the same time, these conditions are determined by dominant interests and by discourses that provide the ideological legitimation for promoting hegemonic classroom practices. In short, such practices not only involve symbolic violence against students by devaluing the cultural capital which they possess, they also tend to restrict teachers to pedagogical models that legitimate their role as white collar clerks. Unfortunately, the notion of teachers as clerks is part of a long tradition of management models of pedagogy and administration that has dominated American public education.

Needless to say, conservative educational discourse is not all of one piece; there is another position within this perspective that does not ignore the relationship between knowledge and student experience. It is to this position that I will now turn.

Schooling and the Ideology of Positive Thinking

In another important variation of conservative educational theory, the analysis and meaning of experience shift from a preoccupation with transmitting positive knowledge to developing forms of pedagogy that recognize and appropriate cultural traditions and experiences that different students bring to the school setting. The theoretical cornerstone of this position is developed around a modified view of the concept of culture. That is, the static notion of culture as a storehouse of traditional knowledge and skills is replaced here by a more anthropological approach.

In its revised form, culture is viewed as a form of production, specifically, as the ways in which human beings make sense of their lives, feelings, beliefs, thoughts, and the wider society. Within this approach, the notion of difference is stripped of its "otherness" and accommodated to the logic of a "polite civic humanism" (Corrigan, 1985, p. 7). Difference no longer symbolizes the threat of disruption. On the contrary, it now signals an invitation for diverse cultural groups to join hands under the democratic banner of an integrative pluralism. The specific ideology that defines the relation between difference and pluralism is central to this version of conservative educational thought in that it legitimates the idea that in spite of differences manifested around race, ethnicity, language, values, and life styles, there is an underlying equality among different cultural groups that allegedly disavows that any one of them is privileged. At work here is an attempt to subsume the notion of difference within a discourse and set of practices that promote harmony, equality, and respect within and between diverse cultural groups.

This is not meant to suggest that conflict is ignored in this approach; I am not suggesting that the social and political antagonisms that characterize the relationship between different cultural groups and the larger society are altogether denied. On the contrary, such problems are generally recognized but as issues to be discussed and overcome in the interest of creating a "happy and cooperative class," which will hopefully play a fundamental role in bringing about a "happy and cooperative world" (Jeffcoate, 1979, p. 122). Within this context, cultural representations of difference as *conflict and tension* only become pedagogically workable within a language of unity and cooperation that legitimates a false and particularly "cheery" view of Western civilization. Consequently, the concept of difference turns into its opposite, for difference now becomes meaningful as something to be resolved within *relevant* forms of exchange and class discussions. Lost here is a respect for the autonomy of different cultural logics and any understanding of how such logics operate within asymmetrical relations of power and domination. In other words, the equality that is associated with different forms of culture serves to displace political considerations regarding the ways in which dominant and subordinate groups interact and struggle both in and outside the schools.

The pedagogical practices deriving from this notion of difference and cultural diversity are suffused with the language of positive thinking. This becomes clear in curriculum projects developed around these practices. These projects generally structure curriculum problems so as to include references to the conflicts and tensions that exist among diverse groups, but rather than educating students to the ways in which various groups struggle within relations of power and domination as these are played out in the larger social arena, they subordinate these issues to pedagogical goals that attempt to foster a mutual respect and understanding in the interest of national unity. The apologetic nature of this discourse is evident in the kinds of educational objectives that structure its classroom practices. The complexity and sweat of social change are quietly ignored.

In more sophisticated versions, conservative educational theory recognizes the existence of racial, gender, ethnic, and other types of conflict among different groups but is more ideologically honest about why they should *not* be emphasized in the school curriculum. Appealing to the interests of a "common culture," this position calls for a pedagogical emphasis on the common interests and ideals that characterize the nation. As one of its spokespersons, Nathan Glazer (1977), puts it, the choice of what is taught "must be guided . . . by our conception of a desirable society, of the relationship between what we select to teach and the ability of people to achieve such a society and live together in it" (p. 51). What is troubling with this position is that it lacks any sense of culture as a terrain of struggle; moreover, it does not pay any attention to the relationship between knowledge and power. In fact, underlying Glazer's statement is a facile egalitarianism that assumes but does not demonstrate that all groups can actively participate in the development of such a society. While appealing to a fictive harmony, his unitary "our" suggests an unwillingness to either indict or interrogate existing structures of domination. This harmony is nothing more than an image in the discourse of those who do not have to suffer the injustices experienced by subordinated groups. In short, this version of conservative educational theory falls prey to a perspective that idealizes the future while stripping the present of its deeply rooted contradictions and tensions. This is not merely the discourse of harmony; it is also a set of interests that refuses to posit the relations between culture and power as a moral question demanding emancipatory political action.

Liberal Discourse and Educational Practice

Liberal discourse in educational theory and practice has a long association with various tenets of what has been loosely called progressive education in the United States. From John Dewey to the free school movement of the sixties and seventies to the present emphasis on multiculturalism, there has been a concern with taking the needs and the cultural experiences of students as a starting point for developing relevant forms of pedagogy.[3] Since it is impossible to analyze in this essay all of the theoretical twists and turns this movement has taken, I want to focus exclusively on some of its dominant ideological tendencies and the way in which its discourses structure the experiences of students and teachers.

Liberal Theory as the Ideology of Deprivation

In its most common-sense form, liberal educational theory favors a notion of experience that is equated either with "fulfilling the needs of kids" or with developing cordial relations with students so as to be able to maintain order and control in the school. In many respects, these two discourses represent different sides of the same educational ideology. In the ideology of "need fulfillment," the category of need represents an *absence* of a particular set of experiences. In most cases, what educators determine as missing are either the culturally specific experiences that school authorities believe students must acquire in order to enrich the quality of their lives or the fundamental skills that they will "need" in order to get jobs once they leave school. Underlying this view of experience is the logic of cultural deprivation theory, which defines education in terms of cultural enrichment, remediation, and basics.

In this version of liberal pedagogy, there is little recognition that what is legitimated as privileged school experience often represents the endorsement of a particular way of life, signified as superior by the "revenge" that befalls those who do not share its attributes. Specifically, the experience of the student as "other" is cast as deviant, underprivileged, or "uncultured." Consequently, not only do students bear the sole responsibility for school failure, but also there is little room for questioning the ways in which administrators and teachers actually create and sustain the problems they attribute to students. This view of students, particularly of those from subordinate groups, is mirrored by a refusal to examine the assumptions and pedagogical practices that legitimate forms of experience embodying the logic of domination. One glaring example of this was brought to me by a secondary school teacher in one of my graduate courses who constantly referred to her working-class students as "low life." In her case, there was no sense of how language was actively constructing her relations with these students, though I am sure the message was not lost on them. One practice that sometimes emerges from this aspect of liberal educational ideology is that of blaming students for their perceived problems while simultaneously humiliating them in an effort to get them to participate in classroom activities. The following incident captures this approach:

The teacher, after taking attendance for fifteen minutes, wrote a few phrases on the board: "Adam and Eve," "spontaneous generation," and "evolution," and told the students that: "For the next forty minutes you are to write an essay on how you think the world started, and here are three possibilities which, you know, we discussed last week. I did this with my college prep class and they liked it. . . . It will do you good. Teach you to think for a change, which is something you don't do often." (Cusick, 1983, p. 55)

Liberal Theory as the Pedagogy of Cordial Relations

When students refuse to surrender to this type of humiliation, teachers and school administrators generally face problems of order and control. One response is to promote a pedagogy of cordial relations. The classic instance of dealing with students in this approach is to try to keep them "happy" by either indulging their personal interests through appropriately developed modes of "low status" knowledge or by developing good rapport with them. Defined as the "other," students now become objects of inquiry in the interest of being understood so as to be more easily controlled. The knowledge, for example, used by teachers with these students is often drawn from cultural forms identified with class-, race-, and gender-specific interests. But relevance, in this instance, has little to do with emancipatory concerns; instead, it translates into pedagogical practices that attempt to appropriate forms of student and popular culture in the interests of maintaining social control. Furthermore, it provides a legitimating ideology for forms of class, race, and gender tracking. The practice of tracking at issue here is developed in its most subtle form through an endless series of school electives that appear to legitimate the cultures of subordinated groups while actually incorporating them in a trivial pedagogical fashion. Thus, working-class girls are "advised" by guidance teachers to take "Girl Talk" while middle-class students have no doubts about the importance of taking classes in literary criticism. In the name of relevance and order, working-class males are encouraged to select "industrial arts" while their middle-class counterparts take courses in advanced chemistry. These practices and social forms along with the divergent interests and pedagogies they produce have been analyzed extensively elsewhere and need not be repeated here.[4]

Liberal Theory and the Pedagogy of Child Centredness

In its theoretical forms, liberal educational discourse provides a "supportive" view of student experience and culture. Within this perspective, student experience is defined by the individualizing psychology of "child centredness." Understood as part of a "natural" unfolding process, it is not tied to the imperatives of rigid disciplinary authority but to the exercise of self-control and self-regulation. The focus of analysis in this discourse is the child as a unitary subject, and pedagogical practices are structured around encouraging "healthy" expression and harmonious social relations. Central to this problematic is an ideology that equates freedom with "the bestowal of love" and with what Carl Rogers (1969) has called "unconditional positive regard" and "emphatic understanding." The liberal pedagogical canon demands that teachers emphasize self-directed learning, link knowledge to the personal experiences of students, and attempt to help students to interact with one another in a positive and harmonious fashion.

How student experiences are developed within this perspective is, of course, directly related to the larger question of how they are constructed and understood within the multiple discourses that embody and reproduce the social and cultural relations of the larger society. This issue is not only ignored in liberal views of educational theory; it is ignored in conservative discourses as well. The silence regarding forms of race, class, and gender discrimination and how these are reproduced in relations between the schools and the larger social order is what links conservative and liberal theories of education, constituting, what I call, the dominant educational discourse. Though I have already criticized some of the assumptions that inform the dominant educational discourses, I want to elaborate on these before I turn to how a radical pedagogy can be fashioned out of a theory of cultural politics.

Dominant Educational Discourse

The dominant educational discourse falls prey to a deeply ingrained ideological tendency in American education as well as in the mainstream social sciences to separate culture from relations of power. By analyzing culture uncritically either as an object of veneration or as a set of practices that embody the traditions and values of diverse groups, this view depoliticizes culture. More specifically, there is no attempt to understand culture as shared and lived principles characteristic of different groups and classes as these emerge within inequitable relations of power and fields of struggle. Actually, culture remains unexplored as a particular relation between dominant and subordinate groups, expressed in antagonistic relations that embody and produce particular forms of meaning and action. In effect, these discourses exclude the concepts of "dominant" and "subordinate" culture altogether and by doing so fail to recognize the effect of wider political and social forces on all aspects of school organization and everyday classroom life.

By refusing to acknowledge the relations between culture and power, the dominant educational discourses fail to understand how schools are implicated in reproducing oppressive ideologies and social practices. Rather, they assume that schools can analyze problems faced by different cultural groups and that out of such analyses students will develop a sense of understanding and mutual respect that will in some way influence the wider society. But schools do more than influence society; they are also shaped by it. That is, schools are inextricably linked to a larger set of political and cultural processes and not only reflect the antagonisms embodied in such processes but also embody and reproduce them. This issue becomes clearer in statistical studies that reveal that "one out of every four students who enrols in ninth grade (in the U.S.) drops out before high school graduation. Drop out rates for Black students are just under twice as great [as those] for White students; those for Hispanic students are just over twice as great. . . . In 1971, 51 percent of all White and 50 percent of all Black high school graduates went to college. In 1981, the rate of young Black high school graduates enrolled in college had fallen to 40 percent, in October of 1982, it fell to 36 percent" (NCAS, 1985, p. x).

The ideological importance of these statistics is that they point to ideological and material practices that are actively produced within the day-to-day activities of schooling but originate in the wider society. They also point to the silence on a number of questions pertaining to how schools produce class, race, and gender differentiations and the fundamental antagonisms that structure them. One issue the statistics point to is how wider forms of political, economic, social, and ideological domination and subordination might be invested in the language, texts, and social practices of the schools as well as in the experiences of the teachers and students themselves. An equally important concern centres around the issue of how power in schools is expressed as a set of relations that treats some groups as privileged while disconfirming others. Some important questions that could be pursued here include: What is the ideology at work when children are tested in a language they do not understand? What interests are being sustained by tracking black children who have no serious intellectual learning disabilities into classes for the educable mentally handicapped? What are the ideologies underlying practices in urban schools where the drop-out rates are 85 percent for Native Americans and between 70 and 80 percent for Puerto Rican students (NCAS, 1985, pp. 10, 14, 16)? The important point illuminated by these figures is that dominant educational discourses lack not only an adequate theory of domination but also a critical understanding of how experience is named, constructed, and legitimated in schools.

Another major criticism of dominant educational discourses focuses on the political nature of school language. Defined primarily in technical terms (mastery) or in terms of its communicative value in developing dialogue and transmitting information, language is abstracted from its political and ideological usage. For instance, language is privileged as a medium for exchanging and presenting knowledge, and, as such, is abstracted from its constitutive role in the struggle of various groups over different meanings, practices, and readings of the world. Within dominant educational theory, there is no sense of how language practices can be used to actively silence some students or of how favoring particular forms of discourse can work to disconfirm the traditions, practices, and values of subordinate language groups; similarly, there is a failure to have teachers acquire forms of language literacy that would translate, pedagogically, into a critical understanding of the structure of language and a capacity to help students validate and critically engage their own experience and cultural milieu.

It is not surprising that within dominant educational discourses, questions of cultural difference are sometimes reduced to a single emphasis on the learning and understanding of school knowledge, in particular, as presented through the form and content of curriculum texts. Lost here are the ways in which power is invested in institutional and ideological forces that bear down on and shape social practices of schooling. There is no clear understanding, for example, of how social relations operate in schools through the organization of time, space, and resources, or the way in which different groups experience these relations via their economic, political, and social locations outside of schools. Dominant educational theory not only fails to understand schooling as a cultural process that is inextricably linked to wider social forces; it also appears incapable of recognizing how teacher and student resistance may emerge in schools as part of a refusal either to teach or to accept the dictates of dominant school culture (Giroux, 1983).

In more specific terms, dominant educational discourses fail to analyze how the school as an agent of social and cultural control is mediated and contested by those whose interests it does not serve. In part, this is due to a functionalist view of schooling which sees schools as serving the needs of the dominant society without questioning either the nature of that society or the effects it has on the daily practices of schooling itself. The theoretical price paid for this type of functionalism is high. One consequence is that schools are seen as if they were removed from the tensions and antagonisms that characterize the wider society. As a result, it becomes impossible to understand schools as sites of struggle over power and meaning. Furthermore, there is no theoretical room in this approach to understand why subordinate groups may actively resist and deny the dominant culture as it is embodied in various aspects of classroom life.

Radical Pedagogy as a Form of Cultural Politics

In this section, I want to develop a perspective that links radical pedagogy with a form of cultural politics. In doing so, I want to draw principally from the works of Paulo Freire and Mikhail Bakhtin and attempt to construct a theoretical model in which the notions of struggle, student voice, and critical dialogue are central to the goal of developing an emancipatory pedagogy.[5] Bakhtin's work is important because he views language usage as an eminently social and political act linked to the ways individuals define meaning and author their relations to the world through an ongoing dialogue with others. As the theoretician of difference, dialogue, and polyphonic voice, Bakhtin rightly emphasizes the need to understand the ongoing struggle between various groups over language and meaning as a moral and epistemological imperative. Accordingly, Bakhtin deepens our understanding of the nature of authorship by providing analyses of how people give value to and operate out of different layers of discourse. He also points to the pedagogical significance of critical dialogue as a form of authorship since it provides the medium and gives meaning to the multiple voices that construct the "texts" constitutive of everyday life.

Paulo Freire both extends and deepens Bakhtin's project. Like Bakhtin, Freire offers the possibility for organizing pedagogical experiences within social forms and practices that "speak" to developing more critical and dialogical modes of learning and struggle. But Freire's theory of experience is rooted in a view of language and culture that links dialogue and meaning to a social project emphasizing the primacy of the political. In this case, "empowerment" is defined as central to the collective struggle for a life without oppression and exploitation.

Both authors employ a view of language, dialogue, chronotype, and difference that rejects a totalizing view of history. Both argue that a critical pedagogy has to begin with a dialectical celebration of the languages of critique and possibility—an approach which finds its noblest expression in a discourse integrating critical analysis with social transformation. Similarly, both authors provide a pedagogical model that begins with problems rooted in the concrete experiences of everyday life. In effect, they provide valuable theoretical models from which radical educators can selectively draw in to develop an analysis of schools as sites of conflict actively involved in the production of lived experiences.

The work of Freire and Bakhtin points to the need to inquire into how human experiences are produced, contested, and legitimated within everyday classroom life. The theoretical importance of this analysis is linked directly to the need for radical educators to fashion a discourse in which a more comprehensive politics of culture, voice, and experience can be developed. At issue here is the recognition that schools are historical and structural embodiments of ideological forms of culture; they signify reality in ways that are often experienced differently and actively contested by various individuals and groups. Schools, in this sense, are ideological and political terrains out of which the dominant culture in part produces its hegemonic "certainties"; but they are also places where dominant and subordinate voices define and constrain each other, in battle and exchange, in response to the socio-historical conditions "carried" in the institutional, textual, and lived practices that define school culture and teacher/student experience. In other words, schools are not ideologically innocent; nor are they simply reproductive of dominant social relations and interests. At the same time, schools produce forms of political and moral regulation intimately connected with the technologies of power that "produce asymmetries in the abilities of individuals and groups to define and realize their needs" (Johnson, 1983, p. 11). More specifically, schools establish the conditions under which some individuals and groups define the terms by which others live, resist, affirm, and participate in the construction of their own identities and subjectivities. Simon (1987) illuminates quite well some of the important theoretical considerations that have to be addressed within a radical pedagogy. He is worth quoting at length on this issue:

> Our concern as educators is to develop a way of thinking about the construction and definition of subjectivity within the concrete social forms of our everyday existence in a way that grasps schooling as a cultural and political site that [embodies] a project of regulation and transformation. As educators we are required to take a position on the acceptability of such forms. We also recognize that while schooling is productive it is not so in isolation, but in complex relations with other forms organized in other sites. . . . [Moreover,] in working to reconstruct aspects of schooling [educators should attempt] to understand how it becomes implicated in the production of subjectivities [and] recognize [how] existing social forms legitimate and produce real inequities which serve the interest of some over others and that a transformative pedagogy is oppositional in intent and is threatening to some in its practice. (pp. 176–177)

Simon rightly argues that as sites of cultural production schools embody representations and practices that construct as well as block the possibilities for human agency among students. This becomes clearer if we recognize that one of the most important elements at work in the construction of experience and subjectivity in schools is language: language intersects with power just as particular linguistic forms structure and legitimate the ideologies of specific groups. Language is intimately related to power, and it constitutes the way that teachers and students define, mediate, and understand their relation to each other and the larger society.

As Bakhtin has pointed out, language is intimately related to the dynamics of authorship and voice.[6] It is within and through language that individuals in particular historical contexts shape values into particular forms and practices. As part of the production of meaning, language represents a central force in the struggle for voice. Schools are one of the primary public spheres where, through the influence of authority, resistance and dialogue, language is able to shape the way various individuals and groups encode and thereby engage the world. In other words, schools are places where language projects, imposes, and constructs particular norms and forms of meaning. In this sense, language does more than merely present "information"; in actuality, it is used as a basis both to "instruct" and to produce subjectivities. For Bakhtin, the issue of language is explored as part of a politics of struggle and representation, a politics forged in the relations of power pertaining to who decides and legislates the territory on which discourse is to be defined and negotiated. The driving momentum of voice and of authorship is inseparable from the relations between individuals and groups. In Bakhtin's terms, "the word is a two-sided act. It is determined . . . by those whose word it is and for whom it is meant. . . . A word is territory shared by both addresser and addressee, by the speaker and his interlocutor" (Volosinov [Bakhtin], 1973, pp. 85–86). At issue here is the critical insight that student subjectivities are developed across a range of discourses and can only be understood within a process of social interaction that "pumps energy from a life situation into the verbal discourse, . . . endow[ing] everything linguistically stable with living historical momentum and uniqueness" (Volosinov [Bakhtin], 1976, p. 106).

With the above theoretical assumptions in mind, I want now to argue in more specific terms for a radical pedagogy as a form of cultural politics. In effect, I want to present the case for constructing this pedagogy on a critically affirmative language that allows us to understand how subjectivities are produced; such a pedagogy makes problematic how teachers and students sustain, or resist, or accommodate those languages, ideologies, social processes, and myths that position them within existing relations of power and dependency. Moreover, this pedagogy points to the need to develop a theory of politics and culture that analyzes discourse and voice as a continually shifting balance of resources and practices in the struggle over specific ways of naming, organizing, and experiencing social reality. Discourse can be recognized as a form of cultural production, linking agency and structure through public and private representations that are concretely organized and structured within schools. Furthermore, discourse is understood as a set of experiences that are lived and suffered by individuals and groups within specific contexts and settings. Within this perspective, the concept of experience is linked to the broader issue of how subjectivities are inscribed within cultural processes that develop with regard to the dynamics of production, transformation, and struggle. Understood in these terms, a pedagogy of cultural politics presents a two-fold set of tasks for radical educators. First, they need to analyze how cultural production is organized within asymmetrical relations of power in schools. Second, they need to construct political strategies for participating in social struggles designed to fight for schools as democratic public spheres.

In order to realize these tasks, it is necessary to assess the political limits and pedagogical potentialities of instances of cultural production that constitute the various processes of schooling. It is important to note that I am calling these social processes "instances of cultural production" rather than using the dominant leftist concept of reproduction. While the notion of reproduction points adequately to the various economic and political ideologies and interests that are reconstituted within the relations of schooling, it lacks a comprehensive, theoretical understanding of how such interests are mediated, worked on, and subjectively produced.

A radical pedagogy that assumes the form of a cultural politics must examine how cultural processes are produced and transformed within three particular, though related, fields of discourse. These are: *the discourse of production, the discourse of text analysis,* and *the discourse of lived cultures.* Each of these discourses has a history of theoretical development in various models of leftist analysis, and each has been subjected to intense discussion and criticism. These need not be repeated here.[7] What I want to do is to look at the potentialities exhibited by these discourses in their interconnections, particularly as they point to a new set of categories for developing educational practices that empower teachers and students to take up emancipatory interests.

Educational Practice and the Discourse of Production

The discourse of production in educational theory has focused on the ways in which the structural forces outside the immediacy of school life construct the objective conditions within which schools function. This strategic framework can provide us with illuminating analyses of the state, the workplace, foundations, publishing companies, and other embodiments of political interest that directly or indirectly influence school policy. Moreover, schools are understood within a larger network that allows us to analyze them as historical and social constructions, as embodiments of social forms that always bear a relationship to the wider society. A fundamental task of the discourse of production is to alert teachers to the primacy of identifying practices and interests that legitimate specific public representations and ways of life. To attempt to understand the process of schooling without taking into consideration how these wider forms of production are constructed, manifested, and contested both in and out of schools is inconceivable within this discourse. This becomes obvious, for instance, if we wish to analyze the ways in which state policy embodies and promotes particular practices that legitimate and render privileged some forms of knowledge over others, or some groups over others.[8] Equally significant would be an analysis of how dominant educational theory and practice are constructed, sustained, and circulated outside of schools. For instance, radical educators need to do more than identify the language and values of corporate ideologies as they are manifested in school curricula; they also need to analyze and transform the processes through which they are produced and circulated. Another important aspect of this approach is that it points to the way in which labor is objectively constructed; that is, it provides the basis for an analysis of the conditions under which educators work and the political importance of these conditions in both limiting and enabling pedagogical practice. This is especially important for analyzing the critical possibilities that exist for public school teachers and students to act and be treated as intellectuals, or, to put it in the words of C. W. Mills, as people who can get "in touch with the realities of themselves and their world" (1979, p. 370).

I would like to stress, however, that if teachers and students work in overcrowded conditions, lack time to work collectively in a creative fashion, or are shackled by rules that disempower them, then these conditions of labor have to be understood and addressed as part of the dynamics of reform and struggle (Aronowitz & Giroux, 1985). The discourse of production represents an important starting point for a pedagogy of cultural politics because it evaluates the relationship between schools and wider structural forces in light of a politics of human dignity—more specifically, a politics fashioned around the ways in which human dignity can be realized in public spheres designed to provide the material conditions for work, dialogue, and self- and social realization. Accordingly, these public spheres represent what Dewey, Mills, and others have called the conditions for freedom and praxis, political embodiments of a social project that takes liberation as its major goal (see Dewey, 1984).

Radical Pedagogy and the Discourse of Textual Analysis

Another important element in the development of a radical pedagogy, which I describe as the discourse of textual analysis, refers to any form of critique capable of analyzing cultural forms as they are produced and used in specific classrooms. The purpose of this approach is to provide teachers and students with the critical tools necessary to analyze those socially constructed representations and interests that organize particular readings of curriculum materials.

The discourse of textual analysis not only draws attention to the ideologies out of which texts are produced, but it also allows educators to distance themselves from the text in order to uncover the layers of meanings, contradictions, and differences inscribed in the form and content of classroom materials. The political and pedagogical importance of this form of analysis is that it opens the text to deconstruction, interrogating it as part of a wider process of cultural production; in addition, by making the text an object of intellectual inquiry, such an analysis posits the reader, not as a passive consumer, but as an active producer of meanings. In this view, the text is no longer endowed with an authorial essence waiting to be translated or discovered. On the contrary, the text becomes an ensemble of discourses constituted by a play of contradictory meanings, some of which are visibly privileged and some of which, in Macherey's terms, represent "a new discourse, the articulation of a silence" (1978, p. 6). Critical to this perspective are the notions of critique, production, and difference, all of which provide important elements for a counterhegemonic pedagogical practice. Belsey (1980) weaves these elements together in her critique of the classical realist text:

> As an alternative it was possible to recognize it [classical realist text] as a construct and so to treat it as available for deconstruction, that is, the analysis of the process and conditions of its construction out of the available discourses. Ideology, masquerading as coherence and plenitude, is in reality inconsistent, limited, contradictory, and the realist text as a crystallization of ideology, participates in this incompleteness even while it diverts attention from the fact in the apparent plenitude of narrative closure. The object of deconstructing the text is to examine the process of its production—not the private experience of the individual author, but the mode of production, the materials and their arrangement in the work. The aim is

to locate the point of contradiction within the text, the point at which it transgresses the limits within which it is constructed, breaks free of the constraints imposed by its own realist form. Composed of contradictions, the text is no longer restricted to a single, harmonious and authoritative reading. Instead, it becomes plural, open to re-reading, no longer an object for passive consumption but an object of work by the reader to produce meaning. (p. 104)

This is a particularly important mode of analysis for radical educators because it argues against the idea that the means of representation in texts are merely neutral conveyors of ideas. Furthermore, such an approach points to the need for careful systematic analyses of the way in which material is used and ordered in school curricula and how its "signifiers" register particular ideological pressures and tendencies. Such an analysis allows teachers and students to deconstruct meanings that are silently built into the structuring principles of classroom meanings, thereby adding an important theoretical dimension to analyzing how the overt and hidden curricula work in schools.

At the day-to-day level of schooling, this type of textual criticism can be used to analyze how the technical conventions or images within various forms such as *narrative, mode of address,* and *ideological* reference attempt to construct a limited range of positions from which they are to be read. Richard Johnson (1983) is worth quoting on this point:

The legitimate object of an identification of "positions" is the pressures or tendencies on the reader, the theoretical problematic which produces subjective forms, the directions in which they move in their force—once inhabited. . . . If we add to this the argument that certain kinds of text ("realism") naturalise the means by which positioning is achieved, we have a dual insight of great force. The particular promise is to render processes hitherto unconsciously suffered (and enjoyed) open to explicit analysis. (pp. 64–65)

Coupled with traditional forms of ideology critique directed at the subject content of school materials, the discourse of text analysis also provides valuable insight into how subjectivities and cultural forms work within schools. The value of this kind of work has been exhibited in analyses which argue that the principles used in the construction of prepackaged curriculum materials utilize a mode of address that positions teachers as mere implementers of knowledge (Apple, 1983). This is clearly at odds with treating teachers and students as critical agents who play an active role in the pedagogical process. In one illuminating display of this approach, Judith Williamson (1978) has provided an extensive study of mass advertising. Similarly, Ariel Dorfman has applied this mode of analysis to various texts in popular culture, including the portrayal of characters such as Donald Duck and Babar the Elephant. It is in his analysis of *Readers Digest* that Dorfman (1983) exhibits a dazzling display of the critical value of text analysis. In one example, he analyzes how *Readers Digest* uses a mode of representation that downplays the importance of viewing knowledge in its historical and dialectical connections. He writes:

> Just as with superheroes, knowledge does not transform the reader; on the contrary, the more he [sic] reads the *Digest*, the less he needs to change. Here is where all that fragmentation returns to play the role it was always meant to play. Prior knowledge is never assumed. From month to month, the reader must purify himself, suffer from amnesia, bottle the knowledge he's acquired and put it on some out-of-the-way shelf so it doesn't interfere with the innocent pleasure of consuming more, all over again. What he learned about the Romans doesn't apply to the Etruscans. Hawaii has nothing to do with Polynesia. Knowledge is consumed for its effect, for "information renewal," for the interchange of banalities. It is useful only insofar as it can be digested anecdotally, but its potential for original sin has been washed clean along with the temptation to generate truth or movement— in other words: change.

Inherent in all of these positions is a call for modes of criticism that promote dialogue as the condition for social action: dialogue, in this case, rooted in a pedagogy informed by a number of assumptions drawn from the works of Bakhtin and Freire. These include: treating the text as a social construct that is produced out of a number of available discourses; locating the contradictions and gaps within an educational text and situating them historically in terms of the interests they sustain and legitimate; recognizing in the text its internal politics of style and how this both opens up and constrains particular representations of the social world; understanding how the text actively works to silence certain voices; and, finally, discovering how to release possibilities from the text that provide new insights and critical readings regarding human understanding and social practices.

I also want to argue that in order to develop a critical pedagogy as a form of cultural politics, it is essential to develop a mode of analysis that does not assume that lived experiences can be inferred automatically from structural determinations. In other words, the complexity of human behavior cannot be reduced to determinants in which such behavior is shaped and against which it constitutes itself, whether these be economic modes of production or systems of textual signification. The way in which individuals and groups both mediate and inhabit the cultural forms presented by such structural forces is in itself a form of production, and needs to be analyzed through related but different modes of analyses. In order to develop this point, I want to present briefly the pedagogical implications of what I call the discourse of lived cultures.

Radical Pedagogy and the Discourse of Lived Cultures

Central to this view is the need to develop what I have termed the theory of self-production (see Touraine, 1977). In the most general sense, this demands an understanding of how teachers and students give meaning to their lives through the complex historical, cultural, and political forms that they both embody and produce. A number of issues need to be developed within a critical pedagogy around this concern. First, it is necessary to acknowledge the subjective forms of political will and struggle that give meaning to the lives of students. Second, as a mode of critique, the discourse of lived cultures should interrogate the ways in which people create stories, memories, and narratives that posit a sense of determination and agency. This is the cultural "stuff" of mediation, the conscious and unconscious material through which members of dominant and subordinate groups offer accounts of who they are in their different readings of the world.

If radical educators treat the histories, experiences, and languages of different cultural groups as particularized forms of production, it becomes less difficult to understand the diverse readings, mediations, and behaviors that, let us say, students exhibit in response to analysis of a particular classroom text. In fact, a cultural politics necessitates that a pedagogy be developed that is attentive to the histories, dreams, and experiences that such students bring to school. It is only by beginning with these subjective forms that critical educators can develop a language and set of practices that engage the contradictory nature of the cultural capital with which students produce meanings that legitimate particular forms of life.

Searching out such elements of self-production is not merely a pedagogical technique for confirming the experiences of students who are silenced by the dominant culture of schooling. It is also part of an analysis of how power, dependence, and social inequality enable and limit students around issues of class, race, and gender. The discourse of lived cultures becomes an "interrogative framework" for teachers, illuminating not only how power and knowledge intersect to disconfirm the cultural capital of students from subordinate groups but also how they can be translated into a language of possibility. The discourse of lived cultures can also be used to develop a radical pedagogy of popular culture, one that engages the knowledge of lived experience through the dual method of confirmation and interrogation. The knowledge of the "other" is engaged in this instance not simply to be celebrated but also to be interrogated with respect to the ideologies it contains, the means of representation it utilizes, and the underlying social practices it confirms. At issue here is the need to link knowledge and power theoretically so as to give students the opportunity to understand more critically who they are as part of a wider social formation and how they have been positioned and constituted through the social domain.

The discourse of lived cultures also points to the need for radical educators to view schools as cultural and political spheres actively engaged in the production and struggle for voice. In many cases, schools do not allow students from subordinate groups to authenticate their problems and experiences through their own individual and collective voices. As I have stressed previously, the dominant school culture generally represents and legitimates the privileged voices of the white middle and upper classes. In order for radical educators to demystify the dominant culture and to make it an object of political analysis, they will need to master the "language of critical understanding." If they are to understand the dominant ideology at work in schools, they will need to attend to the voices that emerge from three different ideological spheres and settings: these include *the school voice, the student voice,* and *the teacher voice.* The interests that these different voices represent have to be analyzed, not so much as oppositional in the sense that they work to counter and disable each other, but as an interplay of dominant and subordinate practices that shape each other in an ongoing struggle over power, meaning, and authorship. This, in turn, presupposes the necessity for analyzing schools in their historical and relational specificity, and it points to the possibility for intervening and shaping school outcomes. In order to understand the multiple and varied meanings that constitute the discourses of student voice, radical educators need to affirm and critically engage the polyphonic languages their students bring to schools. Educators need to learn "the collection and communicative practices associated with particular uses of both written and spoken forms among specific groups" (Sola & Bennett, 1985, p. 89). Moreover, any adequate understanding of this language has to encompass the social and community relations outside of school life that give it meaning and dignity.

Learning the discourse of school voice means that radical educators need to critically analyze the directives, imperatives, and rules that shape particular configurations of time, space, and curricula within the institutional and political settings of schools. The category of school voice, for example, points to sets of practices and ideologies that structure how classrooms are arranged, what content is taught, what general social practices teachers have to follow. Moreover, it is in the interplay between the dominant school culture and the polyphonic representations and layers of meaning of student voice that dominant and oppositional ideologies define and constrain each other.

Teacher voice reflects the values, ideologies, and structuring principles that give meaning to the histories, cultures, and subjectivities that define the day-to-day activities of educators. It is the critical voice of common sense that teachers utilize to mediate between the discourses of production, of texts, and of lived cultures as expressed within the asymmetrical relations of power characterizing such potentially "counterpublic" spheres as schools. In effect, it is through the mediation and action of teacher voice that the very nature of the schooling process is either sustained or challenged; that is, the power of teacher voice to shape schooling according to the logic of emancipatory interests is inextricably related to a high degree of self-understanding regarding values and interests. Teacher voice moves within a contradiction that points to its pedagogical significance for marginalizing as well as empowering students. On the one hand, teacher voice represents a basis in authority that can provide knowledge and forms of self-understanding allowing students to develop the power of critical consciousness. At the same time, regardless of how politically or ideologically correct a teacher may be, his or her "voice" can be destructive for students if it is imposed on them or if it is used to silence them.

Kathleen Weiler (1988), in her brilliant ethnography of a group of feminist school administrators and teachers, illustrates this issue. She reports on one class in which a feminist teacher has read a selection from *The Autobiography of Malcolm X* describing how a young Malcolm is told by one of his public school teachers that the most he can hope for in life is to get a job working with his hands. In reading this story, the teacher's aim is to illustrate a particular theory of socialization. John, a black student in the class, reads the selection as an example of outright racism, one that he fully understands in light of his own experiences. He isn't interested in looking at the more abstract issue of socialization. For him, the issue is naming a racist experience and condemning it forcefully. Molly, the teacher, sees John's questions as disruptive and chooses to ignore him. In response to her action, John drops out of the class the next day. Defending her position, Molly argues that students must learn how the process of socialization works, especially if they are to understand fundamental concepts in sociology. But in teaching this point, she has failed to understand that students inhabit multilayered subjectivities which often promote contradictory and diverse voices and as such present different, if not oppositional, readings of the materials provided in class, in spite of their alleged worth. In this case, the culture of the teacher's voice, which is white and middle class, comes into conflict with that of the student voice, which is black and working class. Rather than mediating this conflict in a pedagogically progressive way, the teacher allowed her voice and authority to silence the student's anger, concern, and interests.

I also want to add that the category of teacher voice points to the need for radical educators to join together in a wider social movement dedicated to restructuring the ideological and material conditions that work both within and outside of schooling. The notion of voice in this case points to a shared tradition as well as a particular form of discourse. It is a tradition that has to organize around the issues of solidarity, struggle, and empowerment in order to provide the conditions for the particularities of teacher and student voice to gain the most emancipatory expression. Thus, the category of teacher voice needs to be understood in terms of its collective political project as well as in relation to the ways it functions to mediate student voices and everyday school life.

In general terms, the discourse of critical understanding not only represents an acknowledgement of the political and pedagogical processes at work in the construction of forms of authorship and voice within different institutional and social spheres; it also constitutes a critical attack on the vertical ordering of reality inherent in the unjust practices that are actively at work in the wider society. To redress some of the problems sketched out in the preceding pages, I believe that schools need to be reconceived and reconstituted as "democratic counterpublic spheres"— as places where students learn the skills and knowledge needed to live in and fight for a viable democratic society. Within this perspective, schools will have to be characterized by a pedagogy that demonstrates its commitment to engaging the views and problems that deeply concern students in their everyday lives. Equally important is the need for schools to cultivate a spirit of critique and a respect for human dignity that will be capable of linking personal and social issues around the pedagogical project of helping students to become active citizens.

In conclusion, each of the three major discourses presented above as part of a radical pedagogy involves a different view of cultural production, pedagogical analysis, and political action. And while each of these radical discourses involves a certain degree of autonomy in both form and content, it is important that a radical pedagogy be developed around the inner connections they share within the context of a cultural politics. For it is within these interconnections that a critical theory of structure and agency can be developed—a theory that engenders a radical educational language capable of asking new questions, making new commitments, and allowing educators to work and organize for the development of schools as democratic counterpublic spheres.

Notes

1. This position has a long history in American public education and is reviewed in Raymond Callahan, *The Cult of Efficiency* (1962); Joel Spring, *Education and the Rise of the Corporate Order* (1972); and Henry A. Giroux, "Public Philosophy and the Crisis in Education" (1984).

2. The most celebrated example of this position can be found in Sam Bowles and Herbert Gintis, *Schooling in Capitalist America* (1976). The literature on schooling and the reproductive thesis is critically reviewed in Stanley Aronowitz and Henry A. Giroux, *Education Under Siege* (1985).

3. I want to make clear that there is a major distinction between the work of John Dewey, especially *Democracy and Education* (1916), and the hybrid discourses of progressive, educational reform that characterized the late 1960s and 1970s in the United States. The discourse of relevance and integration that I am analyzing here bears little resemblance to Dewey's philosophy of experience in that Dewey stressed the relationships among student experience, critical reflection, and learning. In contrast, the call for relevance that has characterized progressive education generally surrenders the concept of systematic knowledge acquisition to an anti-intellectual concept of student experience.

4. For a recent analysis of school tracking, see Jeannie Oakes, *Keeping Track: How Schools Structure Inequality* (1985). See also, Henry A. Giroux and David Purpel, *The Hidden Curriculum and Moral Education* (1983).

5. The works from which I will be drawing for both authors include: Paulo Freire, *Pedagogy of the Oppressed* (1970), *Education for Critical Consciousness* (1973), *The Politics of Education* (1985); and Mikhail Bakhtin, *Rabelais and His World* (1984a), *Problems of Dostoevsky's Poetics* (1984b), V. N. Volosinov (M. M. Bakhtin) *Marxism and the Philosophy of Language* (1973); and *Freudianism: A Marxist Critique* (1976).

6. See Ann Shukman (Ed.), *Bakhtin's School Papers* (1983); V. N. Volosinov (M. M. Bakhtin), *Marxism and the Philosophy of Language* (1973).

7. A major analysis of these discourses and the traditions with which they are generally associated can be found in Richard Johnson, "What is Cultural Studies Anyway?" (1983).

8. Examples of this discourse can be found in Martin Carnoy and Henry Levin, *Schooling and Work in the Democratic State* (1985).

References

Adler, M. (1982). *The paideia proposal.* New York: Macmillan.

Apple, M. (1983). *Education and power.* New York: Routledge & Kegan Paul.

Aronowitz, S., & Giroux, H. A. (1985). *Education under siege.* South Hadley, MA: Bergin & Garvey.

Bakhtin, M. (1981). *The dialogic imagination* (C. Emerson & M. Holquist, Trans.). Austin: University of Texas Press.

Bakhtin, M. (1984a). *Rabelais and his world* (H. Iswolsky, Trans.). Bloomington: Indiana University Press.

Bakhtin, M. (1984b). *Problems of Dostoevsky's poetics* (C. Emerson, Trans.). Minneapolis: University of Minnesota Press.
Belsey, C. (1980). *Critical practice.* New York: Methuen.
Bowles, S., & Gintis, H. (1976). *Schooling in capitalist America.* New York: Basic Books.
Callahan, R. (1962). *The cult of efficiency.* Chicago: University of Chicago Press.
Carnoy, M., & Levin, H. (1985). *Schooling and work in the democratic states.* Stanford: Stanford University Press.
Corrigan, P. (1985). *Race, ethnicity, gender, culture: Embodying differences educationally—An argument.* Unpublished paper. Ontario Institute for Studies in Education, Toronto.
Cusick, P. (1983). *The egalitarian ideal and the American school.* New York: Longman.
Dewey, J. (1916). *Democracy and education.* New York: Free Press.
Dewey, J. (1984). The public and its problems. In J. A. Boydston (Ed.), *John Dewey, the later works* (Vol. 2: 1925–1927). Carbondale, IL: Southern Illinois Press.
Dorfman, A. (1983). *The empire's old clothes.* New York: Pantheon.
Freire, P. (1970). *Pedagogy of the oppressed.* New York: Seabury Press.
Freire, P. (1973). *Education for critical consciousness.* New York: Seabury Press.
Freire, P. (1985). *The politics of education.* South Hadley, MA: Bergin & Garvey.
Giroux, H. A. (1983). *Theory and resistance in education.* South Hadley, MA: Bergin & Garvey.
Giroux, H. A. (1984). Public philosophy and the crisis of education. *Harvard Educational Review, 54*(2), 186–194.
Giroux, H. A., & Purpel, D. (1983). *The hidden curriculum and moral education.* Berkeley: McCutchan.
Glazer, N. (1977). Cultural pluralism: The social aspect. In M. Tumen & W. Plotch (Eds.), *Pluralism in a democratic society.* New York: Prager.
Henriques, J., Holloway, W., Urwin, C., Venn, C., & Walkerdine, V. (1984). *Changing the subject.* New York: Methuen.
Jeffcoate, R. (1979). *Positive image: Towards a multicultural curriculum.* London: Writers & Readers Cooperative.
Johnson, R. (1983). What is Cultural Studies anyway? *Anglistica, 26*(1/2).
Macherey, P. (1978). *A theory of literacy production* (G. Wall, Trans.). London: Routledge & Kegan Paul.
Mills, C. W. (1979). Mass society and liberal education. In I. L. Horowitz (Ed.), *Collected essays of C. W. Mills.* New York: Oxford University Press.
National Coalition of Advocates for Students (NCAS) (1985). *Barriers to excellence: Our children at risk.* Boston: Author.
Oakes, J. (1985). *Keeping track: How schools structure inequality.* New Haven: Yale University Press.
Rogers, C. (1969). *Freedom to learn.* Columbus, OH: Charles Merrill.
Shukman, A. (Ed.). (1983). *Bakhtin's school papers.* Oxford: RPT Publications.
Simon, R. (1987). Work experience as the production of subjectivity. In D. Livingstone (Ed.), *Critical pedagogy and cultural power.* South Hadley, MA: Bergin & Garvey.

Spring, J. (1972). *Education and the rise of the corporate order.* Boston: Beacon Press.

Sola, M., & Bennett, A. (1985). The struggle for voice: Narrative, literacy, and consciousness in an East Harlem school. *Boston University Journal of Education,* 167(1).

Touraine, A. (1977). *The self-production of society.* Chicago: University of Chicago Press.

Volosinov, V. N. (M. M. Bakhtin). (1973). *Marxism and the philosophy of language* (L. Mateyka & I. R. Titunik, Trans.). New York: Seminar Press.

Volosinov, V. N. (M. M. Bakhtin). (1976). *Freudianism: A Marxist critique.* New York: Academic Press.

Weiler, K. (1988). *Women teaching for change.* South Hadley, MA: Bergin & Garvey.

Williamson, J. (1978). *Decoding advertisements.* New York: Marion Boyars.

6 | *Border Pedagogy in the Age of Postmodernism*

Border Pedagogy as a Counter-Text

Border pedagogy offers the opportunity for students to engage the multiple references that constitute different cultural codes, experiences, and languages. This means educating students not only to read these codes critically but also to learn the limits of such codes, including the ones they use to construct their own narratives and histories. Partiality becomes, in this case, the basis for recognizing the limits built into all discourses and necessitates taking a critical view of authority. Within this discourse, a student must engage knowledge as a border-crosser, as a person moving in and out of borders constructed around coordinates of difference and power (Hicks, 1988). These are not only physical borders, they are cultural borders historically constructed and socially organized within maps of rules and regulations that limit and enable particular identities, individual capacities, and social forms. In this case, students cross over into borders of meaning, maps of knowledge, social relations, and values that are increasingly being negotiated and rewritten as the codes and regulations which organize them become destabilized and reshaped. Border pedagogy decenters as it remaps. The terrain of learning becomes inextricably linked to the shifting parameters of place, identity, history, and power.

Within critical social theory, it has become commonplace to argue that knowledge and power are related, though the weight of the argument has often overemphasized how domination works through the intricacies of this relationship (Foucault, 1977b). Border pedagogy offers a crucial theoretical and political corrective to this insight. It does so by shifting the emphasis of the knowledge/power relationship away from the limited emphasis on the mapping of domination to the politically strategic issue of engaging the ways in which knowledge can be remapped, reterritorialized, and decentered in the wider interests of rewriting the borders and coordinates of an oppositional cultural politics. This is not an abandonment of critique as much as it is an extension of its possibilities. In this case, border pedagogy not only incorporates the postmodern emphasis on criticizing official texts and using alternative modes of representation (mixing video, photography, and print), it also incorporates popular culture as a serious object of politics and analysis and makes central to its project the recovery of those forms of knowledge and history that characterize alternative and oppositional Others (Said, 1983). How these cultural practices might be taken up as pedagogical practices has been demonstrated by a number of theorists (Brodkey & Fine, 1988; Cherryholmes, 1988; Giroux & Simon, 1988; Scholes, 1985).

For example, Robert Scholes (1985) develops elements of a "border pedagogy" around the notion of textual power. According to Scholes, texts have to be seen in historical and temporal terms and not treated as a sacred vehicle for producing eternal truths. Instead of simply imparting information to students, Scholes argues that teachers should replace teaching texts with what he calls textuality. What this refers to pedagogically is a process of textual study that can be identified by three forms of practice: reading, interpretation, and criticism, which roughly correspond to what Scholes calls reading within, upon, and against a text. In brief, reading within a text means identifying the cultural codes that structure an author's work. But it also has the pedagogical value of illuminating further how such codes function as part of a student's own attempt "to produce written texts that are 'within' the world constructed by their reading" (p. 27). This is particularly important, Scholes adds, in giving students the opportunity to "retell the story, to summarize it, and to expand it." Interpretation means reading a text along with a variety of diverse interpretations that represent a second commentary on the text. At issue here is the pedagogical task of helping students to analyze texts within "a network of relations with other texts and institutional practices" so as to make available to students "the whole intertextual system of relations that connects one text to others—a system that will finally include the student's own writing" (Scholes, 1985, p. 30). The first two stages of Scholes's pedagogical practice are very important because they demonstrate the need for students to sufficiently engage and disrupt the text. He wants students to read the text in terms that the author might have intended so as not to make the text merely a mirror image of the student's own subjective position, but at the same time he wants students to open the text up to a wide variety of readings so it can be "sufficiently other for us to interpret it and, especially to criticize it" (Scholes, 1985, p. 39). Finally, Scholes wants students to explode the cultural codes of the text through the assertion of the reader's own textual power, to analyze the text in terms of its absences, to free "ourselves from [the] text [by] finding a position outside the assumptions upon which the text is based" (p. 62). Scholes combines the best of postmodern criticism with a notion of modernity in his notion of pedagogy. He wants, on the one hand, to engage texts as semiotic objects, but on the other hand he employs a modernist concern for history by arguing that the point of such an interrogation is to "liberate us from the empirical object— whether institution, even, or individual work—by displacing our attention to its constitution as an object and its relationship to the other objects constituted" (Scholes, 1985, p. 84).

Another example of how a postmodern pedagogy of resistance might inform the notion of border pedagogy can be found in some of the recent work being done on educational theory and popular culture (Giroux & Simon, 1988; Giroux & Simon, 1989). Two important issues are being worked out. First, there is a central concern for understanding how the production of meaning is tied to emotional investments and the production of pleasure. In this view, it is necessary for teachers to incorporate into their pedagogies a theoretical understanding of how the production of meaning and pleasure become mutually constitutive of who students are, how they view themselves, and how they construct a particular vision of their future. Second, rethinking the nature of how students make semantic and emotional investments needs to be theorized within a number of important pedagogical considerations. One such consideration is that the production and regulation of desire must be seen as a crucial aspect of how students mediate, relate, resist, and create particular cultural forms and forms of knowing. Another concern is that popular culture be seen as a legitimate aspect of the everyday lives of students and be analyzed as a primary force in shaping the various and often contradictory subject positions that students take up. Finally, popular culture needs to become a serious object of study in the official curriculum. This can be done by treating popular culture either as a distinct object of study within particular academic disciplines such as media studies or by drawing upon the resources it produces for engaging various aspects of the official curriculum (Giroux & Simon, 1988).

In both of these examples, important elements of a border pedagogy informed by postmodern criticism point to ways in which those master narratives based on white, patriarchal, and class-specific versions of the world can be challenged critically and effectively deterritorialized. That is, by offering a theoretical language for establishing new boundaries with respect to knowledge most often associated with the margins and the periphery of the cultural dominant, postmodern discourses open up the possibility for incorporating into the curriculum a notion of border pedagogy in which cultural and social practices need no longer be mapped or referenced solely on the basis of the dominant models of Western culture. In this case, knowledge forms emanating from the margins can be used to redefine the complex, multiple, heterogeneous realities that constitute those relations of difference that make up the experiences of students who often find it impossible to define their identities through the cultural and political codes of a single, unitary culture.

The sensibility which informs this view of knowledge emphasizes a pedagogy in which students need to develop a relationship of non-identity with respect to their own subject positions and the multiple cultural, political, and social codes which constitute established boundaries of power, dependency, and possibility. In other words, such a pedagogy emphasizes the nonsynchronous relationship between one's social position and the multiple ways in which culture is constructed and read. That is, there is no single, predetermined relationship between a cultural code and the subject position that a student occupies. One's class, racial, gender, or ethnic position may influence but does not irrevocably predetermine how one takes up a particular ideology, reads a particular text, or responds to particular forms of oppression. Border pedagogy recognizes that teachers, students, and others often "read and write culture on multiple levels" (Kaplan, 1987, p. 187). Of course, the different subject positions and forms of subjugation that are constituted within these various levels and relations of culture have the potential to isolate and alienate instead of opening up the possibility for criticism and struggle. What is at stake here is developing a border pedagogy that can fruitfully work to break down those ideologies, cultural codes, and social practices that prevent students from recognizing how social forms at particular historical conjunctures operate to repress alternative readings of their own experiences, society, and the world.

Border Pedagogy as Counter-Memory

Postmodernism charts the process of deterritorialization as part of the breakdown of master narratives. It celebrates, in part, the loss of certainty and experience of defamiliarization even as it produces alienation and the displacement of identities (Deleuze & Guattari, 1986). In opposition to conservative readings of this shifting destabilizing process, I believe that such a disruption of traditional meaning offers important insights for developing a theory of border pedagogy based on a postmodernism of resistance. But this language runs the risk of undercutting its own political possibilities by ignoring how a language of difference can be articulated with critical modernist concerns for developing a discourse of public life. It also ignores the possibilities for developing, through the process of counter-memory, new and emancipatory forms of political identity. In what follows, I address some of the important work being done in radical public philosophy and feminist theory, paying particular attention to the issues of identity and counter-memory. The brief final section of this paper will offer some considerations of how the critical insights of a postmodernism of resistance can be deepened within a theory of border pedagogy.

Postmodernism has launched a major attack on the modernist notion of political universality (Ross, 1988). By insisting on the multiplicity of social positions, it has seriously challenged the political closure of modernity with its divisions between the center and the margins and in doing so has made room for those groups generally defined as the excluded others. In effect, postmodernism has reasserted the importance of the partial, the local, and the contingent, and in doing so it has given general expression to the demands of a wide variety of social movements. Postmodernism has also effectively challenged the ways in which written history has embodied a number of assumptions that inform the discourse of Eurocentrism. More specifically, it has rejected such Eurocentric assumptions as the pretentious claim to "speak" for all of mankind (*sic*) and the epistemological claims to foundationalism.

Laclau (1988) rightfully argues that an adequate approximation of the postmodern experience needs to be seen as part of a challenge to the discourses of modernity, with their "pretension to intellectually dominate the foundation of the social, to give a rational context to the notion of the totality of history, and to base in the latter the project of global human emancipation" (pp. 71–72). But Laclau also points out that the postmodern challenge to modernity does not represent the abandonment of its emancipatory values so much as it opens them up to a plurality of contexts and an indeterminacy "that redefines them in an unpredictable way" (p. 72). Chantal Mouffe (1988) extends this insight and argues that modernity has two contradictory aspects: its political project is rooted in a conception of the struggle for democracy, while its social project is tied to a foundationalism which fuels the process of social modernization under "the growing domination of relations of capitalist production" (p. 32). For Mouffe, the modernist project of democracy must be coupled with an understanding of the various social movements and the new politics that have emerged with the postmodern age. At the heart of this position is the need to rearticulate the tradition of liberty and justice with a notion of radical democracy; similarly, there is a need to articulate the concept of difference as more than a replay of liberal pluralism or a pastiche of diverse strands of interests with no common ground to hold them together.

This is not a liberal call to harmonize and resolve differences, as critics like Elizabeth Ellsworth (1988) wrongly argue, but an attempt to understand differences in terms of the historical and social grounds on which they are organized. By locating differences in a particular historical and

social location, it becomes possible to understand how they are organized and constructed within maps of rules and regulations and located
within dominant social forms which either enable or disable such differences. Differences only exist relative to the social forms in which they
are enunciated, that is, in relation to schools, workplaces, families, as
well as in relationship to the discourses of history, citizenship, sex, race,
gender, and ethnicity. To detach them from the discourse of democracy
and freedom is to remove the possibility of either articulating their particular interests as part of a wider struggle for power or understanding
how their individual contradictory interests are developed with historically specific conjunctures. At stake here is the need for educators to
fashion a critical politics of difference not outside but within a tradition
of radical democracy. Similarly, it is imperative for critical educators to
develop a discourse of counter-memory, not as an essentialist and
closed narrative, but as part of a utopian project that recognizes "the
composite, heterogeneous, open, and ultimately indeterminate character of the democratic tradition" (Mouffe, 1988, p. 41). The pedagogical
issue here is the need to articulate difference as part of the construction
of a new type of subject, one which would be both multiple and democratic. Chantal Mouffe (1988) is worth quoting at length on this issue:

> If the task of radical democracy is indeed to deepen the democratic revolu-
> tion and to link together diverse democratic struggles, such a task requires
> the creation of new subject-positions that would allow the common articu-
> lation, for example, of antiracism, antisexism, and anticapitalism. These
> struggles do not spontaneously converge, and in order to establish demo-
> cratic equivalences, a new "common sense" is necessary, which would
> transform the identity of different groups so that the demands of each
> group could be articulated with those of others according to the principle
> of democratic equivalence. For it is not a matter of establishing a mere al-
> liance between given interests but of actually modifying the very identity of
> these forces. In order that the defense of workers' interests is not pursued at
> the cost of the rights of women, immigrants, or consumers, it is necessary
> to establish an equivalence between these different struggles. It is only
> under these circumstances that struggles against [authoritarian] power be-
> come truly democratic. (p. 42)

How might the issue of democracy and difference be taken up as part
of a border pedagogy informed by a project of possibility? I want to
argue that the discourses of democracy and difference can be taken up
as pedagogical practices through what Foucault calls the notion of
counter-memory. For Foucault (1977a), counter-memory is a practice
which "transforms history from a judgment on the past in the name of
the present truth to a 'counter-memory' that combats our current
modes of truth and justice, helping us to understand and change the

present by placing it in a new relation to the past" (pp. 160, 163–164). Counter-memory represents a critical reading of not only how the past informs the present but how the present reads the past. Counter-memory provides a theoretical tool to restore the connection between the language of public life and the discourse of difference. It represents an attempt to rewrite the language of resistance in terms that connect human beings within forms of remembrance that dignify public life while at the same time allowing people to speak from their particular histories and voices. Counter-memory refuses to treat democracy as merely inherited knowledge; it attempts, instead, to link democracy to notions of public life that "afford both agency and sources of power or empowering investments" (De Lauretis, 1987, p. 25). It also reasserts as a pedagogical practice the rewriting of history through the power of student voice. This points to the practice of counter-memory as a means of constructing democratic social forms that enable and disable particular subjectivities and identities; put another way, democracy in this instance becomes a referent for understanding how public life organizes differences and what this means for the ways in which schools, teachers, and students define themselves as political subjects, as citizens who operate within particular configurations of power.

In effect, the language of radical democracy provides the basis for educators not only to understand how differences are organized but also how the ground for such difference might be constructed within a political identity rooted in a respect for democratic public life (Giroux, 1988b). What is being suggested here is the construction of a project of possibility in pedagogical terms which is connected to a notion of democracy capable of mobilizing a variety of groups to develop and struggle for what Linda Alcoff (1988) calls a positive alternative vision. She writes, "As the Left should by now have learned, you cannot mobilize a movement that is only and always against: you must have a positive alternative, a vision of a better future that can motivate people to sacrifice their time and energy toward its realization" (Alcoff, 1988, pp. 418–419). If the notion of radical democracy is to function as a pedagogical practice, educators need to allow students to comprehend democracy as a way of life that consistently has to be fought for, has to be struggled over, and has to be rewritten as part of an oppositional politics. This means that democracy has to be viewed as a historical and social construction rooted in the tension between what Bruce James Smith (1985) calls remembrance and custom. I want to extend Smith's argument by developing remembrance as a form of counter-memory and custom as a form of reactionary nostalgia rooted in the loss of memory.

Custom, as Smith (1985) argues, constructs subjects within a discourse of continuity in which knowledge and practice are viewed as a matter of inheritance and transmission. Custom is the complex of ideologies and social practices that views counter-memory as subversive and critical teaching as unpatriotic. It is the ideological basis for forms of knowledge and pedagogy which refuse to interrogate public forms and which deny difference as a fundamental referent for a democratic society. According to Smith (1985), custom can be characterized in the following manner:

> The affection it enjoys and the authority it commands are prescriptive. The behavior of the person of custom is, by and large, habitual. To the question "why?" he [*sic*] is apt to respond simply, "This is the way it has always been done." . . . A creature of habit, the person of custom does not reflect upon his condition. To the extent that a customary society "conceives" of its practice, it is likely to see it, says Pocock, as "an indefinite series of repetitions." If the customary society is, in reality, a fluid order always in the process of adaptation, its continuity and incrementalism give rise to perceptions of changelessness and of the simple repetition of familiar motions. . . . Indeed, . . . custom operates as if it were a second nature. . . . Custom is at once both more and less inclusive than remembrance. It includes things that are remembered and things that are forgotten. It is almost a definition of custom that its beginnings are lost. (pp. 15–16)

Remembrance is directed more toward specificity and struggle, it resurrects the legacies of actions and happenings, it points to the multitude of voices that constitute the struggle over history and power. Its focus is not on the ordinary but the extraordinary. Its language presents the unrepresentable, not merely as an isolated voice, but as a subversive interruption, a discursive space, that moves "against the grain" as it occupies "a view . . . carved in the interstices of institutions and in the chinks and cracks of the power-knowledge apparati" (De Lauretis, 1987, p. 25). Remembrance is part of a language of public life that promotes an ongoing dialogue between the past, present, and future. It is a vision of optimism rooted in the need to bear witness to history, to reclaim that which must not be forgotten. It is a vision of public life which calls for an ongoing interrogation of the past that allows different groups to locate themselves in history while simultaneously struggling to make it.

Counter-memory provides the ethical and epistemological grounds for a politics of solidarity within difference. At one level, it situates the notion of difference and the primacy of the political firmly within the wider struggle for broadening and revitalizing democratic public life. At the same time, it strips reason of its universal pretensions and recognizes the partiality of all points of view. In this perspective, the positing of a monolithic tradition that exists simply to be revered, reaffirmed, reproduced, or resisted is unequivocally rejected. Instead, counter-memory attempts to recover communities of memory and narratives of struggle that provide a sense of location, place, and identity to various dominant and subordinate groups. Counter-memory as a form of pedagogical practice is not concerned with simply marking difference as a historical construct; rather, it is concerned with providing the grounds for self-representation and the struggle for justice and a democratic society. Counter-memory resists comparison to either a humanist notion of pluralism or a celebration of diversity for its own sake. As both a pedagogical and political practice, it attempts to alter oppressive relations of power and to educate both teachers and students to the ways in which they might be complicitous with dominant power relations, victimized by them, and how they might be able to transform such relations. Abdul JanMohamed and David Lloyd (1987) are instructive on what counter-memory might mean as part of discourse of critique and transformation:

> Ethnic or gender difference must be perceived as one among a number of residual cultural elements which retain the memory of practices which have had to be and still have to be repressed in order that the capitalist economic subject may be more easily produced. . . . "Becoming minor" is not a question of essence but a question of positions—a subject-position that can only be defined, in the final analysis, in "political" terms, that is, in terms of the effects of economic exploitation, political disfranchisement, social manipulation, and ideological domination on the cultural formation of minority subjects and discourses. It is one of the central tasks of the theory of minority discourse to define that subject-position and explore the strengths and weaknesses, the affirmations and negations that inhere in it. (p. 11)

Remembrance as a form of counter-memory attempts to create for students the limits of any story that makes claims to predetermined endings and to expose how the transgressions in those stories cause particular forms of suffering and hardship. At the same time, remembrance as counter-memory opens up the past not as nostalgia but as the invention of stories, some of which deserve a retelling, and which speak to a very different future—one in which democratic community makes room for a politics of both difference and solidarity, for otherness stripped of subjugation, and for others fighting to embrace their own interests in opposition to sexism, racism, ethnocentrism, and class exploitation. Counter-memory is tied in this sense to a vision of public life that both resurrects the ongoing struggle for difference and situates difference within the broader struggle for cultural and social justice.

Counter-memory provides the basis and rationale for a particular kind of pedagogy but it cannot on its own articulate the specific classroom practices that can be constructed on the basis of such a rationale.

The formation of democratic citizens demands forms of political identity which radically extend the principles of justice, liberty, and dignity to public spheres constituted by difference and multiple forms of community. Such identities have to be constructed as part of a pedagogy in which difference becomes a basis for solidarity and unity rather than for hierarchy, denigration, competition, and discrimination. It is to that issue that I will now turn.

Border Pedagogy and the Politics of Difference

If the concept of border pedagogy is to be linked to the imperatives of a critical democracy, as it must, it is important that educators possess a theoretical grasp of the ways in which difference is constructed through various representations and practices that name, legitimate, marginalize, and exclude the cultural capital and voices of subordinate groups in American society.

As part of this theoretical project, a theory of border pedagogy needs to address the important question of how representations and practices that name, marginalize, and define difference as the devalued Other are actively learned, interiorized, challenged, or transformed. In addition, such a pedagogy needs to address how an understanding of these differences can be used in order to change the prevailing relations of power that sustain them. It is also imperative that such a pedagogy acknowledge and critically interrogate how the colonizing of differences by dominant groups is expressed and sustained through representations: in which Others are seen as a deficit, in which the humanity of the Others is either cynically posited as problematic or ruthlessly denied. At the same time, it is important to understand how the experience of marginality at the level of everyday life lends itself to forms of oppositional and transformative consciousness. This is an understanding based on the need for those designated as Others to both reclaim and remake their histories, voices, and visions as part of a wider struggle to change those material and social relations that deny radical pluralism as the basis of democratic political community. For it is only through such an understanding that teachers can develop a border pedagogy, one which is characterized by what Teresa De Lauretis (1987) calls "an ongoing effort to create new spaces of discourse, to rewrite cultural narratives, and to define the terms of another perspective—a view from 'elsewhere'" (p. 25). This suggests a pedagogy in which occurs a critical questioning of the omissions and tensions that exist between the master narratives and hegemonic discourses that make up the official curriculum and the self-representations of subordinate groups as they might appear in "forgotten" or erased histories, texts, memories, experiences, and community narratives.

Border pedagogy both confirms and critically engages the knowledge and experience through which students author their own voices and construct social identities. This suggests taking seriously the knowledge and experiences that constitute the individual and collective voices by which students identify and give meaning to themselves and others and drawing upon what they know about their own lives as a basis for criticizing the dominant culture. In this case, student experience has to be first understood and recognized as the accumulation of collective memories and stories that provide students with a sense of familiarity, identity, and practical knowledge. Such experience has to be both affirmed and critically interrogated. In addition, the social and historical construction of such experience has to be affirmed and understood as part of a wider struggle for voice. But it must also be understood that while past experiences can never be denied, their most debilitating dimensions can be engaged through a critical understanding of what was at work in their construction. It is in their critical engagement that such experiences can be remade, reterritorialized in the interest of a social imagery that dignifies the best traditions and possibilities of those groups who are learning to speak from a discourse of dignity and self-governance. In her analysis of the deterritorialization of women as Other, Caren Kaplan (1987) astutely articulates this position:

> Recognizing the minor cannot erase the aspects of the major, but as a mode of understanding it enables us to see the fissures in our identities, to unravel the seams of our totalities. . . . We must leave home, as it were, since our homes are often sites of racism, sexism, and other damaging social practices. Where we come to locate ourselves in terms of our specific histories and differences must be a place with room for what can be salvaged from the past and made anew. What we gain is a reterritorialization; we reinhabit a world of our making (here "our" is expanded to a coalition of identities—neither universal nor particular). (pp. 187–188)

Furthermore, it is important to extend the possibilities of the often contradictory values that give meaning to students' lives by making them the object of critical inquiry—and by appropriating in a similarly critical fashion, when necessary, the codes and knowledges that constitute broader and less familiar historical and cultural traditions. At issue here is the development of a pedagogy that replaces the authoritative language of recitation with an approach that allows students to speak from their own histories, collective memories, and voices while simultaneously challenging the grounds on which knowledge and power are constructed and legitimated. Such a pedagogy contributes to making possible a variety of social forms and human capacities which expand the range of social identities that students may carry and become. It points to the importance of understanding in both pedagogical and political terms how subjectivities are produced within those social forms in which people move but of which they are often only partially conscious. Similarly, it raises fundamental questions regarding how students make particular investments of meaning and affect, how they are constituted within a triad of relationships of knowledge, power, and pleasure, and why students should be indifferent to the forms of authority, knowledge, and values that we produce and legitimate within our classrooms and university. It is worth noting that such a pedagogy not only articulates a respect for a diversity of student voices, it also provides a referent for developing a public language rooted in a commitment to social transformation.

Central to the notion of border pedagogy are a number of important pedagogical issues regarding the role that teachers might play within the interface of modern and postmodern concerns that have been taken up in this essay. Clearly, the concept of border pedagogy suggests that teachers exist within social, political, and cultural boundaries that are both multiple and historical in nature and that place particular demands on a recognition and pedagogical appropriation of differences. As part of the process of developing a pedagogy of difference, teachers need to deal with the plethora of voices, and the specificity and organization of differences that constitute any course, class, or curriculum so as to make problematic not only the stories that give meanings to the lives of their students, but also the ethical and political lineaments that inform their students' subjectivities and identities.

In part this suggests a pedagogy which does more than provide students with a language and context by which to critically engage the plurality of habits, practices, experiences, and desires that define them as part of a particular social formation within ongoing relations of domination and resistance. Border pedagogy provides opportunities for teachers to deepen their own understanding of the discourse of various others in order to effect a more dialectical understanding of their own politics, values, and pedagogy. What border pedagogy makes undeniable is the relational nature of one's own politics and personal investments. But at the same time, border pedagogy emphasizes the primacy of a politics in which teachers assert rather than retreat from the pedagogies they utilize in dealing with the various differences represented by the students who come into their classes. For example, it is not enough for teachers to merely affirm uncritically their students' histories, experiences, and stories. To take student voices at face value is to run the risk of idealizing and romanticizing them. The contradictory and complex histories and stories that give meaning to the lives of students are never innocent and it is important that they be recognized for their contradictions as well as for their possibilities. Of course, it is crucial that critical educators provide the pedagogical conditions for students to give voice to how their past and present experiences place them within existing relations of domination and resistance. Central to this pedagogical process is the important task of affirming the voices that students bring to school and challenging the separation of school knowledge from the experience of everyday life (Fine, 1987). But it is crucial that critical educators do more than allow such stories to be heard. It is equally important for teachers to help students find a language for critically examining the historically and socially constructed forms by which they live. Such a process involves more than "speaking" one's history and social formation, it also involves engaging collectively with others within a pedagogical framework that helps to reterritorialize and rewrite the complex narratives that make up one's life. This is more than a matter of rewriting stories as counter-memories, it is what Frigga Haug (1988) and her colleagues call memory-work, a crucial example of how the pedagogical functions to interrogate and retrieve rather than to merely celebrate one's voice. She writes:

> By excavating traces of the motives for our past actions, and comparing these with our present lives, we are able to expand the range of our demands and competences. Admittedly, this is not as easy as it sounds. Our stories are expressed in the language we use today. Buried or abandoned memories do not speak loudly; on the contrary we can expect them to meet us with obdurate silence. In recognition of this, we must adopt some method of analysis suited to the resolution of a key question for women; a method that seeks out the un-named, the silent and the absent. Here too, our experience of education maps out a ready-made path of analysis; we have been taught to content ourselves with decoding texts, with search for truth in textual analysis, complemented at best by the author's own analysis. "Re-learning" in this context means seeing what is *not* said as interesting, and the fact that it was not said as important; it involves a huge methodological leap, and demands more than a little imagination. (p. 65)

The different stories that students from all groups bring to class need to be interrogated for their absences as well as their contradictions, but they also need to be understood as more than simply a myriad of different stories. They have to be recognized as being forged in relations of opposition to the dominant structures of power. At the same time, differences among students are not merely antagonistic as Liz Ellsworth (1988) has argued. She suggests not only that there is little common ground for addressing these differences, but that separatism is the only valid political option for any kind of pedagogical and political action. Regrettably, this represents less an insight than a crippling form of political disengagement. It reduces one to paralysis in the face of such differences. It ignores the necessity of exploring differences for the specific, irreducible interests they represent, for the excesses and reactionary positions they may produce, and for the pedagogical possibilities they contain for helping students to work with other groups as part of a collective attempt at developing a radical language of democratic public life. Moreover, Ellsworth's attempt to delegitimate the work of other critical educators by claiming rather self-righteously the primacy and singularity of her own ideological reading of what constitutes a political project appears to ignore both the multiplicity of contexts and projects that characterize critical educational work and the tension that haunts all forms of teacher authority, a tension marked by the potential contradiction between being theoretically or ideologically correct and pedagogically wrong. By ignoring the dynamics of such a tension and the variety of struggles being waged under historically specific educational conditions, she degrades the rich complexity of theoretical and pedagogical processes that characterize the diverse discourses in the field of critical pedagogy. In doing so, she succumbs to the familiar academic strategy of dismissing others through the use of strawman tactics and excessive simplifications which undermine not only the strengths of her own work, but also the very nature of social criticism itself. This is "theorizing" as a form of "bad faith," a discourse imbued with the type of careerism that has become all too characteristic of many left academics.

At stake here is an important theoretical issue that is worth repeating. Knowledge and power come together not merely to reaffirm difference but also to interrogate it, to open up broader theoretical considerations, to tease out its limitations, and to engage a vision of community in which student voices define themselves in terms of their distinct social formations and their broader collective hopes. As teachers we can never inclusively speak *as* the Other (though we may be the Other with respect to issues of race, class, or gender), but we can certainly work *with* diverse Others to deepen their understanding of the complexity of the traditions, histories, knowledges, and politics that they bring to the schools. This means, as Abdul JanMohamed and David Lloyd (1987) point out, that educators need to recognize the importance of developing a theory of minority discourse which not only explores the strengths and weaknesses, affirmations and negations that inhere in the subject positions of subordinate groups but also "involves drawing our solidarities in the form of similarities between modes of repression and modes of struggle which all minorities separately experience, and experience precisely as minorities" (JanMohamed & Lloyd, 1987, p. 11). To assume such a position is not to practice forms of gender, racial, or class-specific imperialism as Ellsworth suggests; rather, it is to create conditions within particular institutions that allow students to locate themselves and others in histories that mobilize rather than destroy their hopes for the future.

The theoretical sweep may be broad, the sentiment utopian, but it is better than wallowing in guilt or refusing to fight for the possibility of a better world. Sentimentality is no excuse for the absence of any vision for the future. Like Klee's angel in the painting "Angelus Novus," modernity provides a faith in human agency while recognizing that the past is often built on the suffering of others. In the best of the Enlightenment tradition, reason at least offers the assumption and hope that men and women can change the world in which they live. Postmodernism frays the boundaries of that world and makes visible what has often been seen as unrepresentable. The task of modernity with its faith in reason and emancipation can perhaps renew its urgency in a postmodern world, a world where difference, contingency, and power can reassert, redefine, and in some instances collapse the monolithic boundaries of nationalism, sexism, racism, and class oppression. In a world whose borders have become chipped and porous, new challenges present themselves not only to educators but to all those for whom contingency and loss of certainty do not mean the inevitable triumph of nihilism and despair but rather a state of possibility in which destiny and hope can be snatched from the weakening grasp of modernity. We live in a postmodern world that no longer has any firm—but has ever flexing—boundaries. It is a time when reason is in crisis and new political and ideological conditions exist for fashioning forms of struggle defined in a radically different conception of politics. For educators, this is as much a pedagogical issue as it is a political one. At best, it points to the importance of rewriting the relationship between knowledge, power, and desire. It points as well to the necessity of redefining the importance of difference while at the same time seeking articulations among subordinate groups and historically privileged groups committed to social transformations that deepen the possibility for radical democracy and human survival.

References

Alcoff, L. (1988). Cultural feminism vs. poststructuralism: The identity crisis in feminist theory. *Signs, 13,* 405–436.

Apple, M., & Beyer, L. (Eds.) (1988). *The curriculum: Problems, politics and possibilities.* Albany: State University of New York Press.

Brodkey, L., & Fine, M. (1988). Presence of mind in the absence of body. *Boston University Journal of Education 170,* No. 3 (1988), 84–99.

Cherryholmes, C. (1988). *Power and criticism: Poststructural investigations in education*. New York: Teachers College Press.

Deleuze, G., & Guattari, F. (1986). *Toward a minor literature*. Minneapolis: University of Minnesota Press.

De Lauretis, T. (1987). *Technologies of gender*. Bloomington: Indiana University Press.

Dews, P. (1987). *Logics of disintegration*. London: Verso Books.

Dienske, I. (1988). Narrative knowledge and science. *Journal of Learning About Learning, 1*(1), 19–27.

Ellsworth, E. (1988). *Why doesn't this feel empowering? Working through the repressive myths of critical pedagogy*. Paper presented at the Tenth Conference on Curriculum Theory and Classroom Practice, Bergamo Conference Center, Dayton, Ohio, October 26–29, 1988.

Fine, M. (1987). Silencing in the public schools. *Language Arts, 64*(2), 157–174.

Foucault, M. (1977a). *Language, counter-memory, practice: Selected essays and interviews* (D. Bouchard, Ed.). Ithaca: Cornell University Press.

Foucault, M. (1977b). *Power and knowledge: Selected interviews and other writings* (G. Gordon, Ed.). New York: Pantheon.

Giroux, H. (1988a). *Schooling and the struggle for public life*. Minneapolis: University of Minnesota Press.

Giroux, H. (1988b). *Teachers as intellectuals*. Granby, MA: Bergin & Garvey.

Giroux, H., & McLaren, P. (1989). Introduction. In H. Giroux & P. McLaren (Eds.), *Critical pedagogy, the state, and cultural struggle*. Albany: State University of New York Press.

Giroux, H., & Simon, R. (1988). Critical pedagogy and the politics of popular culture. *Cultural Studies, 2*, 294–320.

Giroux, H., & Simon, R. (1989). *Popular culture, schooling, and everyday life*. South Hadley, Mass.: Bergin & Garvey Press.

Haug, F., et al. (1987). *Female sexualization: A collective work of memory*. London: Verso Press.

Hicks, E. (1988). Deterritorialization and border writing. In R. Merrill (Ed.), *Ethics/aesthetics: Post-modern positions* (pp. 47–58). Washington, DC: Maisonneuve Press.

Jameson, F. (1984). Postmodernism or the cultural logic of late capitalism. *New Left Review*, No. 146, pp. 53–93.

JanMohamed, A. (1987). Introduction: Toward a theory of minority discourse. *Cultural Critique*, No. 6, pp. 5–11.

JanMohamed, A., & Lloyd, D. (1987). Introduction: Minority discourse—what is to be done? *Cultural Critique*, No. 7, 5–17.

Kaplan, C. (1987). Deterritorialisations: The rewriting of home and exile in western feminist discourse. *Cultural Critique*, No. 6, 187–198.

Kellner, D. (1988). Postmodernism as social theory: Some challenges and problems. *Theory, Culture and Society, 5*(2 & 3), 239–269.

Kellner, D. (n.d.). Boundaries and borderlines: Reflections on Jean Baudrillard and critical theory.

Kolb, D. (1986). *The critique of pure modernity: Hegel, Heidegger, and after*. Chicago: University of Chicago Press.

Laclau, E. (1988). Politics and the limits of modernity. In A. Ross (Ed.), *Universal abandon? The politics of postmodernism* (pp. 63–82). Minneapolis: University of Minnesota Press.

Laclau, E., & Mouffe, C. (1985). *Hegemony and socialist strategy.* London: Verso Books.

Lash, S., & Urry, J. (1987). *The end of organized capitalism.* Madison: University of Wisconsin Press.

Lunn, E. (1982). *Marxism and modernism.* Berkeley: University of California Press.

Lyotard, J. (1984). *The postmodern condition.* Minneapolis: University of Minnesota Press.

McLaren, P. (1986). Postmodernism and the death of politics: A Brazilian reprieve. *Educational Theory, 36,* 389–401.

McLaren, P. (1988). *Life in schools.* New York: Longman.

Morris, M. (1988). *The pirate's fiancee: Feminism, reading, postmodernism.* London: Verso Press.

Mouffe, C. (1988). Radical democracy: Modern or postmodern? In A. Ross (Ed.), *Universal abandon? The politics of postmodernism* (pp. 31–45). Minneapolis: University of Minnesota Press.

Peller, G. (1987). Reason and the mob: The politics of representation. *Tikkun, 2*(3), 28–31, 92–95.

Pinar, W. (Ed.). (1988). *Contemporary curriculum discourses.* Scottsdale, AZ: Gorsuch Scarisbrick.

Pinon, N. (1982). La contaminacion de La Languaje: Interview with Nelida Pinon. *13th Moon,* No. 6(1 & 2), 72–76.

Richard, N. (1987/1988). Postmodernism and periphery. *Third Text,* No. 2, pp. 5–12.

Ross, A. (Ed.). (1988). *Universal abandon? The politics of postmodernism.* Minneapolis: University of Minnesota Press.

Said, E. (1983). Opponents, audiences, constituencies, and community. In H. Foster (Ed.), *The anti-aesthetic: Essays on postmodern culture* (pp. 135–139). Port Townsend, WA: Bay Press.

Scholes, R. (1985). *Textual power.* New Haven: Yale University Press.

Shor, I. (1979). *Critical teaching and everyday life.* Boston: South End Press.

Smith, B. J. (1985). *Politics and remembrance.* Princeton: Princeton University Press.

7 Disturbing the Peace: Writing in the Cultural Studies Classroom

IT IS BECOMING INCREASINGLY MORE difficult to assess what Cultural Studies is either as a political project or as a postdisciplinary practice.[1] For some theorists, it is precisely the emergence of Cultural Studies outside of the university and its articulation with various social movements such as feminism, rather than its academic location, that have helped to prevent it from being incorporated into the university as merely an additive to the established canon.[2] For others, Cultural Studies must be developed with regard not only to the changing nature and specificity of the problems and conflicts it addresses, but also to the legacy of its history as a preeminently political and oppositional practice.[3]

It is not my intention here to replay the debate regarding the real history of Cultural Studies, though this is an important issue. Instead, I want to analyze how certain features of the history of Cultural Studies might inform its present and future politics. More specifically, I want to focus on the importance of pedagogy as a central aspect of Cultural Studies and writing as a pedagogical practice. In doing so, I want to develop a notion of border writing as a form of cultural production forged among the shifting borderlands of a politics of representation, identity, and struggle. In part, I am concerned with a notion of cultural recovery in which the production of knowledge, subjectivity, and agency can be addressed as ethical, political, and pedagogical issues. In part, this suggests critically appropriating from Cultural Studies the insights it has accrued as it has moved historically from its narrow concerns with class and language to its more recent analysis of the politics of race, gender, and colonialism. This is not meant to suggest that the history of Cultural Studies needs to be laid out in great detail as some sort of foundational exegesis. On the contrary, Cultural Studies needs to be approached historically as a mix of founding moments, transformative challenges, and self-critical interrogations (Nelson 32). It is precisely the rupturing spirit

164

informing elements of its postdisciplinary practice, social activism, and historical awareness that prompts my concern for the current lacunae in Cultural Studies regarding the theoretical and political importance of pedagogy as a founding moment in its legacy. At the same time, it is important to stress that the general indifference of many theorists to pedagogy as a form of cultural practice does an injustice to the politically charged legacy of Cultural Studies, one that points to the necessity for combining self-criticism with a commitment to transforming existing social and political problems.

Neither critical educators nor Cultural Studies theorists can ignore the relationship of pedagogy to Cultural Studies in the current historical juncture. Indeed, such indifference warrants a deep suspicion of the viability of the political project that informs such a view of Cultural Studies. Central to my analysis as well as to the politics of my own location as a teacher and cultural worker is the assumption that Cultural Studies must be grounded, in part, in a project that deepens and expands the possibilities for radical democracy both in the United States and abroad. Democracy in this sense is the discursive face and lived experiences of struggling to expand the conditions for social justice, freedom, and equality across all the major political and economic spheres that shape, position, and locate people in everyday life. It is within this project that I want to address the importance of writing and pedagogy as central elements of an insurgent Cultural Studies.

In what follows, I want to argue that while Cultural Studies represents an ensemble of diverse discourses, it is an important historical, political, and cultural formation that points to a number of issues that need to be addressed in pedagogical terms. I then want to provide a rationale for re-inserting the language of pedagogy and politics back into the discourse of Cultural Studies as part of a broader attempt to expand and deepen what I will call a pedagogy of Cultural Studies. Finally, I will explore how I take up the issue of pedagogy as a cultural practice through the use of writing in my class. In part, this section not only discusses border writing as a form of pedagogical practice, but also suggests a connection between some of the central themes of Cultural Studies and writing as a cultural practice.

Cultural Studies and the Absence of Pedagogy

It is generally argued that Cultural Studies is largely defined through its analysis of the interrelationship between culture and power, particularly with regard to the production, reception, and diverse use of texts. Texts in this case constitute a wide range of aural, visual, and printed signifiers. These are often taken up as part of a broader attempt to analyze how individual and social identities are mobilized, engaged, and transformed within circuits of power informed by issues of race, gender, class, ethnicity, and other social formations. All of these concerns point to the intellectual and institutional borders that police, contain, and engage meaning as a site of social struggle. Moreover, one of the emerging theoretical features of Cultural Studies is to refute the notion that the struggle over meaning is primarily about the struggle over language and textuality.[4] On the contrary, a number of Cultural Studies theorists have named terror and oppression in concrete terms and have addressed how domination is manifested in a variety of sites, on a number of different levels, and how it can be understood in historical and relational terms through a variety of articulations and categories.[5] In fact, Cultural Studies draws its theoretical inspiration from feminism, postmodernism, postcolonialism, and a host of other areas. Lawrence Grossberg claims that Cultural Studies as a strategic practice performs two functions: first, it keeps alive the importance of political work in an "age of diminishing possibilities." That is, it radicalizes the notion of hope by politicizing rather than romanticizing it. Second, it refuses to immobilize a commitment to political work in the frozen theoretical winter of orthodoxy. By responding to the specificity of history it leaves open the political cartography that informs how it names both its own strategies and the "world of political struggle" (*We Gotta Get Out* 18). For Grossberg, the notion that Cultural Studies is unstable, open, and always contested becomes the basis for its rewriting as both the condition for ideological self-criticism and constructing social agents within rather than outside historical struggles. Grossberg writes:

> [C]ultural studies assumes that history—its shape, its seams, its outcomes—is never guaranteed. As a result, doing cultural studies takes work, including the kind of work deciding what cultural studies is, of making cultural studies over again and again. Cultural studies constructs itself as it faces new questions and takes up new positions. In that sense, doing cultural studies is always risky and never totally comfortable. It is fraught with inescapable tensions (as well as with real pleasures). In the U.S., the rapid institutional success of cultural studies has made it all a bit too easy. Cultural studies has to be wary of anything that makes its work too easy, that erases the real battles, both theoretical and political, that have to be waged, that defines the answers before it even begins. (18–19)

I want to take Grossberg at his word and argue that Cultural Studies is still too rigidly tied to the modernist, academic disciplinary structures that it often criticizes. This is not to suggest that it does not adequately engage the issue of academic disciplines. In fact, this is one of its most salient characteristics.[6] What it fails to do is critically address a major prop of disciplinarity, which is the notion of pedagogy as an unproblematic vehicle for transmitting knowledge. Lost here is the attempt to understand pedagogy as a mode of cultural criticism for questioning the very conditions under which knowledge and identities are produced. Of course, theorists such as Larry Grossberg, Stanley Aronowitz, and others do engage the relationship between Cultural Studies and pedagogy, but they constitute a small minority.[7] The haunting issue here is, what is it about pedagogy that allows Cultural Studies theorists to ignore it?

One answer may lie in the refusal of Cultural Studies theorists either to take schooling seriously as a site of struggle or to probe how traditional pedagogy produces particular forms of subjectification, how it constructs students through a range of subject positions. Of course, within radical educational theory, there is a long history of developing critical discourses of the subject around pedagogical issues.[8]

Another reason Cultural Studies theorists have devoted little attention to pedagogy may be the disciplinary terrorism that leaves the marks of its legacy on all areas of the humanities and liberal arts. Pedagogy is often deemed unworthy of being taken up as a serious subject. Even popular culture has more credibility than pedagogy. This can be seen not only in the general absence of any discussion of pedagogy in Cultural Studies texts, but also in those studies in the humanities that have begun to engage pedagogical issues. Even in these works there is a willful refusal to acknowledge some of the important theoretical gains in pedagogy that have been made in the last twenty years.[9] Within this silence lurk the imperatives of a disciplinary policing, a refusal to cross academic borders, and a shoring up of the imperatives of originality, competitiveness, and elitism. Of course, composition studies, one of the few fields in the humanities that does take pedagogy seriously, occupies a status as disparaged as the field of education.[10] The legacy of academic elitism and professionalism still exercises a strong influence in the field of Cultural Studies, in spite of its alleged democratization of social knowledge.

Reclaiming Pedagogy

In making my case for the importance of pedagogy as a central aspect of Cultural Studies, I first want to analyze the role that pedagogy played in the early founding stages of the Birmingham Centre for Cultural Studies. I then want to define more specifically the central dimensions of pedagogy as a cultural practice. But before I address these two important moments of critical pedagogy as a form of cultural politics, I think it is important to stress that the concept of pedagogy must be used with respectful caution. Not only are there different versions of what constitutes critical pedagogy, but there is no generic definition that can be applied to the term. At the same time, there are important theoretical insights and practices that weave through various approaches to critical pedagogy. It is precisely these insights, which often define a common set of problems, that serve to delineate critical pedagogy as a set of conditions articulated within the context of a particular political project—a project that takes up these problems differently within the specificity of particular contexts. These problems include but are not limited to the relationships between knowledge and power, language and experience, ethics and authority, student agency and transformative politics, and teacher location and student formations.

This is precisely how Raymond Williams addressed the issue of pedagogy in his discussion of the emergence of Cultural Studies in Britain. For Williams, pedagogy offered the opportunity to link cultural practice with the development of radical cultural theories. Not only did pedagogy connect questions of form and content, it also introduced a sense of how teaching, learning, textual studies, and knowledge could be addressed as a political issue that foregrounded considerations of power and social agency. According to Williams, Cultural Studies in the 1930s and 1940s emerged directly from the pedagogical work that was going on in Adult Education. The specificity of the content and context of adult education provided Cultural Studies with a number of issues that were to direct its subsequent developments in Birmingham. These included the refusal to accept the limitations of established academic boundaries and power structures, the demand for linking literature to the life situations of the adult learners, and the call that schooling be empowering rather than merely humanizing. Williams is quite adamant in refuting "encyclopedia articles dating the birth of Cultural Studies from this or that book in the late 'fifties." He goes on to say that:

> the shift of perspective about the teaching of art and literature and their relation to history and to contemporary society began in Adult Education, it didn't happen anywhere else. It was when it was taken across by people with that experience to the Universities that it was suddenly recognized as a subject. It is in these and other similar ways that the contribution of the process itself to social change itself, and specifically to learning, has happened. ("Adult Education"; see also "Future" 151–62)

For Williams there is more at stake here than reclaiming the history of Cultural Studies. He is most adamant in making clear that the "deepest impulse [informing Cultural Studies] was the desire to make learning part of the process of social change itself" ("Future" 158). It is precisely this attempt to broaden the notion of the political by making it more pedagogical that reminds us of the importance of pedagogy as a cultural practice. In this context, pedagogy deepens and extends the study of culture and power by addressing not only how culture is shaped, produced, circulated, and transformed, but also how it is actually taken up by human beings within specific settings and circumstances. It becomes an act of cultural production, a form of "writing" in which the process by which power is inscribed on the body and implicated in the production of desire, knowledge, and values begins not with a particular claim to postdisciplinary knowledge but with real people articulating and rewriting their lived experiences within, rather than outside, history.

The importance of pedagogy to the content and context of Cultural Studies lies in the relevance it has for illuminating how knowledge and subjectivities are produced in a variety of sites including schools. Pedagogy, in this sense, offers an articulatory concept for understanding how power and knowledge configure in the production, reception, and transformation of subject positions, forms of ethical address, and "desired versions of a future human community" (Simon 15). By refuting the objectivity of knowledge and asserting the partiality of all forms of pedagogical authority, critical pedagogy initiates an inquiry into the relationship between cultural work, authority, and the securing of particular cultural practices, and as a mode of cultural politics takes as an object of study the relationship between the possibilities for social agency expressed in a range of human capacities and the social forms that often constrain or enable them.

The politics of critical pedagogy are radical but not doctrinaire. That is, critical pedagogy self-consciously operates from a perspective in which teaching and learning are committed to expanding rather than restricting the opportunities for students and others to be social, political, and economic agents. As agents, students and others need to learn how to take risks, to understand how power works differently as both a productive and dominating force, to be able to "read" the world from a variety of perspectives, and to be willing to think beyond the commonsense assumptions that govern everyday existence. Critical pedagogy engages experience in order to inquire into the conditions of its production, authorization, and effects. What is radical about the relationship between pedagogy and the issue of experience is that it addresses the inner workings of experience, how it functions to produce knowledge, and how it might be implicated in the construction of forms of subjectification. Politicizing the relationship between thought and experience points to a pedagogical practice in which cultural workers can offer "questions, analyses, visions and practical options that people can pursue in their attempts to participate in the determination of various aspects of their lives. . . . Required is a practice rooted in an ethical-political vision that attempts to take people beyond the world they already

know but in a way that does not insist on a fixed set of altered meanings"
(Simon 46–47).

Defined as an attempt to alter experience in the interest of expanding
the possibilities for human agency and social justice, critical pedagogy
makes visible the need for social relations that inform a number of considerations that cut across the diverse terrain of Cultural Studies.

Writing as a Pedagogical Practice

In what follows, I want to describe how I use writing as a pedagogical
practice to transgress certain dominant assumptions about the meaning
of schooling, the discourse of authority, the relationship between language and experience, and the role of social responsibility within the
politics of my own location as a university teacher. Most of the classes I
teach at Penn State University are graduate courses in education and
Cultural Studies. The students who take my courses are mostly working-
class males and females, generally between the ages of 25 and 60. Very
few of the students are familiar with the theoretical discourses of Cultural Studies and critical pedagogy. In the past, I have tried to organize
my courses around selected critical texts, combining introductory lectures with a seminar format in which students were asked to engage the
texts actively by reading them oppositionally. Though this approach attempted to make the class more democratic, it failed to unsettle the
kinds of social relations that characterize teacher-centered environments. The reasons are numerous and they include the following. First,
many students felt intimidated by the language of theory. They often
noted at some point in the class that the assigned texts were too difficult
to read, they didn't understand their practical application to education,
or they simply did not feel comfortable speaking through a discourse
that seemed foreign to them. Second, many students have not prob-
lematized the ways in which traditional schooling has shaped their perceptions of power, learning, and identity. Many of the students in my
classes believed that either their own voices did not count for much or
that the only role for students in the class was to accept what was dispensed to them as knowledge rather than either raise questions about
taking control over the conditions of the production of knowledge or engage the classroom texts critically in light of their own experiences, histories, and concerns. Thirdly, whenever class discussion did occur it was
more often than not dominated by males, especially white males, in
spite of the fact that women often constituted over 50% of my classes.
Moreover, when students did speak they often looked at me rather than
direct their remarks to other students. In this instance, they were posi-

tioning me as the authorizing agent for their discourse and for some feedback.

It became clear to me very quickly that in spite of my use of oppositional material and the seminar format of the class, I was reproducing a set of pedagogical relations that did not decenter authority, that, on the contrary, undermined my efforts both to provide students with the opportunity to speak in a safe space and to appropriate power in the class in order to deconstruct the texts and engage in collective self-criticism and a critique of the politics of my location as a teacher.

In the first semester of the 1992–1993 school year, I taught a new course called Postcolonialism, Race, and Critical Pedagogy. In this course, I attempted to address some of the above problems by organizing a series of pedagogical practices around particular writing assignments that helped to create what can be called, to use Homi Bhabha's phrase, a "third space" in the classroom. But before I articulate the specifics of the pedagogical practices that I employed, I want to mention a specific tension that I had to address in the classroom and in my own teaching.

Like many teachers, academics, and other cultural workers, I felt that the most substantive aspect of my pedagogy centered on defining my own goals for education along with the politics of my own location as a teacher. For example, my overriding pedagogical project was rooted in an attempt at majority democratic education, that is, an education whose aim was to advance the ideological and lived relations necessary for students at least to interrogate the possibility of addressing schooling as a site of ongoing struggle over the "social and political task of transformation, resistance, and radical democratization" (Butler 13). This is a project that has continually driven my own politics and pedagogy regardless of the specific courses I have taught in the university. In looking back at this project, I have fewer reservations about its political importance than I do about the pedagogical practice of removing it from the actual social formations that shaped students' histories and lived experiences, which served to undo its most promising possibilities. In other words, by not paying more attention to what it meant to give students more control over the conditions of their own knowledge production, I reproduced the binarism of being politically enlightened in my theorizing and pedagogically wrong in my organization of concrete class relations. Overcoming this binarism was a major goal behind the reorganization of my pedagogy in the Postcolonialism, Race, and Critical Pedagogy class. Developing a series of reading and writing activities as the basis of the new course helped me to work through and resist the negative effects of my own authority as a teacher. In what follows, I want to spell out how I used border writing less as technical exercise in skill development than as a form of cultural production that more closely articulated the relationship between my political project as a progressive teacher and the underlying principles and practices that informed the organization and character of my class.

My use of writing assignments was closely linked to getting students to theorize their own experiences rather than articulate the meaning of other peoples' theories. The assignments were designed to get students to examine how representations signify and position students through the institutional and ideological authority they carry in the dominant culture. Moreover, the writing assignments were constructed so as to give students the opportunity to acknowledge their own emotional and affective investments in issues regarding race, colonialism, and the politics of representation. In addition, writing was used not merely as an ideological marker for locating specific biographical interests and forms of identification; it was also viewed as a rupturing practice, as an oppositional pedagogy in which one pushes against the grain of traditional history, disciplinary structures, dominant readings, and existing relations of power.

Raymond Williams has rightly pointed out the need for cultural workers to be attentive to the formations out of which specific projects arise. As part of an attempt not to reproduce the legacy of those pedagogical practices that positioned students as objects rather than as subjects of learning, I attempted to organize the writing assignments in my seminar around a number of structuring principles necessary for the success of my own political and pedagogical project. For instance, I introduced the course by talking about power in the classroom and how it was implicated in all aspects of classroom teaching, including the development of a syllabus, the organization of classroom relations, and the method of evaluation. I also made clear the rationale for the authority I exercised in the course and how that authority was intended to be used to expand rather than restrict the possibility for student agency. In part, I made the form and content of my authority as a teacher visible in order to problematize and debate the moral vision and social ethic I used to justify my organization of the syllabus and the pedagogical practices that informed my class.

In doing so, I relinquished all claims to objectivity, and I attempted to refute the traditional notion that teachers were disinterested, that knowledge was unproblematic, and that teaching was merely a methodology for transmitting information to students. I argued that the latter positions were often used to obscure the ideological and political interests that regulated dominant versions of schooling and the role that teachers play in actively regulating the production of knowledge and values. By presenting a view of schools as a site of conflict and contestation, I attempted to open a space for students to engage political, social, and cultural differences in ways that highlighted pedagogy as an oppositional rather than merely a dominating practice.

In addition, I stressed the need for social relations in the class that would give students the opportunity to produce and appropriate knowledge as part of an ongoing struggle to represent themselves in terms of their interests, lived experiences, and wider political concerns. Two issues derived from the more political and emancipatory theoretical insights of Cultural Studies guided my pedagogical concerns. First, I wanted to make clear that no pedagogical process could be located outside of the intellectual and affective investments I brought to the class. Hence, the politics of my own location had to be subjected to extensive critique and dialogue in the written assignment and class debates. Second, the class had to become a site where writing offered the opportunity to "engage rather than displace the voices of aggressive, theorizing subjects [students]."[11] I further suggested that some of the major elements structuring teacher-student relations in the class would be taken up around some of the following considerations: How do language and experience intersect? That is, how do different discourses shape, engage, and deconstruct the experiences and stories told by ourselves and others? Second, what conditions are necessary to develop a sense of political, moral, and social agency in the class? For example, what pedagogical practices might be necessary to promote collaborative work? To engage dominant and subordinate traditions critically? To get students to question the partiality of both their own knowledge and the knowledge presented by the teacher? Third, how might teacher authority be manifested without being inimical to the issue and practice of student freedom?

By making my own theoretical and pedagogical concerns visible at the beginning of the course, I attempt to be up-front about the parameters of the course, especially in a school of education where students often believe that they will not have to read intellectually challenging work or that educational theory is mainly about learning methodologies. But there is more at stake here than exercising authority in the spirit of promoting rigorous intellectual work and providing a call for self-discipline. I also posit the goals and project of the course as an invitation for the students to rethink how they might want to take up and transform certain aspects of their own learning. For instance, in an effort not to remove all traces of their own socially constructed voices, I asked students to form groups after my introductory remarks in order to respond to the issues I raised. I was particularly interested in whether the principles and rationale I offered for the course were suitable to their own perception of the course. I also invited the students to suggest specific readings outside of the assigned texts that we might take up in the class.

Within an hour the students convened their respective groups and a debate took place over the shape and format of the class. It became instantly clear to me that the students also wanted the class to be participatory, critical, and attentive to immediate and global concerns regarding racial politics, and that they wanted both to provide their own list of readings for the course and to evaluate their own performance for a course grade. Gently exercising my own authority I mediated their concerns with three qualifications. First, I suggested that the course had to be organized around a series of writing assignments that reproduced the principles they had articulated in the discussion. Second, in order to relieve the immediate fear that students often express about writing in a class, I suggested that as a major precondition for discussing the student writing presented to the class it was imperative for all of us to create the conditions for a "safe space" for each other. This means that since students often feel that their identities are on trial when they either speak from their writing or share it with the rest of the class, it is imperative that each student be given every opportunity to speak, argue, take risks, and position him/herself without fear of intimidation, humiliation, or outright pedagogical terrorism from either the teacher or other students. In this case, issues of trust and respect for difference become paramount in structuring classroom relations. In addition, it was suggested that every attempt be made to use student writing as a pedagogical tool to present one's theoretical position, to promote class discussions, to engage other texts, and to work collaboratively with others. Third, while they would be given the opportunity to evaluate their own final projects, the projects should be organized around an attempt to integrate the theoretical discourses taken up in the class with an analysis of some aspect of popular culture. For example, an individual or a group might decide to write about how the legacy of colonialism frames much of the racial discourse in a film like *Grand Canyon*. Students might also want to mix media in compiling a critical commentary on racism in the university, town, or in the national media. They might also want to focus on popular magazines as a source of social knowledge, use ethnographic approaches to conducting oral histories, or construct their own video, etc.

As part of an attempt to pay close attention to the political and pedagogical dynamics that structured the class, three major writing assignments were used to organize how texts were to be taken up and rewritten as part of a larger attempt to register differences, analyze diverse arguments, and cross disciplinary borders.

The writing assignments were organized in the following ways. The initial three weeks of the course were developed around analyzing the reading material largely selected by the class. The readings were taken up through the thematics of "Orientalism, Difference, and Multiculturalism," "Postcolonialism, Race, and Feminism," and "Nationalism and the Politics of Speaking for Others." The class was divided into three groups. Each group was assigned the task of developing position paper(s) on the readings for one of the three themes. The papers would then be duplicated for the rest of the class and used as a basis for class discussion.

Each group worked collaboratively to produce a paper that was duplicated and read by the rest of the class the evening their respective reading assignment was due. The group assigned to present a paper for that class first talked about how they came to address a particular aspect of the assignment, how they worked out the collaborative process, and why they thought the issues they addressed were important to them in terms of their own experiences. For example, the first group developed a paper that was a transcript of a dialogue they collectively held in analyzing certain aspects of the readings on Orientalism and the politics of multiculturalism. The paper clearly demonstrated those issues over which individual members of the group disagreed, what concerns they shared, and what questions they wanted to take up with the rest of the class. It is important to note that students who did not present a group paper during any one class meeting had to prepare journal entries on the readings assigned, and in doing so worked from their own notes in responding to both the group paper and other questions that arose from the readings. Since the readings ranged from sources as diverse as Cornel West's "The New Politics of Difference" to Diane Ravitich's "Multiculturalism," there was a range of ideological positions to engage and make for a lively discussion.

But in discussing the papers the emphasis was not merely on taking up conflicting positions. Students had to insert themselves into the texts by taking a position on the readings, talking about the consequences of their positions in terms of how they addressed questions of race, freedom, justice, and so on. Moreover, the group constantly talked about how the university itself was implicated in reproducing some of the racial problems they discussed and how the racial problems in the school articulated with and mutually reinforced larger societal problems.

During the second part of the course, students paired up in groups of two and for the remainder of the course each group taught a particular text that was assigned for any one particular week. Books discussed ranged from *There Ain't No Black in the Union Jack* by Paul Gilroy to *Black Looks* by bell hooks and *Learning to Question* by Paulo Freire and Antonio Faundez. In this assignment, students had to "write" the book; that is, they had to present a paper that provided an exegesis, offer a critical reading of the text's major assumptions, and analyze the relevance of the text to their own experiences as future educators. Moreover, they could present the analysis in a variety of mixed formats but had to use a substantial portion of their time for dialogue with the rest of the class. The presentations were on the whole amazingly imaginative. Most students combined a short lecture with some other form of media to illustrate their analysis of the texts. Most prepared open questions to partly structure the debates, and in some cases provided the rest of the class with alternative or supplementary readings.

The third writing assignment was organized around a collaborative position paper based on applying some aspect of what they learned about race and pedagogy in the class to a particular problem in the wider university community. The activities undertaken ranged from an analysis of the textbooks used in the local secondary school to an interrogation of the racial sensitivity seminars conducted by some faculty in the university. In each case, the students had little trouble in applying some of the theoretical issues they addressed in the class to wider practical and pedagogical concerns.

The final writing project in the class engaged writing as a pedagogical practice by getting students not only to analyze popular texts that extend the range of what constitutes social knowledge but also to be self-reflective about their own engagement with the course and what its implications were for rethinking the ways in which power works through diverse regimes of representation, institutional structures, and the larger spaces of social power.

All of these writing assignments positioned students as cultural producers and enabled them to rewrite their own experiences and perceptions through an engagement with various texts, ideological positions, and theories. In all cases, there was an ongoing attempt to get the students to learn from each other, to decenter the power in the classroom, to challenge disciplinary borders, to create a borderland where new hybridized identities might emerge, to take up in a problematic way the relationship between language and experience, and to appropriate knowledge as part of a broader effort at self-definition and ethical responsibility. Border writing in this case became a type of hybridized, border literacy, a form of cultural production and pedagogical practice where otherness becomes comprehensible, collective memory rewrites the narratives of insurgent social movements, and students travel between diverse theoretical and cultural zones of difference, and, in doing so, generate a space where new intersections between identity and culture emerge. It is precisely in this space informed by the critical imperatives of Cultural Studies, the ongoing demands of a restless critical pedagogy, and faith in a project of possibility that teachers and students can rewrite, reaffirm, and struggle over the assumption that the goal of achieving a multicultural, multiracial democracy in the United States remains the critical issue of modern politics and life.

Notes

1. One of the most important critiques of Cultural Studies treating this issue of purpose and meaning has been made by Meaghan Morris.

2. This issue is taken up in Franklin, Lury, and Stacey; see also Clarke, esp. chapt. 2; Parry; and Hall, "Cultural Studies and its Theoretical Legacies."

3. See, for example, Nelson, "Always Already"; Nelson et al., "Cultural Studies: An Introduction"; and Bennett.

4. For expressions of this position see Grossberg, *We Gotta Get Out;* Hall, "Cultural Studies and its Theoretical Legacies"; and Grossberg, "The Formation."

5. A number of writers in the Grossberg et al. anthology take this position.

6. As a representative of this type of critique, see any of the major theoretical sources of Cultural Studies, especially the Centre for Contemporary Cultural Studies in Birmingham. See Hall, "Cultural Studies: Two Paradigms" and "Cultural Studies and the Centre"; Richard Johnson; and Morris.

7. See Grossberg et al. for examples; also, various issues of *College Literature* under the editorship of Kostas Myrsiades. It is quite revealing to look into some of the latest books on Cultural Studies and see no serious engagement of pedagogy as a site of theoretical and practical struggle. For example see Brantlinger; Turner; Clarke; Franklin et al. In Punter there is one chapter on identifying racism in textbooks.

8. While there are too many sources to cite here, see Connell et al.; Henriques et al.; Sears; Fine; Simon; and Donald.

9. For instance, while theorists such as Jane Tompkins, Gerald Graff, Gregory Ulmer, and others address pedagogical issues, they do it solely within the referenced terrain of literary studies. Moreover, even those theorists in literary studies who insist on the political nature of pedagogy generally ignore, with few exceptions, the work that has gone on in the field for twenty years. See, for example, Felman and Lamb; Henricksen and Morgan; Donahue and Quahndahl; Ulmer; and Barbara Johnson.

10. One interesting example of this occured when Gary Olson, the editor of the *Journal of Advanced Composition,* interviewed Jacques Derrida. He asked Derrida, in the context of a discussion about pedagogy and teaching, if he knew of the work of Paulo Freire. Derrida responded, "This is the first time I've heard his name" (Olson 133). It is hard to imagine that a figure of Freire's international stature would not be known to someone in literary studies who is one of the major proponents of deconstruction. So much for crossing boundaries. Clearly, Derrida does not read the radical literature in composition studies, because if he did he could not miss the numerous references to the work of Freire and other critical educators. See, for instance, Atkins and Johnson; Brodkey; and Hurlbert and Blitz.

11. The two considerations and quotation come from Morris (20).

Works Cited

Aronowitz, Stanley. *Roll Over Beethoven: Return of Cultural Strife*. Hanover: UP of New England, 1993.

Atkins, C. Douglas, and Michael L. Johnson. *Writing and Reading Differently: Deconstruction and the Teaching of Composition and Literature*. Lawrence: U of Kansas P, 1985.

Bennett, Tony. "Putting Policy into Cultural Studies." Grossberg, Nelson, and Treichler, *Cultural Studies* 23–34.

Brantlinger, Patrick. *Crusoe's Footprints: Cultural Studies in Britain and America*. New York: Routledge, 1990.

Brodkey, Linda. *Academic Writing as a Social Practice*. Philadelphia: Temple UP, 1987.

Butler, Judith. "Contingent Foundations: Feminism and the Question of Postmodernism." *Feminists Theorizing the Political*. Ed. Judith Butler and Joan Scott. New York: Routledge, 1992.

Clarke, John. *New Times and Old Enemies: Essays on Cultural Studies and America*. London: Harper Collins, 1991.

Connell, R. W., D. J. Ashenden, S. Kessler, and G. W. Dowsett. *Making the Difference*. Boston: Allen and Unwin, 1982.

Donahue, Patricia, and Ellen Quahndahl, eds. *Reclaiming Pedagogy: The Rhetoric of the Classroom*. Carbondale: Southern Illinois UP, 1989.

Donald, James. *Sentimental Education*. London: Verso, 1992.

Felman, Shoshana, and Dori Lamb. *Testimony: Crisis of Witnessing in Literature, Psychoanalysis, and History*. New York: Routledge, 1992.

Fine, Michelle. *Framing Dropouts*. Albany: SU of New York P, 1991.

Franklin, Sarah, Celia Lury, and Jackie Stacey. "Feminism and Cultural Studies: Pasts, Presents, Futures." *Off-Centre: Feminism and Cultural Studies*. Ed. Sarah Franklin, et al. London: Harper Collins, 1991. 1–19.

Grossberg, Lawrence. "The Formation of Cultural Studies: An American in Birmingham." *Strategies* 2 (1989): 114–49.

_____. *We Gotta Get Out of This Place*. New York: Routledge, 1992.

_____, Cary Nelson, and Paula A. Treichler, eds. *Cultural Studies*. New York: Routledge, 1992.

Hall, Stuart. "Cultural Studies and its Theoretical Legacies." Grossberg, Nelson, and Treichler, *Cultural Studies* 277–86.

_____. "Cultural Studies and the Centre: Some Problematics and Problems." *Culture, Media, Language: Working Papers in Cultural Studies*. Ed. Stuart Hall, et al. London: Hutchinson, 1980.

_____. "Cultural Studies: Two Paradigms." *Media, Culture, and Society* 2 (1980): 57–72.

Henricksen, Bruce, and Thais E. Morgan. *Reorientations: Critical Theories and Pedagogies*. Urbana: U of Illinois P, 1990.

Henriques, Julian, Wendy Hollway, Cathy Unwin, Couze Venn, and Valerie Walkerdine. *Changing the Subject*. London: Methuen, 1984.

Hurlbert, C. Mark, and Michael Blitz, eds. *Composition and Resistance*. Portsmouth: Heinemann, 1991.

Johnson, Barbara, ed. *The Pedagogical Imperative: Teaching as a Literary Genre.* New Haven: Yale UP, 1983.

Johnson, Richard. "What Is Cultural Studies, Anyway?" *Social Text* 6.1 (1987): 38–40.

Morris, Meaghan. "Banality in Cultural Studies." *Discourse* 10.2 (1988): 3–29.

Nelson, Cary. "Always Already Cultural Studies: Two Conferences and a Manifesto." *Journal of Midwest Modern Language Association* 24.1 (Spring 1991): 24–38.

_____, Paula A. Treichler, and Lawrence Grossberg. "Cultural Studies: An Introduction." *Cultural Studies.* Ed. Cary Nelson, Paula A. Treichler, and Lawrence Grossberg. New York: Routledge, 1991.

Olson, Gary. "Jacques Derrida on Rhetoric and Composition: A Conversation." *(Inter)views: Cross-Disciplinary Perspectives on Rhetoric and Literacy.* Ed. Gary Olson and Irene Gale. Carbondale: Southern Illinois UP, 1991.

Parry, Benita. "The Contradictions of Cultural Studies." *Transitions* 53 (1991): 37–45.

Punter, David, ed. *Introduction to Contemporary Cultural Studies.* New York: Longman, 1986.

Sears, James T. *Growing Up Gay in the South: Race, Gender, and Journeys of the Spirit.* New York: Harrington Park, 1991.

Simon, Roger I. *Teaching against the Grain.* New York: Bergin and Garvey, 1992.

Turner, Graeme. *British Cultural Studies.* London: Unwin Hyman, 1990.

Ulmer, Gregory. *Applied Grammatology.* Baltimore: Johns Hopkins UP, 1985.

Williams, Raymond. "Adult Education and Social Change." *What I Came to Say.* London: Hutchinson-Radus, 1989. 157–66.

_____. "The Future of Cultural Studies." *The Politics of Modernism.* London: Verso, 1989. 151–62.

PART THREE

Contemporary Concerns

8 Rethinking the Boundaries of Educational Discourse: Modernism, Postmodernism, and Feminism

Mapping the Politics of Modernism

To invoke the term modernism is immediately to place oneself in the precarious position of suggesting a definition that is itself open to enormous debate and little agreement (Groz et al. 7–17; Newman, "Revising Modernism"). Not only is there a disagreement regarding the periodization of the term, there is enormous controversy regarding what it actually refers to.[1] To some it has become synonymous with terroristic claims of reason, science, and totality (Lyotard). To others it embodies, for better or worse, various movements in the arts (Newman, *Post-Modern Aura*). And to some of its more ardent defenders, it represents the progressive rationality of communicative competence and support for the autonomous individual subject (Habermas, "Modernity versus Postmodernity"; "Modernity"; *Discourse*). It is not possible within the context of this essay to provide a detailed history of the various historical and ideological discourses of modernism, even though such an analysis is essential to provide a sense of the complexity of both the category and the debates that have emerged around modernism.[2] Instead I want to focus on some of the central assumptions of modernism. The value of this approach is that it not only serves to highlight some of the more important arguments that have been made in the defense of modernism, but also provides a theoretical and political backdrop for understanding some of the central features of various postmodernist and feminist discourses. This is particularly important with respect to postmodernism, which presupposes some idea of the modern and also of various feminist discourses, which have increasingly been forged largely in opposition to some of modernism's major assumptions, particularly as these relate to notions such as rationality, truth, subjectivity, and progress.

The theoretical, ideological, and political complexity of modernism can be grasped by analyzing its diverse vocabularies with respect to three traditions: the social, the aesthetic, and the political. The notion of social modernity corresponds with the tradition of the new, the process of economic and social organization carried out under the growing relations of capitalist production. Social modernity approximates what Matei Calinescu calls the bourgeois idea of modernity, which is characterized by

> The doctrine of progress, the confidence in the beneficial possibilities of science and technology, the concern with time (a measurable time, a time that can be bought and sold and therefore has, like any other commodity, a calculable equivalent in money), the cult of reason, and the ideal of freedom defined within the framework of an abstract humanism, but also the orientation toward pragmatism and the cult of action and success. (41)

Within this notion of modernism, the unfolding of history is linked to the "continual progress of the sciences and of techniques, the rational division of industrial work, [which] introduces into social life a dimension of permanent change, of destruction of customs and traditional culture" (Baudrillard 65). At issue here is a definition of modernity that points to the progressive differentiation and rationalization of the social world through the process of economic growth and administrative rationalization. Another characteristic of social modernism is the epistemological project of elevating reason to an ontological status. Modernism in this view becomes synonymous with civilization itself, and reason is universalized in cognitive and instrumental terms as the basis for a model of industrial, cultural, and social progress. At stake in this notion of modernity is a view of individual and collective identity in which historical memory is devised as a linear process, the human subject becomes the ultimate source of meaning and action, and a notion of geographical and cultural territoriality is constructed in a hierarchy of domination and subordination marked by a center and margin legitimated through the civilizing knowledge/power of a privileged Eurocentric culture (Aronowitz).

The category of aesthetic modernity has a dual characterization that is best exemplified in its traditions of resistance and formal aestheticism (Newman, "Revising Modernism"). But it is in the tradition of opposition, with its all-consuming disgust with bourgeois values and its attempt through various literary and avant-garde movements to define art as a representation of criticism, rebellion, and resistance, that aesthetic modernism first gains a sense of notoriety. Fueling this aesthetic modernism of the nineteenth and early twentieth centuries is an alienation and negative passion whose novelty is perhaps best captured in

Bakunin's anarchist maxim, "To destroy is to create" (quoted in Calinescu 117). The cultural and political lineaments of this branch of aesthetic modernism are best expressed in avant-garde movements ranging from the surrealists and the futurists to the conceptualist artists of the 1970s. Within this movement, with its diverse politics and expressions, there is an underlying commonality, an attempt to collapse the distinction between art and politics and to blur the boundaries between life and aesthetics. But in spite of its oppositional tendencies, aesthetic modernism has not fared well in the latter part of the twentieth century. Its critical stance, its aesthetic dependency on the presence of bourgeois norms, and its apocalyptic tone have increasingly become recognized as artistically fashionable by the very class it attacks (Barthes).

The central elements that bring these two traditions of modernism together constitute a powerful force not only for shaping the academic disciplines and the discourse of educational theory and practice, but also for providing a number of points where various ideological positions share a common ground. This is especially true in modernism's claim for the superiority of high culture over popular culture; its affirmation of a centered if not unified subject; its faith in the power of the highly rational, conscious mind; and its belief in the unequivocal ability of human beings to shape a better world. There is a long tradition of support for modernism, and some of its best representatives are as diverse as Marx, Baudelaire, and Dostoevsky. This notion of the self based on the universalization of reason and the totalizing discourses of emancipation have provided a cultural and political script for celebrating Western culture as synonymous with civilization itself, and for regarding progress as a terrain that only needed to be mastered as part of the inexorable march of science and history. Marshall Berman exemplifies the dizzying heights of ecstasy made possible by the script of modernism in his own rendition of the modernist sensibility:

> Modernists, as I portray them, are simultaneously at home in this world and at odds with it. They celebrate and identify with the triumphs of modern science, art, technology, communications, economics, politics—in short, with all the activities, techniques, and sensibilities that enable mankind to do what the Bible said God could do—to "make all things new." At the same time, however, they oppose modernization's betrayal of its own human promise and potential. Modernists demand more profound and radical renewals: modern men and women must become the subjects as well as the objects of modernization; they must learn to change the world that is changing them and to make it their own. The modernist knows this is possible: the fact that the world has changed so much is proof that it can change still more. The modernist can, in Hegel's phrase, "look the negative in the face and live with it." The fact that "all that is solid melts into air" is a

> source not of despair, but of strength and affirmation. If everything must go, then let it go: modern people have the power to create a better world than the world they have lost. ("Why Modernism" 11)

Of course, for many critics of modernism, the coupling of social and aesthetic modernism reveals itself quite differently. Modernist art is criticized for having become nothing more than a commercial market for the museums and the corporate boardrooms and a depoliticized discourse institutionalized within the universities. In addition, many critics have argued that under the banner of modernism, reason and aesthetics often come together in a technology of self and culture that combines a notion of beauty that is white, male, and European with a notion of mastery that legitimates modern industrial technologies and the exploitation of vast pools of labor from the "margins" of second- and third-world economies. Robert Merrill gives this argument a special twist in claiming that the modernist ego, with its pretensions to infallibility and unending progress, has actually come to doubt its own promises. For example, he argues that many proponents of modernism increasingly recognize that what has been developed by the West in the name of mastery actually indicates the failure of modernism to produce a technology of self and power that can deliver on the promises to provide freedom through science, technology, and control. He writes:

> [A loss of faith in the promises of modernism] . . . is no less true for corporate and governmental culture in the United States which displays a . . . desperate quest for aestheticization of the self as modernist construct—white, male, Christian, industrialist—through monumentally styled office buildings, the Brooks Brothers suit (for male and female), designer food, business practices which amount only to the exercise of symbolic power, and most of all, the Mercedes Benz which as the unification in design of the good (here functional) and the beautiful and in production of industrial coordination and exploitation of human labor is pre-eminently the sign that one has finally achieved liberation and mastery, "made it to the top" (even if its stylistic lines thematize what can only be called a fascist aesthetics). (ix)

It is against the claims of social and aesthetic modernism that the diverse discourses of postmodernism and feminism have delivered some of their strongest theoretical and political criticism, and these will be taken up shortly. But there is a third tradition of modernism that has been engaged by feminism but generally ignored by postmodernism. This is the tradition of political modernism. Political modernism, unlike its related aesthetic and social traditions, does not focus on epistemological and cultural issues so much as it develops a project of possibility out of a number of Enlightenment ideals (Laclau, "Politics"; Mouffe,

"Radical Democracy" 32–34). It should be noted that political modernism constructs a project that rests on a distinction between political liberalism and economic liberalism. In the latter, freedom is conflated with the dynamics of the capitalist marketplace, whereas in the former, freedom is associated with the principles and rights embodied in the democratic revolution that has progressed in the West over the last three centuries. The ideals that have emerged out of this revolution include "the notion that human beings ought to use their reason to decide on courses of action, control their futures, enter into reciprocal agreements, and be responsible for what they do and who they are" (Warren ix–x). In general terms, the political project of modernism is rooted in the capacity of individuals to be moved by human suffering so as to remove its causes; to give meaning to the principles of equality, liberty, and justice; and to increase those social forms that enable human beings to develop the capacities needed to overcome ideologies and material forms that legitimate and are embedded in relations of domination.

The tradition of political modernism has largely been taken up and defended in opposition to and against the discourse of postmodernism. Consequently, when postmodernism is defined in relation to the discourse of democracy, it is either pitted against the Enlightenment project and seen as reactionary in its political tendencies (Berman, *Air;* Habermas, "Modernity," *Discourse*), grafted onto a notion of economic liberalism that converts it into an apology for rich Western democracies (Rorty, "Habermas" 174–75), or portrayed in opposition to the emancipatory projects of Marxism (Eagleton; Anderson) and feminism (Hartsock 190–91; Christian). In what follows, I want to examine some of the challenges that Jürgen Habermas presents to various versions of postmodernism and feminism through his defense of modernity as an unfinished emancipatory project.

Habermas and the Challenge of Modernism

Habermas has been one of the most vigorous defenders of the legacy of modernism. His work is important because in forging his defense of modernism as part of a critique of the postmodernist and poststructuralist discourses that have emerged in France since 1968, he has opened up a debate between these seemingly opposing positions. Moreover, Habermas has attempted to revise and reconstruct the earlier work of his Frankfurt School colleagues, Theodor Adorno and Max Horkheimer, by revising their pessimistic views of rationality and democratic struggle.

Habermas identifies postmodernity less as a question of style and culture than as one of politics. Postmodernism's rejection of grand narratives, its denial of epistemological foundations, and its charge that reason and truth are always implicated in relations of power are viewed by Habermas as both a retreat from and a threat to modernity. For him, postmodernism has a paradoxical relation with modernism. On the one hand, it embodies the worst dimensions of an aesthetic modernism. That is, it extends those aspects of the avant-garde which "live [in] the experience of rebelling against all that is normative" ("Modernity" 5). In this sense, postmodernism echoes surrealism's attempt to undermine the cultural autonomy of art by removing the boundaries that separate it from everyday life. On the other hand, postmodernism represents the negation of the project of social modernity by rejecting the latter's language of universal reason, rights, and autonomy as a foundation for modern social life. According to Habermas, postmodernism's argument that realism, consensus, and totality are synonymous with terror represents a form of political and ethical exhaustion that unjustifiably renounces the unfinished task of the rule of reason (*Communication* 3–13).

In Habermas's terms, the postmodernist thinkers are conservatives whose philosophical roots are to be found in various irrationalist and counter-Enlightenment theories that suggest a peculiar political kinship with fascism. Hence postmodernism undermines the still unfolding project of modernity, with its promise of democracy through the rule of reason, communicative competence, and cultural differentiation. Postmodernism is guilty of the dual crime, in this case, of rejecting the most basic tenets of the modernist ethos and failing to recognize its most emancipatory contributions to contemporary life. In the first instance, postmodernism recklessly overemphasizes the play of difference, contingency, and language against all appeals to universalized and transcendental claims. For the postmodernist, theory without the guarantee of truth redefines the relationship between discourse and power and in doing so destabilizes the modernist faith in consensus and reason. For Habermas, postmodernism represents a revolt against a substantive view of reason and subjectivity and negates the productive features of modernism.

Modernity offers Habermas the promise of integrating the differentiating spheres of science, morality, and art back into society, not through an appeal to power, but through the rule of reason, the application of a universal pragmatics of language, and the development of forms of learning based on dictates of communicative competence. While he accepts the excesses of technological rationality and substantive reason, he believes that only through reason can the logic of scientific/technological rationality and domination be subordinated to the imperatives of modernist justice and morality (Kellner 262–66). Habermas admires Western culture and argues that "bourgeois ideals" contain elements of reason that should be at the center of a democratic society. By these ideals, he writes,

> I mean the internal theoretical dynamic which constantly propels the sciences—and the self-reflection of the sciences as well—beyond the creation of merely technologically exploitable knowledge; furthermore, I mean the universalist foundations of law and morality which have also been embodied (in no matter how distorted and imperfect a form) in the institutions of constitutional states, in the forms of democratic decisionmaking, and in individualistic patterns of identity formation; finally, I mean the productivity and the liberating force of an aesthetic experience with a subjectivity set free from the imperatives of purposive activity and from the conventions of everyday perception. ("Entwinement" 18)

Central to Habermas's defense of modernity is his important distinction between instrumental and communicative rationality. Instrumental rationality represents those systems or practices embodied in the state, money, and various forms of power which work through "steering mechanisms" to stabilize society. Communicative rationality refers to the world of common experience and discursive intersubjective interaction, a world characterized by various forms of socialization mediated through language and oriented toward social integration and consensus. Habermas accepts various criticisms of instrumental rationality, but he largely agrees that capitalism, in spite of its problems, represents more acceptable forms of social differentiation, rationalization, and modernization than have characterized past stages of social and instrumental development. On the other hand, he is adamant about the virtues of communicative rationality, with its emphasis on the rules of mutual understanding, clarity, consensus, and the force of argument. Habermas views any serious attack on this form of rationality as in itself being irrational. In effect, his notion of communicative rationality provides the basis not only for his ideal speech situation but also for his broader view of social reconstruction. Rationality, in this case, with its distinctions between an outer world of systemic steering practices and a privileged inner world of communicative process, represents in part a division between a world saturated with material power expressed in the evolution of ever-growing and complex subsystems of rational modernization and one shaped by universal reason and communicative action. At the core of this distinction is a notion of democracy in which struggle and conflict are not based on a politics of difference and power, but on a conceptual and linguistic search for defining the content of what is rational (Ryan 27–45).

Habermas's defense of modernity is not rooted in a rigorous questioning of the relationship among discourses, institutional structures, and the interests they produce and legitimate within specific social conditions. Instead he focuses on linguistic competence and the principle of consensus, with its guiding problematic defined by the need to uproot the obstacles to "distorted communication." This not only points to a particular view of power, politics, and modernity; it also legitimates, as Stanley Aronowitz points out, a specific notion of reason and learning:

> He [Habermas] admonishes us to recognize [modernity's] unfinished tasks: the rule of reason. Rather than rules of governance based on power or discursive hegemonies, we are exhorted to create a new imaginary, one that would recognize societies able to resolve social conflicts, at least provisionally, so as to permit a kind of collective reflexivity. Characteristically, Habermas finds that the barriers to learning are not found in the exigencies of class interest, but in distorted communication. The mediation of communication by interest constitutes here an obstacle to reflexive knowledge. "Progressive" societies are those capable of learning—that is, acquiring knowledge that overcomes the limits of strategic or instrumental action. (103)

Habermas's work has been both opposed and taken up by a number of critical and radical groups. He has been criticized by feminists such as Nancy Fraser ("Critical Theory") and embraced by radicals who believe that his search for universal values represents a necessary ingredient in the struggle for human emancipation (Epstein 54–56). In many respects his writing provides a theoretical marker for examining how the debate over foundationalism and democracy on the one hand, and over a politics of difference and contingency on the other, has manifested itself on the left as a debate among those who line up for or against different versions of modernism or postmodernism.

A more constructive approach, both to the specifics of Habermas's work and to the larger issue of modernism, is that neither should be accepted or rejected as if the only choice were complete denial or conversion. Habermas, for example, is both right and wrong in his analyses of modernism and postmodernism. He is right in attempting to salvage the productive and emancipatory aspects of modernism and to develop a unifying principle that provides a referent point for engaging and advancing a democratic society. He is also right in claiming that postmodernism is as much about politics and culture as it is about aesthetics and style (Huyssen). In this sense, Habermas provides a theoretical service by trying to keep alive as part of a modernist discourse the categories of critique, agency, and democracy. For better or worse, Habermas injects into the modernist-versus-postmodernist debate the primacy of politics and of the role that rationality might play in the service of human freedom and the imperatives of democratic ideology and struggle. As Thomas McCarthy points out, Habermas believes that the defects of the Enlightenment can only be made good by further enlightenment. The totalized critique of reason undercuts the capacity of reason to be critical. It refuses to acknowledge that modernization bears developments as well as distortions of reason. Among the former, he mentions the "unthawing" and "reflective refraction" of cultural traditions, the universalization of norms and generalization of values, and the growing individuation of personal identities—all prerequisites for that effectively democratic organization of society through which alone reason can, in the end, become practical. (xvii)

It is around these concerns that postmodern theorists have challenged some of the basic assumptions of modernism. For Habermas, these challenges weaken rather than mobilize the democratic tendencies of modernism. But as I hope to demonstrate in the remainder of this essay, Habermas is wrong in simply dismissing all forms of postmodernism as antimodernist and neoconservative. Moreover, given his own notions of consensus and social action, coupled with his defense of Western tradition, his view of modernity is too complicitous with a notion of reason that is used to legitimate the superiority of a culture primarily white, male, and Eurocentric. Habermas's position is susceptible to the charge not only of being patriarchal but also of not adequately engaging the relationship between discourse and power and the messy material relations of class, race, and gender. Postmodern and feminist critiques of his work cannot be dismissed simply because they might be labeled antimodern or antirationalist. In what follows, I want to take up some of the challenges that postmodernism has developed in opposition to some of the central assumptions of modernism.

Postmodern Negations

If postmodernism means putting the World in its place . . . if it means the opening up to critical discourse of lines of enquiry which were formerly prohibited, of evidence which was previously inadmissible so that new and different questions can be asked and new and other voices can begin asking them; if it means the opening up of institutional and discursive spaces within which more fluid and plural social and sexual identities may develop; if it means the erosion of triangular formations of power and knowledge with the expert at the apex and the "masses" at the base, if, in a word, it enhances our collective (and democratic) sense of *possibility,* then I for one am a postmodernist. (Hebdige, *Hiding* 226)

Dick Hebdige's guarded comments regarding his own relationship to postmodernism suggest some of the problems that have to be faced in using the term. As the term is increasingly employed both in and out of the academy to designate a variety of discourses, its political and semantic currency repeatedly becomes an object of conflicting forces and divergent tendencies. Postmodernism has not only become a site of conflicting ideological struggles—denounced by different factions on both the left and the right, supported by an equal number of diverse progressive groups, and appropriated by interests that would renounce any claim to politics—its varied forms also produce both radical and reactionary elements. Postmodernism's diffuse influence and contradictory character are evident within many cultural fields—painting, architecture, photography, video, dance, literature, education, music, mass communications—and in the varied contexts of its production and exhibition. Such a term does not lend itself to the usual topology of categories that serve to inscribe it ideologically and politically within traditional binary oppositions. In this case the politics of postmodernism cannot be neatly labeled under the traditional categories of left and right.

That many groups are making a claim for its use should not suggest that the term has no value except as a buzzword for the latest intellectual fashions. On the contrary, its widespread appeal and conflict-ridden terrain indicate that something important is being fought over, that new forms of social discourse are being constructed at a time when the intellectual, political, and cultural boundaries of the age are being refigured amidst significant historical shifts, changing power structures, and emergent alternative forms of political struggle. Of course, whether these new postmodernist discourses adequately articulate rather than simply reflect these changes is the important question.

I believe that the discourse of postmodernism is worth struggling over, and not merely as a semantic category that needs to be subjected to ever more precise definitional rigor. As a discourse of plurality, difference, and multinarratives, postmodernism resists being inscribed in any single articulating principle in order to explain either the mechanics of domination or the dynamic of emancipation. At issue here is the need to mine its contradictory and oppositional insights so that they might be appropriated in the service of a radical project of democratic struggle. The value of postmodernism lies in its role as a shifting signifier that both reflects and contributes to the unstable cultural and structural relationships that increasingly characterize the advanced industrial countries of the West. The important point here is not whether postmodernism can be defined within the parameters of particular politics, but how its best insights might be appropriated within a progressive and emancipatory democratic politics.

I want to argue that while postmodernism does not suggest a particular ordering principle for defining a particular political project, it does have a rudimentary coherence with respect to the set of "problems and basic issues that have been created by the various discourses of post-modernism, issues that were not particularly problematic before but certainly are now" (Hutcheon, "Problematic" 5). Postmodernism raises questions and problems so as to redraw and re-present the boundaries of discourse and cultural criticism. The issues that postmodernism has brought into view can be seen, in part, through its various refusals of all "natural laws" and transcendental claims that by definition attempt to "escape" from any type of historical and normative grounding. In fact, if there is any underlying harmony to various discourses of postmod-ernism, it is in their rejection of absolute essences. Arguing along similar lines, Laclau claims that postmodernity as a discourse of social and cul-tural criticism begins with a form of epistemological, ethical, and politi-cal awareness based on three fundamental negations:

> The beginning of postmodernity can . . . be conceived as the achievement of multiple awareness: epistemological awareness, insofar as scientific progress appears as a succession of paradigms whose transformation and replacement is not grounded in any algorithmic certainty; ethical aware-ness, insofar as the defense and assertion of values is grounded on argu-mentative movements (conservational movements, according to Rorty), which do not lead back to any absolute foundation; political awareness, in-sofar as historical achievements appear as the product of hegemonic and contingent—and as such, always reversible—articulations and not as the result of immanent laws of history. ("Building" 21)

Laclau's list does not exhaust the range of negations that postmod-ernism has taken up as part of the increasing resistance to all totalizing explanatory systems and as part of the growing call for a language that offers the possibility of addressing the changing ideological and struc-tural conditions of our time. In what follows, I will address some of the important thematic considerations that cut across postmodernism, what I define as a series of postmodern negations. I will address these negations in terms of the challenge they present to what can be prob-lematized as either oppressive or productive features of modernism.

Postmodernism and the Negation of Totality, Reason, and Foundationalism

A central feature of postmodernism has been its critique of totality, rea-son, and universality. This critique has been most powerfully developed in the work of Jean-François Lyotard. In developing his attack on En-lightenment notions of totality, Lyotard argues that the very notion of the postmodern is inseparable from an incredulity toward metanarra-tives. In Lyotard's view, "The narrative view is losing its functors, its great hero, its great dangers, its great voyages, its great goal. It is being dispersed in clouds of narrative language elements—narrative, but also denotative, prescriptive, descriptive, and so on" (xxiv). For Lyotard, grand narratives do not problematize their own legitimacy; they deny the historical and social construction of their own first principles, and in doing so wage war on difference, contingency, and particularity. Against Habermas and others, Lyotard argues that appeals to reason and consensus, when inserted within grand narratives that unify history, emancipation, and knowledge, deny their own implications in the production of knowledge and power. More emphatically, Lyotard claims that within such narratives are elements of mastery and control in which "we can hear the mutterings of the desire for a return of terror, for the realization of the fantasy to seize reality" (82). Against metanarratives that totalize historical experience by reducing its diversity to a one-dimensional, all-encompassing logic, he posits a discourse of multiple horizons, the play of language games, and the terrain of micropolitics. Against the formal logic of identity and the transhistorical subject, he invokes a dialectics of indeterminacy, varied discourses of legitimation, and a politics based on the "permanence of difference."

Lyotard's attack on metanarratives represents both a trenchant form of social criticism and a philosophical challenge to all forms of foundationalism that deny the historical, the normative, and the contingent. Nancy Fraser and Linda Nicholson articulate this connection well:

> For Lyotard, postmodernism designates a general condition of contemporary Western civilization. The postmodern condition is one in which "grand narratives of legitimation" are no longer credible. By "grand narratives" he means, in the first instance, overarching philosophies of history like the Enlightenment story of the gradual but steady progress of reason and freedom, Hegel's dialectic of Spirit coming to know itself, and, most important, Marx's drama of the forward march of human productive capacities via class conflict culminating in proletarian revolution. . . . For what most interests [Lyotard] about the Enlightenment, Hegelian, and Marxist stories is what they share with other nonnarrative forms of philosophy. Like ahistorical epistemologies and moral theories, they aim to show that specific first-order discursive practices are well formed and capable of yielding true and just results. True and just here mean something more than results reached by adhering scrupulously to the constitutive rules of some given scientific and political games. They mean, rather, results that correspond to Truth and Justice as they really are in themselves independent of contingent, historical social practices. Thus, in Lyotard's view, a metanarrative. . . . purports to be a privileged discourse capable of situating, characterizing, and evaluating all other discourses, but not itself infected by the historicity and contingency that render first-order discourses potentially distorted and in need of legitimation. (86–87)

What Fraser and Nicholson point out by implication is that postmodernism does more than wage war on totality; it also calls into question the use of reason in the service of power, the role of intellectuals who speak through authority invested in a science of truth and history, and the forms of leadership that demand unification and consensus within centrally administered chains of command. Postmodernism rejects a notion of reason that is disinterested, transcendent, and universal. Rather than separating reason from the terrain of history, place, and desire, postmodernism argues that reason and science can only be understood as part of a broader historical, political, and social struggle over the relationship between language and power. Within this context, the distinctions between passion and reason, objectivity and interpretation no longer exist as separate entities, but represent instead the effects of particular discourses and forms of social power. This issue is not merely epistemological, but deeply political and normative. Gary Peller makes this point clear by arguing that what is at stake in this form of criticism is nothing less than the dominant and liberal commitment to Enlightenment culture. He writes:

> Indeed the whole way that we conceive of liberal progress (overcoming prejudice in the name of truth, seeing through the distortions of ideology to get at reality, surmounting ignorance and superstition with the acquisition of knowledge) is called into question. [Postmodernism] suggests that what has been presented in our social-political and our intellectual traditions as knowledge, truth, objectivity, and reason are actually merely the effects of a particular form of social world that then presents itself as beyond mere interpretation, as truth itself. (30)

By asserting the primacy of the historical and the contingent in the construction of reason, authority, truth, ethics, and identity, postmodernism provides a politics of representation and a basis for social struggle. Laclau argues that the postmodern attack on foundationalism is an eminently political act since it expands the possibility for argumentation and dialogue. Moreover, by acknowledging questions of power and value in the construction of knowledge and subjectivities, postmodernism helps to make visible important ideological and structural forces, such as race, gender, and class. For theorists such as Laclau, the collapse of foundationalism does not suggest a banal relativism or the onset of a dangerous nihilism. On the contrary, he argues that the lack of ultimate meaning radicalizes the possibilities for human agency and a democratic politics:

> Abandoning the myth of foundations does not lead to nihilism, just as uncertainty as to how an enemy will attack does not lead to passivity. It leads, rather, to a proliferation of discursive interventions and arguments that are

necessary, because there is no extradiscursive reality that discourse might simply reflect. Inasmuch as argument and discourse constitute the social, their open-ended character becomes the source of a greater activism and a more radical libertarianism. Humankind, having always bowed to external forces—God, Nature, the necessary laws of History—can now, at the threshold of postmodernity, consider itself for the first time the creator and constructor of its own history. ("Politics" 79–80)

The postmodern attack on totality and foundationalism is not without its drawbacks. While it rightly focuses on the importance of local narratives and rejects the notion that truth precedes the notion of representation, it also runs the risk of blurring the distinction between master narratives that are monocausal and formative narratives that provide the basis for historically and relationally placing different groups or local narratives within some common project. To draw out this point further, it is difficult to imagine any politics of difference as a form of radical social theory if it doesn't offer a formative narrative capable of analyzing difference within rather than against unity. I will develop these criticisms in more detail in another section.

Postmodernism as the Negation of Border Cultures

Postmodernism offers a challenge to the cultural politics of modernism at a number of different levels. That is, it not only provides a discourse for retheorizing culture as fundamental to the construction of political subjects and collective struggle, it also theorizes culture as a politics of representation and power. Emily Hicks has presented the postmodern challenge to modernist culture as one framed within the contexts of shifting identities, the remapping of borders, and nonsynchronous memory. In her terms, modernist culture negates the possibility of identities created within the experience of multiple narratives and "border" crossings; instead, modernism frames culture within rigid boundaries that both privilege and exclude around the categories of race, class, gender, and ethnicity. Within the discourse of modernism, culture in large part becomes an organizing principle for constructing borders that reproduce relations of domination, subordination, and inequality. In this case, borders do not offer the possibility of experiencing and positioning ourselves within a productive exchange of narratives. Instead, modernism constructs borders framed in the language of universals and oppositions. Within the cultural politics of modernism, European culture becomes identified with the center of civilization, high culture is defined in essentialist terms against the popular culture of the everyday, and history as the reclaiming of critical memory is displaced by the prolifera-tion of images. In effect, postmodernism constitutes a general attempt to transgress the borders sealed by modernism, to proclaim the arbi-trariness of all boundaries, and to call attention to the sphere of culture as a shifting social and historical construction.

I want to approach the postmodern challenge to a modernist cultural politics by focusing briefly on a number of issues. First, postmodernism has broadened the discussion regarding the relationship between cul-ture and power by illuminating the changing conditions of knowledge embedded in the age of electronically mediated information systems, cybernetic technologies, and computer engineering (Lyotard). In doing so, it has pointed to the development of new forms of knowledge that significantly shape traditional analyses relevant to the intersection of culture, power, and politics. Second, postmodernism raises a new set of questions about how culture is inscribed in the production of center/margin hierarchies and the reproduction of postcolonial forms of subjugation. At stake here is not only a reconsideration of the inter-section of race, gender, and class but also a new way of reading history; that is, postmodernism provides forms of historical knowledge as a way of reclaiming power and identity for subordinate groups (Spivak; Minh-ha). Third, postmodernism breaks down the distinction between high and low culture and makes the everyday an object of serious study (Collins).

In the first instance, postmodernism points to the increasingly power-ful and complex role of the new electronic medium in constituting indi-vidual identities, cultural languages, and new social formations. In ef-fect, postmodernism has provided a new discourse that enables us to understand the changing nature of domination and resistance in late capitalist societies (Lash and Urry). This is particularly true in its analy-ses of how the conditions for the production of knowledge have changed within the last two decades with respect to the electronic information technologies of production, the types of knowledge produced, and the impact they have had at both the level of everyday life and in larger global terms (Poster). Postmodern discourses highlight radical changes in the ways in which culture is produced, circulated, read, and con-sumed; moreover, it seriously challenges those theoretical models that have inadequately analyzed culture as a productive and constituting force within an increasingly global network of scientific, technological, and information-producing apparatuses.

In the second instance, postmodernism has provided an important theoretical service in mapping the relations of the center and the pe-riphery with respect to three related interventions into cultural politics. First, it has offered a powerful challenge to the hegemonic notion that

Eurocentric culture is superior to other cultures and traditions by virtue of its canonical status as a universal measure of Western civilization. In exposing the particularity of the alleged universals that constitute Eurocentric culture, postmodernism has revealed that the "truth" of Western culture is by design a metanarrative that ruthlessly expunges the stories, traditions, and voices of those who by virtue of race, class, and gender constitute the "Other." Postmodernism's war on totality is defined, in this case, as a campaign against Western patriarchal culture and ethnocentricity (McLaren and Hammer). To the extent that postmodernism has rejected the ethnocentricism of Western culture, it has also waged a battle against those forms of academic knowledge that serve to reproduce the dominant Western culture as a privileged canon and tradition immune from history, ideology, and social criticism (Aronowitz and Giroux, *Education*). Central to such a challenge is a second aspect of postmodernism's refiguring of the politics of the center and the margins. That is, postmodernism not only challenges the form and content of dominant models of knowledge, it also produces new forms of knowledge through its emphasis on breaking down disciplines and taking up objects of study that were unrepresentable in the dominant discourses of the Western canon.

Postmodern criticism provides an important theoretical and political service in assisting those deemed "Other" to reclaim their own histories and voices. By problematizing the dominant notion of tradition, postmodernism has developed a power-sensitive discourse that helps subordinated and excluded groups to make sense out of their own social worlds and histories while simultaneously offering new opportunities to produce political and cultural vocabularies by which to define and shape their individual and collective identities (Lipsitz 211–31). At stake here is the rewriting of history within a politics of difference that substitutes for totalizing narratives of oppression local and multiple narratives that assert their identities and interests as part of a broader reconstruction of democratic public life. Craig Owens captures the project of possibility that is part of reclaiming voices that have been relegated to the marginal and therefore seem to be unrepresentable. While women emerge as the privileged force of the marginal in this account, his analysis is equally true for a number of subordinated groups:

> It is precisely at the legislative frontier between what can be represented and what cannot that the postmodernist operation is being staged—not in order to transcend representation, but in order to expose that system of power that authorizes certain representations while blocking, prohibiting or invalidating others. Among those prohibited from Western representation, whose representations are denied all legitimacy, are women. Excluded

from representation by its very structure, they return within it as a figure for—a presentation of—the unrepresentable. (59)

Postmodernism's attempt to explore and articulate new spaces is not without its problems. Marginality as difference is not an unproblematic issue, and differences have to be weighed against the implications they have for constructing multiple relations between the self and the "Other." Moreover, resistance not only takes place on the margins but also at various points of entry within dominant institutions. Needless to say, any notion of difference and marginality runs the risk of mystifying as well as enabling a radical cultural politics. But what is crucial is that postmodernism does offer the possibility for developing a cultural politics that focuses on the margins, for reclaiming, as Edward Said points out, "the right of formerly un- or misrepresented human groups to speak for and represent themselves in domains defined, politically and intellectually, as normally excluding them, usurping their signifying and representing functions, over-riding their historical reality" (quoted in Connor 233).

This leads to a third dimension of a postmodern cultural politics. As part of a broader politics of difference, postmodernism has also focused on the ways in which modernity functions as an imperialist master narrative that links Western models of industrial progress with hegemonic forms of culture, identity, and consumption. Within this context, the project of modernity relegates all non-Western cultures to the periphery of civilization, outposts of insignificant histories, cultures, and narratives.

In the discourse of postcolonial modernism, the culture of the "Other" is no longer inscribed in imperialist relations of domination and subordination through the raw exercise of military or bureaucratic power. Power now inscribes itself in apparatuses of cultural production that easily transgress national and cultural borders. Data banks, radio transmissions, and international communications systems become part of the vanguard of a new global network of cultural and economic imperialism. Modernity now parades its universal message of progress through the experts and intellectuals it sends to Third World universities, through the systems of representations that it produces to saturate billboards all over Latin America, and/or through the advertising images it sends out from satellites to the television sets of inhabitants of Africa, India, and Asia.

Postmodernism makes visible both the changing technological nature of postcolonial imperialism and the new forms of emerging resistance that it encounters. On the one hand, it rejects the notion that the colonial relationship is an "uninterrupted psychodrama of repression and subjugation" (Roth 250). In this perspective, there is an attempt to understand how power is not only administered, but also taken up, resisted, and struggled over. The "Other" in this scenario does not suffer the fate of being generalized out of existence, but bears the weight of historical and cultural specificity. In part, this has resulted in a radical attempt to read the culture of the "Other" as a construction rather than a description, as a form of text that evokes rather than merely represents (Tyler; Clifford and Marcus; Clifford). Within this scenario, the relationship between the subject and the object, between invention and construction, is never innocent and is always implicated in theorizing about the margins and the center. At issue here is an attempt to make problematic the voices of those who try to describe the margins, even when they do so in the interests of emancipation and social justice (Minh-ha). This suggests yet another aspect of postcolonial discourse that postmodernism has begun to analyze as part of its own cultural politics.

In the postmodern age, the boundaries that once held back diversity, otherness, and difference, whether in domestic ghettoes or through national borders policed by custom officials, have begun to break down. The Eurocentric center can no longer absorb or contain the culture of the "Other" as something threatening and dangerous. As Renato Rosaldo points out, "the Third World has imploded into the metropolis. Even the conservative national politics of containment, designed to shield 'us' from 'them,' betray the impossibility of maintaining hermetically sealed cultures" (44). Culture in postcolonial discourse becomes something that "Others" have; it is the mark of ethnicity and difference. What has changed in this hegemonic formulation/strategy is that diversity is not ignored in the dominant cultural apparatus, but promoted in order to be narrowly and reductively defined through dominant stereotypes. Representation does not merely exclude, it also defines cultural difference by *actively* constructing the identity of the "Other" for dominant and subordinate groups. Postmodernism challenges postcolonial discourse by bringing the margins to the center in terms of their own voices and histories. Representation, in this sense, gives way to opposition and the struggle over questions of identity, place, and values (Spivak; Minh-ha). Difference in this context holds out the possibility of not only bringing the voices and politics of the "Other" to the centers of power, but also understanding how the center is implicated in the margins. It is an attempt to understand how the radicalizing of difference can produce new forms of displacement and more refined forms of racism and sexism. Understandably, the best work in this field is being done by writers from the "margins."

Finally, it is well known that postmodernism breaks with dominant forms of representation by rejecting the distinction between elite and popular culture and by arguing for alternative sites of artistic engagement and forms of experimentation (Hebdige, *Hiding* 116–43). As an anti-aesthetic, postmodernism rejects the modernist notion of privileged culture or art; it renounces "official" centers for "housing" and displaying art and culture along with their interests in origins, periodization, and authenticity (Foster xv–xvi; Crimp). Moreover, postmodernism's challenge to the boundaries of modernist art and culture has, in part, resulted in new forms of art, writing, film-making, and various types of aesthetic and social criticism. For example, films like *Wetherby* (1985) deny the structure of plot and seem to have no recognizable beginning or end; photographer Sherrie Levine uses a "discourse of copy" in her work in order to transgress the notions of origin and originality. Writer James Sculley blurs the lines between writing poetry and producing it within a variety of representational forms. The American band Talking Heads adopts an eclectic range of aural and visual signifiers to produce a pastiche of styles in which genres are mixed, identities shift, and the lines between reality and image are purposely blurred (Hebdige, *Hiding* 233–44).

Most importantly, postmodernism conceives of the everyday and the popular as worthy of serious *and* playful consideration. In the first instance, popular culture is analyzed as an important sphere of contestation, struggle, and resistance. In doing so, postmodernism does not abandon the distinctions that structure varied cultural forms within and among different levels of social practice; instead it deepens the possibility for understanding the social, historical, and political foundations for such distinctions as they are played out within the intersection of power, culture, and politics. In the second instance, postmodernism cultivates a tone of irony, parody, and playfulness as part of an aesthetic that desacralizes cultural aura and "greatness" while simultaneously demonstrating that "contingency penetrates all identity" and that "the primary and constitutive character of the discursive is . . . the condition of any practice" (Laclau, "Building" 17). Richard Kearney has noted that the postmodern notion of play, with its elements of undecidability and poetical imagining, challenges constricted and egocentric levels of selfhood and allows us to move toward a greater understanding of the "Other":

> The ex-centric characteristics of the play paradigm may be construed as tokens of the poetical power of imagination to transcend the limits of egocentric, and indeed anthropocentric, consciousness—thereby exploring different possibilities of existence. Such "possibilities" may well be deemed impossible at the level of the established reality. (366–67)

Central to the postmodern rejection of elite culture as a privileged domain of cultural production and repository of "truth" and civilization is

an attempt to understand modernist cultural practices in their hegemonic and contradictory manifestations. Similarly, postmodernism rejects the notion of popular culture as structured exclusively through a
combination of commodity production and audience passivity, a site
both for dumping commercial junk and for creating consumer robots.
Instead, postmodernism views popular culture as a terrain of accommodation and struggle, a terrain whose structuring principles should not
be analyzed in the reductionistic language of aesthetic standards but
rather through the discourse of power and politics (Giroux and Simon,
"Pedagogy"). Of course, it must be stated that the postmodern elements
of a cultural politics that I have provided need to be interrogated more
closely for their excesses and absences, and I will take up this issue in
another section; but in what follows I will analyze the third postmodern
negation, that regarding language and subjectivity.

Postmodernism, Language, and the
Negation of the Humanist Subject

Within the discourse of postmodernism, the new social agents become
plural; that is, the universal agent, such as the working class, is replaced
by multiple agents forged in a variety of struggles and social movements.
Here we have a politics that stresses differences among groups. But it is
worth noting that subjectivities are also constituted within difference.
This is an important distinction and offers an important challenge to the
humanist notion of the subject as a free, unified, stable, and coherent
self. In fact, one of the most important theoretical and political advances
of postmodernism is its stress on the centrality of language and subjectivity as new fronts from which to rethink the issues of meaning, identity, and politics. This issue can best be approached by analyzing the
ways in which postmodernism has challenged the conventional view of
language.

Postmodern discourse has retheorized the nature of language as a system of signs structured in the infinite play of difference, and in doing so
has undermined the dominant, positivist notion of language as either a
genetic code structured in permanence or simply a linguistic, transparent medium for transmitting ideas and meaning. Theorists such as
Jacques Derrida, Michel Foucault, Jacques Lacan, and Laclau and
Mouffe, in particular, have played a major role in retheorizing the relationship among discourse, power, and difference. For example, Derrida
has brilliantly analyzed the issue of language through the principle of
what he calls "*différance*." This view suggests that meaning is the product of a language constructed out of and subject to the endless play of
differences among signifiers. What constitutes the meaning of a signifier

is defined by the shifting, changing relations of difference that characterize the referential play of language. What Derrida, Laclau and Mouffe, and a host of other critics have demonstrated is "the increasing difficulty of defining the limits of language, or, more accurately, of defining the specific identity of the linguistic object" (Laclau, "Politics" 67). But more is at stake here than theoretically demonstrating that meaning can never be fixed once and for all.

The postmodern emphasis on the importance of discourse has also resulted in a major rethinking of the notion of subjectivity. In particular, various postmodern discourses have offered a major critique of the liberal humanist notion of subjectivity, which is predicated on the notion of a unified, rational, self-determining consciousness. In this view, the individual subject is the source of self-knowledge, and his or her view of the world is constituted through the exercise of a rational and autonomous mode of understanding and knowing. What postmodern discourse challenges is liberal humanism's notion of the subject "as a kind of free, autonomous, universal sensibility, indifferent to any particular or moral contents" (Eagleton 101). Teresa Ebert, in her discussion of the construction of gender differences, offers a succinct commentary on the humanist notion of identity:

> Postmodern feminist cultural theory breaks with the dominant humanist view . . . in which the subject is still considered to be an autonomous individual with a coherent, stable self constituted by a set of natural and pre-given elements such as biological sex. It theorizes the subject as produced through signifying practices which precede her and not as the originator of meaning. One acquires specific subject positions—that is, existence in meaning, in social relations—being constituted in ideologically structured discursive acts. Subjectivity is thus the effect of a set of ideologically organized signifying practices through which the individual is situated in the world and in terms of which the world and one's self are made intelligible. (22–23)

The importance of postmodernism's retheorizing of subjectivity cannot be overemphasized. In this view, subjectivity is no longer assigned to the apolitical waste land of essences and essentialism. Subjectivity is now read as multiple, layered, and nonunitary; rather than being constituted in a unified and integrated ego, the "self" is seen as being "constituted out of and by difference and remains contradictory" (quoted in Grossberg 56). No longer viewed as merely the repository of consciousness and creativity, the self is constructed as a terrain of conflict and struggle, and subjectivity is seen as site of both liberation and subjugation. How subjectivity relates to issues of identity, intentionality, and desire is a deeply political issue that is inextricably related to social and cultural forces that extend far beyond the self-consciousness of the so-called humanist subject. Both the very nature of subjectivity and its capacities for self- and social determination can no longer be situated within the guarantees of transcendent phenomena or metaphysical essences. Within this postmodern perspective, the basis for a cultural politics and the struggle for power has been opened up to include the issues of language and identity. In what follows, I want to take up how various feminist discourses reinscribe some of the central assumptions of modernism and postmodernism as part of a broader cultural practice and political project.

Postmodern Feminism as Political and Ethical Practice

Feminist theory has always engaged in a dialectical relationship with modernism. On the one hand, it has stressed modernist concerns with equality, social justice, and freedom through an ongoing engagement with substantive political issues, specifically the rewriting of the historical and social construction of gender in the interest of an emancipatory cultural politics. In other words, feminism has been quite discriminating in its ability to sift through the wreckage of modernism in order to liberate modernism's victories, particularly the unrealized potentialities that reside in its categories of agency, justice, and politics. On the other hand, postmodern feminism has rejected those aspects of modernism that exalt universal laws at the expense of specificity and contingency. More specifically, postmodern feminism opposes a linear view of history which legitimates patriarchal notions of subjectivity and society; moreover, it rejects the notion that science and reason have a direct correspondence with objectivity and truth. In effect, postmodern feminism rejects the binary opposition between modernism and postmodernism in favor of a broader theoretical attempt to situate both discourses critically within a feminist political project.

Feminist theory has both produced and profited from a critical appropriation of a number of assumptions central to modernism and postmodernism. The feminist engagement with modernism has been primarily a discourse of self-criticism and has served to expand radically a plurality of positions within feminism itself. Women of color, lesbians, poor and working-class women have challenged the essentialism, separatism, and ethnocentricism that have been expressed in feminist theorizing, and in doing so have seriously undermined the Eurocentrist and totalizing discourse that has become a political straitjacket within the movement. Fraser and Nicholson offer a succinct analysis of some of the issues involved in this debate, particularly in relation to the appropriation by some feminists of "quasi metanarratives":

> They tacitly presuppose some commonly held but unwarranted and essentialist assumptions about the nature of human beings and the conditions for social life. In addition, they assume methods and/or concepts that are uninflected by temporality or historicity and that therefore function de facto as permanent, neutral matrices for inquiry. Such theories, then, share some of the essentialist and ahistorical features of metanarratives: they are insufficiently attentive to historical and cultural diversity; and they falsely universalize features of the theorist's own era, society, culture, class, sexual orientation, and/or ethnic or racial group. . . . It has become clear that quasi metanarratives hamper, rather than promote, sisterhood, since they elide differences among women and among the forms of sexism to which different women are differentially subject. Likewise, it is increasingly apparent that such theories hinder alliances with other progressive movements, since they tend to occlude axes of domination other than gender. In sum, there is a growing interest among feminists in modes of theorizing that are attentive to differences and to cultural and historical specificity. (92, 99)

Fashioning a language that has been highly critical of modernism has not only served to make problematic what can be called totalizing feminisms; it has also called into question the notion that sexist oppression is at the root of all forms of domination (Malson, et al. 5–9). Implicit in this position are two assumptions that have significantly shaped the arguments of mostly white, Western women. The first argument inverts the orthodox Marxist position that regards class as the primary category of domination, with all other modes of oppression being relegated to second place. In this instance, patriarchy becomes the primary form of domination, while race and class are reduced to its distorted reflection. The second assumption recycles another aspect of orthodox Marxism, which assumes that the struggle over power is exclusively waged among opposing social classes. The feminist version of this argument simply substitutes gender for class, and in doing so reproduces a form of "us-against-them" politics that is antithetical to developing community within a broad and diversified public culture. Both of these arguments represent the ideological baggage of modernism. In both cases, domination is framed in binary oppositions which suggest that workers or women cannot be complicit in their own oppression and that domination assumes a form that is singular and uncomplicated. The feminist challenge to this ideological straitjacket of modernism is well expressed by bell hooks, who avoids the politics of separatism by invoking an important distinction between the role feminists might play in asserting their own particular struggle against patriarchy and the role they can play as part of a broader struggle for liberation:

> Feminist effort to end patriarchal domination should be of primary concern precisely because it insists on the eradication of exploitation and oppression in the family context and in all other intimate relationships. . . . Feminism, as liberation struggle, must exist apart from and as a part of the larger struggle to eradicate domination in all of its forms. We must understand that patriarchal domination shares an ideological foundation with racism and other forms of group oppression, that there is no hope that it can be eradicated while these systems remain intact. This knowledge should consistently inform the direction of feminist theory and practice. Unfortunately, racism and class elitism among women [have] frequently led to the suppression and distortion of this connection so that it is now necessary for feminist thinkers to critique and revise much feminist theory and the direction of the feminist movement. This effort at revision is perhaps most evident in the current widespread acknowledgement that sexism, racism, and class exploitation constitute interlocking systems of domination—that sex, race, and class, and not sex alone, determine the nature of any female's identity, status, and circumstance, the degree to which she will or will not be dominated, the extent to which she will have the power to dominate. (22)

I invoke the feminist critique of modernism to make visible some of the ideological territory it shares with certain versions of postmodernism and to suggest the wider implications that a postmodern feminism has for developing and broadening the terrain of political struggle and transformation. It is important to note that this encounter between feminism and postmodernism should not be seen as an effort to displace a feminist politics with a politics and pedagogy of postmodernism. On the contrary, I think feminism provides postmodernism with a politics, and with a great deal more. What is at stake here is using feminism, in the words of Meaghan Morris, as "a context in which debates about postmodernism might further be considered, developed, transformed (or abandoned)" (16). Critical to such a project is the need to analyze the ways in which feminist theorists have used postmodernism to fashion a form of social criticism whose value lies in its critical approach to gender issues and in the theoretical insights it provides for developing broader democratic and pedagogical struggles.

The theoretical status and political viability of various postmodern discourses regarding the issues of totality, foundationalism, culture, subjectivity, and language are a matter of intense debate among diverse feminist groups. I am little concerned with charting this debate or focusing on those positions that dismiss postmodernism as antithetical to feminism. Instead I want to focus primarily on those feminist discourses that acknowledge being influenced by postmodernism but at the same time deepen and radicalize the assumptions most important in the interest of a theory and practice of transformative feminist, democratic struggles.[3]

Feminism's relationship with postmodernism has been fruitful but problematic (E. Kaplan 1–6). Postmodernism shares a number of assumptions with various feminist theories and practices. For example, both discourses view reason as plural and partial, define subjectivity as multilayered and contradictory, and posit contingency and difference against various forms of essentialism.

At the same time, postmodern feminism has criticized and extended a number of assumptions central to postmodernism. First, it has asserted the primacy of social criticism, and in doing so has redefined the significance of the postmodern challenge to founding discourses and universal principles in terms that prioritize political struggles over epistemological engagements. Donna Haraway puts it well in her comment that "the issue is ethics and politics perhaps more than epistemology" (579). Second, postmodern feminism has refused to accept the postmodern view of totality as a wholesale rejection of all forms of totality or metanarratives. Third, it has rejected the postmodern emphasis on erasing human agency by decentering the subject; in related fashion it has resisted defining language as the only source of meaning, and in doing so has linked power not merely to discourse but also to material practices and struggles. Fourth, it has asserted the importance of difference as part of a broader struggle for ideological and institutional change rather than emphasized the postmodern approach to difference as either an aesthetic (pastiche) or an expression of liberal pluralism (the proliferation of difference without recourse to the language of power). Since it is impossible within this essay to analyze all of these issues in great detail, I will take up some of the more important tendencies implied in these positions.

Postmodern Feminism and the Primacy of the Political

Working collectively to confront difference, to expand our awareness of sex, race, and class as interlocking systems of domination, of the ways we reinforce and perpetuate these structures, is the context in which we learn the true meaning of solidarity. It is this work that must be the foundation of feminist movement. Without it, we cannot effectively resist patriarchal domination; without it, we remain estranged and alienated from one another. Fear of painful confrontation often leads women and men active in feminist movement to avoid rigorous critical encounter, yet if we cannot engage dialectically in a committed, rigorous, humanizing manner, we cannot hope to change the world. . . . While the struggle to eradicate sexism and sexist oppression is and should be the primary thrust of feminist movement, to prepare ourselves politically for this effort we must first learn how to be in solidarity, how to struggle with one another. (hooks 25)

hooks speaks eloquently to the issue of constructing a feminism that is self-consciously political. In solidarity with a number of feminists, she provides a much-needed corrective to the postmodern tendency to eclipse the political and ethical in favor of epistemological and aesthetic concerns. Not only does she assert that intellectual and cultural work must be driven by political questions and issues, she also performs the theoretically important task of affirming a feminist politics that attempts to understand and contest the various ways in which patriarchy is inscribed at every level of daily life. But what is different and postmodern about hooks's commentary is that she not only argues for a postmodern feminist practice that is oppositional in its appeal "to end sexism and sexist oppression" (23), she also calls into question those feminisms that reduce domination to a single cause, focus exclusively on sexual difference, and ignore women's differences as they intersect across other vectors of power, particularly with regard to race and class. What is at stake in this version of postmodern feminist politics is an attempt to reaffirm the centrality of gender struggles while simultaneously broadening the issues associated with such struggles. Similarly, there is an attempt to connect gender politics to a broader politics of solidarity. Let me be more specific about some of these issues.

Central to the feminist movement in the United States since the 1970s has been the important notion that the personal is political. This argument suggests a complex relationship between material social practices and the construction of subjectivity through the use of language. Within this context, subjectivity was analyzed as a historical and social construction, en-gendered through the historically weighted configurations of power, language, and social formations. The problematization of gender relations in this case has often been described as the most important theoretical advance made by feminists (Showalter). Postmodern feminism has extended the political significance of this issue in important ways.

First, it has strongly argued that feminist analyses cannot downplay the dialectical significance of gender relations. That is, such relations have to focus not only on the various ways in which women are inscribed in patriarchal representations and relations of power, but also on how gender relations can be used to problematize the sexual identities, differences, and commonalities of both men and women. To suggest that masculinity is an unproblematic category is to adopt an essentialist position that ultimately reinforces the power of patriarchal discourse (Showalter 1–3).

Second, feminist theorists have redefined the relationship between the personal and the political in ways that advance some important postmodern assumptions. In part, this redefinition has emerged out of a growing feminist criticism that rejects the notions that sexuality is the only axis of domination and that the study of sexuality should be limited theoretically to an exclusive focus on how women's subjectivities are constructed. For example, theorists such as Teresa de Lauretis have argued that central to feminist social criticism is the need for feminists to maintain a "tension between [the personal and the political] precisely through the understanding of identity as multiple and even self-contradictory" ("Feminist" 9). To ignore such a tension often leads to the trap of collapsing the political into the personal and limiting the sphere of politics to the language of pain, anger, and separatism. hooks elaborates on this point by arguing that when feminists reduce the relationship between the personal and the political to the mere naming of one's pain in relation to structures of domination, they often undercut the possibilities of understanding domination's multifaceted nature and creating a politics of possibility. She writes:

> That powerful slogan, "the personal is political," addresses the connection between the self and political reality. Yet it was often interpreted as meaning that to name one's personal pain in relation to structures of domination was not just a beginning stage in the process of coming to political consciousness, to awareness, but all that was necessary. In most cases, naming one's personal pain was not sufficiently linked to overall education for critical consciousness of collective political resistance. Focussing on the personal in a framework that did not compel acknowledgement of the complexity of structures of domination could easily lead to misnaming, to the creation of yet another sophisticated level of non or distorted awareness. This often happens in a feminist context when race and/or class are not seen as factors determining the social construction of one's gendered reality and most importantly, the extent to which one will suffer exploitation and domination. (32)

In this case, the construction of gender must be seen in the context of the wider relations in which it is structured. At issue here is the need to deepen the postmodern notion of difference by radicalizing the notion of gender through a refusal to isolate it as a social category while simultaneously engaging in a politics that aims at transforming self, community, and society. Within this context, postmodern feminism offers the possibility of going beyond the language of domination, anger, and critique.

Third, postmodern feminism attempts to understand the broader workings of power by examining how it functions through means other than specific technologies of control and mastery (de Lauretis, *Technologies*). At issue here is understanding how power is constituted productively. De Lauretis develops this insight by arguing that while postmodernism provides a theoretical service in recognizing that power is "productive of knowledges, meanings, and values, it seems obvious enough that we have to make distinctions between the positive effects and the oppressive effects of such production" ("Feminist" 18). Her point is important because it suggests that power can work in the interests of a politics of possibility, that it can be used to rewrite the narratives of subordinate groups not merely in reaction to the forces of domination but in response to the construction of alternative visions and futures. The exclusive emphasis on power as oppressive always runs the risk of developing as its political equivalent a version of radical cynicism and antiutopianism. Postmodern feminism offers the possibility for redefining both a negative feminist politics (Kristeva) and a more general postmodern inclination toward a despair that dresses itself up in irony, parody, and pastiche. Linda Alcoff puts it well in arguing, "As the Left should by now have learned, you cannot mobilize a movement that is only and always against: you must have a positive alternative, a vision of a better future that can motivate people to sacrifice their time and energy toward its realization" (418–19). Central to this call for a language of possibility are the ways in which a postmodern feminism has taken up the issue of power in more expansive and productive terms, one that is attentive to the ways in which power inscribes itself through the force of reason, and constructs itself at the levels of intimate and local associations (Diamond and Quinby).

Postmodern Feminism and the Politics of Reason and Totality

Various feminist discourses have provided a theoretical context and politics for enriching postmodernism's analyses of reason and totality. Whereas postmodern theorists have stressed the historical, contingent, and cultural construction of reason, they have failed to show how reason has been constructed as part of a masculine discourse (Diamond and Quinby 194–97). Postmodern feminists have provided a powerful challenge to this position, particularly in their analyses of the ways in which reason, language, and representation have produced knowledge/power relations, legitimated in the discourse of science and objectivity, to silence, marginalize, and misrepresent women (Jagger; Keller; Harding; Birke). Feminist theorists have also modified the postmodern discussion of reason in another two important ways. First, while recognizing that all claims to reason are partial, they have argued for the emancipatory possibilities that exist in reflective consciousness and critical reason as a basis for social criticism (Welch; de Lauretis, "Feminist"). In these terms, reason is not merely about a politics of representation structured in domination or a relativist discourse that abstracts itself from the dynamics of power and struggle; it also offers the possibility for self-representation and social reconstruction. For example, Haraway has qualified the postmodern turn toward relativism by theorizing reason within a discourse of partiality that "privileges contestation, deconstruction, passionate construction, webbed connections, and hope for transformation of systems of knowledge and ways of seeing" (585). Similarly, hooks (105–19) and others have argued that feminists who deny the power of critical reason and abstract discourse often reproduce a cultural practice that operates in the interest of patriarchy. That is, this culture serves to silence women and others by positioning them in ways that cultivate a fear of theory, which positions in turn often produce a form of powerlessness buttressed by a powerful anti-intellectualism. Second, feminists such as Jane Flax have modified postmodernism's approach to reason by arguing that reason is not the only locus of meaning:

> I cannot agree . . . that liberation, stable meaning, insight, self-understanding and justice depend above all on the "primacy of reason and intelligence." There are many ways in which such qualities may be attained—for example, political practices; economic, racial and gender equality; good childrearing; empathy; fantasy; feelings; imagination; and embodiment. On what grounds can we claim reason is privileged or primary for the self or justice? ("Reply" 202)

At issue here is the rejection not of reason but of a modernist version of reason that is totalizing, essentialist, and politically repressive. Postmodern feminism has challenged and modified the postmodern approach to totality or master narratives on similar terms. While accepting the postmodern critique of master narratives that employ a single standard and claim to embody a universal experience, postmodern feminism does not define all large or formative narratives as oppressive. At the same time, postmodern feminism recognizes the importance of grounding narratives in the contexts and specificities of people's lives, communities, and cultures, but supplements this distinctly postmodern emphasis on the contextual with an argument for metanarratives that employ forms of social criticism that are dialectical, relational, and holistic. Metanarratives play an important theoretical role in placing the particular and the specific in broader historical and relational contexts. To reject all notions of totality is to risk being trapped in particularistic theories that cannot explain how the various diverse relations that constitute larger social, political, and global systems interrelate or mutually determine and constrain one another. Postmodern feminism recognizes that we need a notion of large narratives that privileges forms of analyses in which it is possible to make visible those mediations, interrelations, and interdependencies that give shape and power to larger political and social systems. Fraser and Nicholson make very clear the importance of such narratives to social criticism:

> Effective criticism . . . requires an array of different methods and genres. It requires, at minimum, large narratives about changes in social organization and ideology, empirical and social-theoretical analyses of macrostructures and institutions, interactionist analyses of the micropolitics of everyday life, critical-hermeneutical and institutional analyses of cultural production, historically and culturally specific sociologies of gender. . . . The list could go on. (91)

Postmodern Feminism and the Politics of Difference and Agency

Feminists share a healthy skepticism about the postmodern celebration of difference. Many feminist theorists welcome the postmodern emphasis on the proliferation of local narratives, the opening up of the world to cultural and ethnic differences, and the positing of difference as a challenge to hegemonic power relations parading as universals (Flax, "Reply"; McRobbie; Nicholson; E. Kaplan; Lather). But at the same time, postmodern feminists have raised serious questions about how differences are to be understood so as to change rather than reproduce prevailing power relations. This is particularly important since difference in the postmodern sense often slips into a theoretically harmless and politically deracinated notion of pastiche. For many postmodern feminists, the issue of difference has to be interrogated around a number of concerns. These include questions about how a politics of difference can be constructed that will not simply reproduce forms of liberal individualism, or how a politics of difference can be "re-written as a refusal of the terms of radical separation" (C. Kaplan 194). Also at issue is how to develop a theory of difference that is not at odds with a politics of solidarity. Equally important is how a theory of the subject constructed in difference might sustain or negate a politics of human agency. Relatedly, there is the question of how a postmodern feminism can redefine the knowledge/power relationship in order to develop a theory of difference that is not static, one that is able to make distinctions between differenccs that matter and those that do not. All these questions have been addressed in a variety of feminist discourses, not all of which support postmodernism. What has increasingly emerged out of this engagement is a discourse that radically complicates and amplifies the possibilities for reconstructing difference within a radical political project and set of transformative practices.

In the most general sense, the postmodern emphasis on difference serves to dissolve all pretensions to an undifferentiated concept of truth, man, woman, and subjectivity, while at the same time refusing to reduce difference to "opposition, exclusion, and hierarchic arrangement" (Malson, et al. 4). Postmodern feminism has gone a long way in framing the issue of difference in terms that give it an emancipatory grounding, that identify the "differences that make a difference" as an important political act. In what follows, I want briefly to take up the issues of difference and agency that have been developed within a postmodern feminist discourse.

Joan Wallach Scott has provided a major theoretical service in dismantling one of the crippling dichotomies in which the issue of difference has been situated. Rejecting the idea that difference and equality constitute an opposition, she argues that the opposite of equality is inequality. In this sense, the issue of equality depends on an acknowledgment of which differences promote inequality and which do not. In this case, the category of difference is central as a political construct to the notion of equality itself. The implication this has for a feminist politics of difference, according to Scott, involves two important theoretical moves:

> In histories of feminism and in feminist political strategies there needs to be at once attention to the operations of difference and an insistence on differences, but not a simple substitution of multiple for binary difference, for it is not a happy pluralism we ought to invoke. The resolution of the "difference dilemma" comes neither from ignoring nor embracing difference as it is normatively constituted. Instead it seems to me that the critical feminist position must always involve two moves: the first, systematic criticism of the operations of categorical difference, exposure of the kinds of exclusions and inclusions—the hierarchies—it constructs, and a refusal of their ultimate "truth." A refusal, however, not in the name of an equality that implies sameness or identity but rather (and this is the second move) of an equality that rests on differences—differences that confound, disrupt, and render ambiguous the meaning of any fixed binary opposition. To do anything else is to buy into the political argument that sameness is a requirement for equality, an untenable position for feminists (and historians) who know that power is constructed on, and so must be challenged from, the ground of difference. (176–77)

According to Scott, to challenge power from the ground of difference by focusing on both exclusions and inclusions is to avoid slipping into a facile and simple elaboration or romanticization of difference. In more concrete terms, E. Ann Kaplan takes up this issue in arguing that the postmodern elimination of all distinctions between high and low culture is important but erases the important differences at work in the production and exhibition of specific cultural works. By not discriminating among differences of context, production, and consumption, postmodern discourses run the risk of suppressing the differences at work in the power relations that characterize these different spheres of cultural production. For example, to treat all cultural products as texts may situate them as historical and social constructions, but it is imperative that the institutional mechanisms and power relations in which different texts are produced be distinguished so that it becomes possible to understand how such texts, in part, make a difference in terms of reproducing particular meanings, social relations, and values.

A similar issue is at work regarding the postmodern notion of subjectivity. The postmodern notion that human subjectivities and bodies are constructed in the endless play of difference threatens to erase not only any possibility for human agency or choice, but also the theoretical means for understanding how the body becomes a site of power and struggle around specific differences that do matter with respect to the issues of race, class, and gender. There is little sense in many postmodern accounts of the ways in which different historical, social, and gendered representations of meaning and desire are actually mediated and taken up subjectively by real individuals. Individuals are positioned within a variety of "subject positions," but there is no sense of how they actually make choices, promote effective resistance, or mediate between themselves and others. Feminist theorists have extended the most radical principles of modernism in modifying the postmodern view of the subject. Theorists such as de Lauretis (*Alice*, "Feminist," *Technologies*) insist that the construction of female experience is not constructed outside of human intentions and choices, however limited. She argues that the agency of subjects is made possible through shifting and multiple forms of consciousness, which are constructed through available discourses and practices but are always open to interrogation through self-analysis. For de Lauretis and others, such as Alcoff, such a practice is theoretical and political. Alcoff's own attempt to construct a feminist identity-politics draws on de Lauretis's work and is insightful in its attempt to develop a theory of positionality:

> The identity of a woman is the product of her own interpretation and reconstruction of her history, as mediated through a cultural discursive context to which she has access. Therefore, the concept of positionality in-

cludes two points: First . . . the concept of woman is a relational term identifiable only with a (constantly moving) context; but second . . . the position that women find themselves in can be actively utilized (rather than transcended) as a location for the construction of meaning, a place where a meaning can be discovered (the meaning of femaleness). The concept . . . of positionality shows how women use their positional perspective as a place from which values are interpreted and constructed rather than as a locus of an already determined set of values. (434)

Feminists have also voiced concern about the postmodern tendency to portray the body as so fragmented, mobile, and boundaryless that it invites confusion over how the body is actually engendered and positioned within concrete configurations of power and forms of material oppression. The postmodern emphasis on the proliferation of ideas, discourses, and representations underplays both the different ways in which bodies are oppressed and the manner in which bodies are constructed differently through specific material relations. Feminists such as Sandra Lee Bartky have provided a postmodern reading of the politics of the body by extending Foucault's notion in *Discipline and Punish* and *The History of Sexuality* of how the growth of the modern state has been accompanied by an unprecedented attempt at disciplining the body. Bartky differs from Foucault in that she employs a discriminating notion of difference by showing how gender is implicated in the production of the body as a site of domination, struggle, and resistance. For example, Bartky points to the disciplinary measures of dieting, the tyranny of fashion and the insistence on slenderness, the discourse of exercise, and other technologies of control. She also goes beyond Foucault in arguing that the body must be seen as a site of resistance and linked to a broader theory of agency.

Postmodern feminism provides a grounded politics that employs the most progressive aspects of modernism and postmodernism. In the most general sense, it reaffirms the importance of difference as part of a broader political struggle for the reconstruction of public life. It rejects all forms of essentialism but recognizes the importance of certain formative narratives. Similarly, it provides a language of power that engages the issues of inequality and struggle. In recognizing the importance of institutional structures and language in the construction of subjectivities and political life, it promotes social criticism that acknowledges the interrelationship between human agents and social structures, rather than succumbing to a social theory that lacks agents or one in which agents are simply the product of radical social theory imbued with a language of critique and possibility. Implicit in its various discourses are new relations of parenting, work, schooling, play, citizenship, and joy. These relations link a politics of intimacy and solidarity, the concrete and the general; it is a politics which in its various forms needs to be taken up as central to the development of a critical pedagogy. That is, critical educators need to provide a sense of how the most critical elements of modernism, postmodernism, and postmodern feminism might be taken up by teachers and educators so as to create a postmodern pedagogical practice. In ending I want to outline briefly what some of the principles are that inform such a practice.

Toward a Postmodern Pedagogy

As long as people are people, democracy in the full sense of the word will always be no more than an ideal. One may approach it as one would a horizon, in ways that may be better or worse, but it can never be fully attained. In this sense, you, too, are merely approaching democracy. You have thousands of problems of all kinds, as other countries do. But you have one great advantage: You have been approaching democracy uninterrupted for more than 200 years. (Vaclav Havel, quoted in Oreskes 16)

How on earth can these prestigious persons in Washington ramble on in their sub-intellectual way about the "end of history"? As I look forward into the twenty-first century I sometimes agonize about the times in which my grandchildren and their children will live. It is not so much the rise in population as the rise in universal material expectations of the globe's huge population that will be straining its resources to the very limits. North-South antagonisms will certainly sharpen, and religious and national fundamentalisms will become more intransigent. The struggle to bring consumer greed within moderate control, to find a level of low growth and satisfaction that is not at the expense of the disadvantaged and poor, to defend the environment and to prevent ecological disasters, to share more equitably the world's resources and to insure their renewal—all this is agenda enough for the continuation of "history." (Thompson 120)

A striking characteristic of the totalitarian system is its peculiar coupling of human demoralization and mass depoliticizing. Consequently, battling this system requires a conscious appeal to morality and an inevitable involvement in politics. (Michnik 44)

All these quotations stress, implicitly or explicitly, the importance of politics and ethics to democracy. In the first, the newly elected president of Czechoslovakia, Vaclav Havel, reminds the American people while addressing a joint session of Congress that democracy is an ideal that is filled with possibilities but that always has to be seen as part of an ongoing struggle for freedom and human dignity. As a playwright and former political prisoner, Havel is a living embodiment of such a struggle. In the second, E. P. Thompson, the English peace activist and historian, reminds the American public that history has not ended but needs to be opened up in order to engage the many problems and possibilities that human beings will have to face in the twenty-first century. And in the third, Adam Michnik, a founder of Poland's Workers' Defense Committee and an elected member of the Polish parliament, provides an ominous insight into one of the central features of totalitarianism, whether on the Right or the Left. He points to a society that fears democratic politics while simultaneously reproducing in people a sense of massive collective despair. None of these writers is from the United States, and all of them are caught up in the struggle to recapture the Enlightenment model of freedom, agency, and democracy while at the same time attempting to deal with the conditions of a postmodern world.

All these statements serve to highlight the inability of the American public to grasp the full significance of the democratization of Eastern Europe in terms of what it reveals about the nature of our own democracy. In Eastern Europe and elsewhere there is a strong call for the primacy of the political and the ethical as a foundation for democratic public life, whereas in the United States there is an ongoing refusal of the discourse of politics and ethics. Elected politicians from both established parties in Congress complain that American politics is about "trivialization, atomization, and paralysis." Politicians as diverse as Lee Atwater, the Republican Party chairman, and Walter Mondale, the former Vice President, agree that we have entered into a time in which much of the American public believes that "Bull permeates everything ... [and that] we've got a kind of politics of irrelevance" (Oreskes 16). At the same time, a number of polls indicate that while the youth of Poland, Czechoslovakia, and East Germany are extending the frontiers of democracy, American youth are both poorly motivated and largely ill-prepared to struggle for and keep democracy alive in the twenty-first century.

Rather than being a model of democracy, the United States has become indifferent to the need to struggle for the conditions that make democracy a substantive rather than lifeless activity. At all levels of national and daily life, the breadth and depth of democratic relations are being rolled back. We have become a society that appears to demand less rather than more of democracy. In some quarters, democracy has actually become subversive. What does this suggest for developing some guiding principles in order to rethink the purpose and meaning of education and critical pedagogy within the present crises? In what follows, I want to situate some of the work I have been developing on critical pedagogy over the last decade by placing it within a broader political context. That is, the principles that I develop below represent educational issues that must be located in a larger framework of politics. Moreover, these principles emerge out of a convergence of various tendencies within modernism, postmodernism, and postmodern feminism. What is important to note here is the refusal simply to play off these various theoretical tendencies against each other. Instead, I try to appropriate critically the most important aspects of these theoretical movements by raising the question of how they contribute to creating the conditions for deepening the possibilities for a radical pedagogy and a political project that aims at reconstructing democratic public life so as to extend the principles of freedom, justice, and equality to all spheres of society.

At stake here is the issue of retaining modernism's commitment to critical reason, agency, and the power of human beings to overcome human suffering. Modernism reminds us of the importance of constructing a discourse that is ethical, historical, and political (Giddens 151–73). At the same time, postmodernism provides a powerful challenge to all totalizing discourses, places an important emphasis on the contingent and the specific, and provides a new theoretical language for developing a politics of difference. Finally, postmodern feminism makes visible the importance of grounding our visions in a political project, redefines the relationship between the margins and the center around concrete political struggles, and offers the opportunity for a politics of voice that links rather than severs the relationship between the personal and the political as part of a broader struggle for justice and social transformation. All the principles developed below touch on these issues and recast the relationship between the pedagogical and the political as central to any social movement that attempts to effect emancipatory struggles and social transformations.

1. Education must be understood as producing not only knowledge but also political subjects. Rather than rejecting the language of politics, critical pedagogy must link public education to the imperatives of a critical democracy (Dewey; Giroux). Critical pedagogy needs to be informed by a public philosophy dedicated to returning schools to their primary task: furnishing places of critical education that serve to create a public sphere of citizens who are able to exercise power over their own lives and especially over the conditions of knowledge production and acquisition. This is a critical pedagogy defined, in part, by the attempt to create the lived experience of empowerment for the vast majority. In other words, the language of critical pedagogy needs to construct schools as democratic public spheres. In part, this means that educators need to develop a critical pedagogy in which the knowledge, habits, and skills of critical rather than simply good citizenship are taught and practiced. This means providing students with the opportunity to develop the critical capacity to challenge and transform existing social and political forms, rather than simply adapt to them. It also means providing

students with the skills they will need to locate themselves in history, find their own voices, and provide the convictions and compassion necessary for exercising civic courage, taking risks, and furthering the habits, customs, and social relations that are essential to democratic public forms.

In effect, critical pedagogy needs to be grounded in a keen sense of the importance of constructing a political vision from which to develop an educational project as part of a wider discourse for revitalizing democratic public life. A critical pedagogy for democracy cannot be reduced, as some educators, politicians, and groups have argued, to forcing students to say the pledge of allegiance at the beginning of every school day or to speak and think only in the dominant English (Hirsch). A critical pedagogy for democracy does not begin with test scores but with these questions: What kinds of citizens do we hope to produce through public education in a postmodern culture? What kind of society do we want to create in the context of the present shifting cultural and ethnic borders? How can we reconcile the notions of difference and equality with the imperatives of freedom and justice?

2. Ethics must be seen as a central concern of critical pedagogy. This suggests that educators should attempt to understand more fully how different discourses offer students diverse ethical referents for structuring their relationship to the wider society. But it also suggests that educators should go beyond the postmodern notion of understanding how student experiences are shaped within different ethical discourses. Educators must also come to view ethics and politics as a relationship between the self and the other. Ethics, in this case, is not a matter of individual choice or relativism but a social discourse grounded in struggles that refuse to accept needless human suffering and exploitation. Thus ethics is taken up as a struggle against inequality and as a discourse for expanding basic human rights. This points to a notion of ethics attentive to both the issue of abstract rights and those contexts that produce particular stories, struggles, and histories. In pedagogical terms, an ethical discourse needs to regard the relations of power, subject positions, and social practices it activates (Simon). This is an ethics of neither essentialism nor relativism. It is an ethical discourse rooted in historical struggles and attentive to the construction of social relations free of injustice. The quality of ethical discourse, in this case, is not simply grounded in difference but in the issue of how justice arises out of concrete historical circumstances (Shapiro).

3. Critical pedagogy needs to focus on the issue of difference in an ethically challenging and politically transformative way. There are at least two notions of difference at work here. First, difference can be incorporated into a critical pedagogy as part of an attempt to understand

how student identities and subjectivities are constructed in multiple and contradictory ways. In this case, identity is explored through its own historicity and complex subject positions. The category of student experience should not be limited pedagogically to students exercising self-reflection but opened up as a race-, gender-, and class-specific construct to include the diverse historical and social ways in which their experiences and identities have been constructed. Second, critical pedagogy can focus on how differences among groups develop and are sustained around both enabling and disempowering sets of relations. In this instance, difference becomes a marker for understanding how social groups are constituted in ways that are integral to the functioning of any democratic society. Examining difference in this context does not only mean charting spatial, racial, ethnic, or cultural differences, but also analyzing historical differences that manifest themselves in public struggles.

As part of their use of a language of critique, teachers can make problematic how different subjectivities are positioned within a historically specific range of ideologies and social practices that inscribe students in modes of behavior that subjugate, infantilize, and corrupt. Similarly, such a language can analyze how differences within and among social groups are constructed and sustained both within and outside schools in webs of domination, subordination, hierarchy, and exploitation. As part of their use of a language of possibility, teachers can explore creating knowledge/power relations in which multiple narratives and social practices are constructed around a politics and pedagogy of difference that offers students the opportunity to read the world differently, resist the abuse of power and privilege, and envision alternative democratic communities. Difference in this case cannot be seen as simply a politics of assertion, of simply affirming one's voice or sense of the common good; it must be developed within practices in which differences can be affirmed *and* transformed in their articulation with categories central to public life: democracy, citizenship, public spheres. In both political and pedagogical terms, the category of difference must be central to the notion of democratic community.

4. Critical pedagogy needs a language that allows for competing solidarities and political vocabularies that do not reduce the issues of power, justice, struggle, and inequality to a single script, a master narrative that suppresses the contingent, the historical, and the everyday as serious objects of study (Cherryholmes). This suggests that curriculum knowledge should not be treated as a sacred text but developed as part of an ongoing engagement with a variety of narratives and traditions that can be reread and reformulated in politically different terms. At issue here is constructing a discourse of textual authority that is power-

sensitive and that has developed as part of a wider analysis of the struggle over culture fought out at the levels of curricula knowledge, pedagogy, and the exercise of institutional power (Aronowitz and Giroux). This is not merely an argument against a canon, but one that disavows the very category. Knowledge has to be reexamined constantly in terms of its limits and rejected as a body of information that only has to be passed down to students. As Laclau has pointed out, setting limits to the answers given by what can be judged as a valued tradition (a matter of argument also) is an important political act ("Politics" 77–78). What Laclau is suggesting is the possibility for students creatively to appropriate the past as part of a living dialogue, an affirmation of the multiplicity of narratives, and the need to judge these narratives not as timeless or as monolithic discourses, but as social and historical inventions that can be refigured in the interests of creating more democratic forms of public life. This points to the possibility of creating pedagogical practices characterized by the open exchange of ideas, the proliferation of dialogue, and the material conditions for the expression of individual and social freedom.

5. Critical pedagogy needs to create new forms of knowledge through its emphasis on breaking down disciplinary boundaries and creating new spaces where knowledge can be produced. In this sense, critical pedagogy must be reclaimed as a cultural politics and a form of counter-memory. This is not merely an epistemological issue, but one of power, ethics, and politics. Critical pedagogy as a cultural politics points to the necessity of inserting the struggle over the production and creation of knowledge into a broader attempt to create a public sphere of citizens who are able to exercise power over their lives and especially over the conditions of knowledge production and acquisition. As a form of counter-memory, critical pedagogy starts with the everyday and the particular as a basis for learning; it reclaims the historical and the popular as part of an ongoing effort to legitimate the voices of those who have been silenced, and to inform the voices of those who have been located within monolithic and totalizing narratives. At stake here is a pedagogy that provides the knowledge, skills, and habits for students and others to read history in ways that enable them to reclaim their identities in the interests of constructing forms of life that are more democratic and more just.

This struggle deepens the pedagogical meaning of the political and the political meaning of the pedagogical. In the first instance, it raises important questions about how students and others are constructed as agents within particular histories, cultures, and social relations. Against the monolith of culture, it posits the conflicting terrain of cultures shaped within asymmetrical relations of power, grounded in diverse historical struggles. Similarly, culture has to be understood as part of the discourse of power and inequality. As a pedagogical issue, the relationship between culture and power is evident in questions such as "Whose cultures are appropriated as our own? How is marginality normalized?" (Popkewitz 77). To insert the primacy of culture as a pedagogical and political issue is to make central how schools function in the shaping of particular identities, values, and histories by producing and legitimating specific cultural narratives and resources. In the second instance, asserting the pedagogical aspects of the political raises the issue of how difference and culture can be taken up as pedagogical practices and not merely as political categories. For example, how does difference matter as a pedagogical category if educators and cultural workers have to make knowledge meaningful before it can become critical and transformative? Or what does it mean to engage the tension between being theoretically correct and being pedagogically wrong? These concerns and tensions offer the possibility for making the relationship between the political and the pedagogical mutually informing and problematic.

6. The Enlightenment notion of reason needs to be reformulated within a critical pedagogy. First, educators need to be skeptical regarding any notion of reason that purports to reveal the truth by denying its own historical construction and ideological principles. Reason is not innocent, and any viable notion of critical pedagogy cannot exercise forms of authority that emulate totalizing forms of reason that appear to be beyond criticism and dialogue. This suggests that we reject claims to objectivity in favor of partial epistemologies that recognize the historical and socially constructed nature of their own knowledge claims and methodologies. In this way, curriculum can be viewed as a cultural script that introduces students to particular forms of reason that structure specific stories and ways of life. Reason in this sense implicates and is implicated in the intersection of power, knowledge, and politics. Second, it is not enough to reject an essentialist or universalist defense of reason. Instead, the limits of reason must be extended to recognizing other ways in which people learn or take up particular subject positions. In this case, educators need to understand more fully how people learn through concrete social relations, through the ways in which the body is positioned (Grumet), through the construction of habit and intuition, and through the production and investment of desire and affect.

7. Critical pedagogy needs to regain a sense of alternatives by combining the languages of critique and possibility. Postmodern feminism exemplifies this combination in its critique of patriarchy and its search to construct new forms of identity and social relations. It is worth noting that teachers can take up this issue around a number of considerations. First, educators need to construct a language of critique that combines

the issue of limits with the discourse of freedom and social responsibility. In other words, the question of freedom needs to be engaged dialectically, not only as a matter of individual rights but also as part of the discourse of social responsibility. That is, whereas freedom remains an essential category in establishing the conditions for ethical and political rights, it must also be seen as a force to be checked if it is expressed in modes of individual and collective behavior that threaten the ecosystem or produce forms of violence and oppression against individuals and social groups. Second, critical pedagogy needs to explore in programmatic terms a language of possibility that is capable of thinking risky thoughts, engages a project of hope, and points to the horizon of the "not yet." A language of possibility does not have to dissolve into a reified form of utopianism; instead, it can develop as a precondition for nourishing the courage to imagine a different and more just world and to struggle for it. A language of moral and political possibility is more than an outmoded vestige of humanist discourse. It is central to responding not only with compassion to human beings who suffer and agonize but also with a politics and a set of pedagogical practices that can refigure and change existing narratives of domination into images and concrete instances of a future worth fighting for.

A certain cynicism characterizes the language of the Left at the present moment. Central to this mindset is the refusal of all utopian images, all appeals of "a language of possibility." Such refusals are often made on the grounds that "utopian discourse" is a strategy employed by the Right and therefore is ideologically tainted. Or the very notion of possibility is dismissed as an impractical and therefore useless category. To my mind, this dismissiveness represents less a serious critique than a refusal to move beyond the language of exhaustion and despair. What it is essential to develop in response to this position is a discriminating notion of possibility, one that makes a distinction between "dystopian" and utopian language. In the former, the appeal to the future is grounded in a form of nostalgic romanticism, with its call for a return to a past, which more often than not serves to legitimate relations of domination and oppression. Similarly, in Constance Penley's terms a "dystopian" discourse often "limits itself to solutions that are either individualist or bound to a romanticized notion of guerrilla-like small-group resistance. The true atrophy of the utopian imagination is this: we can imagine the future but we *cannot* conceive the kind of collective political strategies necessary to change or ensure that future" (122). In contrast to the language of dystopia, a discourse of possibility rejects apocalyptic emptiness and nostalgic imperialism and sees history as open and society worth struggling for in the image of an alternative future. This is the language of the "not yet," one in which the imagination is redeemed and nourished in the effort to construct new relationships fashioned out of strategies of collective resistance based on a critical recognition of both what society is and what it might become. Paraphrasing Walter Benjamin, this is a discourse of imagination and hope that pushes history against the grain. Fraser illuminates this sentiment by emphasizing the importance of a language of possibility to the project of social change: "It allows for the possibility of a radical democratic politics in which immanent critique and transfigurative desire mingle with one another" (*Unruly Practices* 107).

8. Critical pedagogy needs to develop a theory of teachers as transformative intellectuals who occupy specifiable political and social locations. Rather than defining teachers' work through the narrow language of professionalism, a critical pedagogy needs to ascertain more carefully what the role of teachers might be as cultural workers engaged in the production of ideologies and social practices. This is not a call for teachers to become wedded to some abstract ideal that removes them from everyday life or turns them into prophets of perfection and certainty; on the contrary, it is a call for teachers to undertake social criticism not as outsiders but as public intellectuals who address the social and political issues of their neighborhood, their nation, and the wider global world. As public and transformative intellectuals, teachers have an opportunity to make organic connections with the historical traditions that provide them and their students with a voice, history, and sense of belonging. It is a position marked by a moral courage and criticism that does not require educators to step back from society in the manner of the "objective" teacher, but to distance themselves from those power relations that subjugate, oppress, and diminish other human beings. Teachers need to take up criticism from within, to develop pedagogical practices that heighten the possibilities not only for critical consciousness but also for transformative action. In this perspective, teachers would be involved in the invention of critical discourses and democratic social relations. Critical pedagogy would represent itself as the active construction rather than the transmission of particular ways of life. More specifically, as transformative intellectuals, teachers could engage in the invention of languages so as to provide spaces for themselves and their students to rethink their experiences in terms that both name relations of oppression and offer ways in which to overcome them.

9. Central to the notion of critical pedagogy is a politics of voice that combines a postmodern notion of difference with a feminist emphasis on the primacy of the political. This politics entails taking up the relationship between the personal and the political in a way that does not collapse the political into the personal but strengthens the relationship between the two so as to engage in rather than withdraw from address-

ing those institutional forms and structures that contribute to forms of racism, sexism, and class exploitation. This engagement suggests some important pedagogical interventions. First, the self must be seen as a primary site of politicization. That is, the issue of how the self is constructed in multiple and complex ways must be analyzed as part of both a language of affirmation and a broader understanding of how identities are inscribed in and among various social, cultural, and historical formations. To engage issues regarding the construction of the self is to address questions of history, culture, community, language, gender, race, and class. It is to raise questions regarding what pedagogical practices will allow students to speak in dialogical contexts that affirm, interrogate, and extend their understandings of themselves and the global contexts in which they live. Such a position recognizes that students have several or multiple identities, but also affirms the importance of offering students a language that allows them to reconstruct their moral and political energies in the service of creating a more just and equitable social order, one that undermines relations of hierarchy and domination.

Second, a politics of voice must offer pedagogical and political strategies that affirm the primacy of the social, intersubjective, and collective. To focus on voice is not meant simply to affirm the stories that students tell, it is not meant simply to glorify the possibility for narration. Such a position often degenerates into a form of narcissism, a cathartic experience that is reduced to naming anger without the benefit of theorizing in order to understand both its underlying causes and what it means to work collectively to transform the structures of domination responsible for oppressive social relations. Raising one's consciousness has increasingly become a pretext for legitimating hegemonic forms of separatism buttressed by self-serving appeals to the primacy of experience. What is often expressed in such appeals is an anti-intellectualism that retreats from any viable form of political engagement, especially one willing to address and transform diverse forms of oppression. The call simply to affirm one's voice has increasingly been reduced to a pedagogical process that is as reactionary as it is inward-looking. A more radical notion of voice should begin with what hooks calls a critical attention to theorizing experience as part of a broader politics of engagement. Referring specifically to feminist pedagogy, she argues that the discourse of confession and memory can be used to "shift the focus away from mere naming of one's experience. . . . to talk about identity in relation to culture, history, politics" (110). For hooks, the telling of tales of victimization, the use of one's voice, is not enough; it is equally imperative that such experiences be the object of theoretical and critical analyses so that they can be connected to rather than severed from broader notions of solidarity, struggle, and politics.

Conclusion

This essay attempts to introduce readers to some of the central assumptions that govern the discourses of modernism, postmodernism, and postmodern feminism. But in doing so, it rejects pitting these movements against each other and tries instead to see how they converge as part of a broader political project linked to the reconstruction of democratic public life. Similarly, I have attempted here to situate the issue of pedagogical practice within a wider discourse of political engagement. Pedagogy, in this case, is not defined as simply something that goes on in schools. On the contrary, it is posited as central to any political practice that takes up questions of how individuals learn, how knowledge is produced, and how subject positions are constructed. In this context, pedagogical practice refers to forms of cultural production that are inextricably historical and political. Pedagogy is, in part, a technology of power, language, and practice that produces and legitimates forms of moral and political regulation that construct and offer human beings particular views of themselves and the world. Such views are never innocent and are always implicated in the discourse and relations of ethics and power. To invoke the importance of pedagogy is to raise questions not simply about how students learn but also about how educators (in the broad sense of the term) construct the ideological and political positions from which they speak. At issue here is a discourse that both situates human beings within history and makes visible the limits of their ideologies and values. Such a position acknowledges the partiality of all discourses so that the relationship between knowledge and power will always be open to dialogue and critical self-engagement. Pedagogy is about the intellectual, emotional, and ethical investments we make as part of our attempt to negotiate, accommodate, and transform the world in which we find ourselves. The purpose and vision that drive such a pedagogy must be based on a politics and view of authority that link teaching and learning to forms of self- and social empowerment, that argue for forms of community life that extend the principles of liberty, equality, and justice to the widest possible set of institutional and lived relations.

Pedagogy as defined within the traditions of modernism, postmodernism, and postmodern feminism offers educators an opportunity to develop a political project that embraces human interests that move beyond the particularistic politics of class, ethnicity, race, and gender. This is not a call to dismiss the postmodern emphasis on difference so much as it is an attempt to develop a radical democratic politics that stresses difference within unity. This effort means developing a public language that can transform a politics of assertion into one of democratic struggle. Central to such a politics and pedagogy is a notion of community developed around a shared conception of social justice, rights, and entitlement. Such a notion is especially necessary at a time in our history in which such concerns have been subordinated to the priorities of the market and used to legitimate the interests of the rich at the expense of the poor, the unemployed, and the homeless. A radical pedagogy and a transformative democratic politics must go hand in hand in constructing a vision in which liberalism's emphasis on individual freedom, postmodernism's concern with the particularistic, and feminism's concern with the politics of the everyday are coupled with democratic socialism's historic concern with solidarity and public life.

We live at a time in which the responsibilities of citizens transcend national borders. The old modernist notions of center and margin, home and exile, and familiar and strange are breaking apart. Geographic, cultural, and ethnic borders are giving way to shifting configurations of power, community, space, and time. Citizenship can no longer ground itself in forms of Eurocentrism and the language of colonialism. New spaces, relationships, and identities have to be created which allow us to move across borders, to engage difference and otherness as part of a discourse of justice, social engagement, and democratic struggle. Academics can no longer retreat into their classrooms or symposia as if these were the only public spheres available for engaging the power of ideas and the relations of power. Foucault's notion of the specific intellectual, who takes up struggles connected to particular issues and contexts, must be combined with Gramsci's notion of the engaged intellectual, who connects his or her work to broader social concerns that deeply affect how people live, work, and survive.

But there is more at stake here than defining the role of the intellectual or the relationship of teaching to democratic struggle. The struggle against racism, class structures, and sexism needs to move away from being simply a language of critique, and redefine itself as part of a language of transformation and hope. This shift suggests that educators must combine with others engaged in public struggles in order to invent languages and provide spaces both in and out of schools that offer new opportunities for social movements to come together. By doing this we can rethink and reexperience democracy as a struggle over values, practices, social relations, and subject positions that enlarge the terrain of human capacities and possibilities as a basis for a compassionate social order. At issue here is the need to create a politics that contributes to the multiplication of sites of democratic struggles, sites that affirm specific struggles while recognizing the necessity to embrace broader issues that both enhance the life of the planet and extend the spirit of democracy to all societies.

Rejecting certain conservative features of modernism, the apolitical nature of some postmodern discourses, and the separatism characteristic of some versions of feminism, I have attempted in this essay to appropriate critically the most emancipatory features of these discourses in the interest of developing a postmodern feminist pedagogy. Of course, the list of principles I provide is far from complete, but it does offer the opportunity for educators to analyze how it might be possible to reconceive as pedagogical practice some of the insights that have emerged from the discourses I analyze in this essay. Far from being exhaustive, the principles offered are only meant to provide some "fleeting images" of a pedagogy which can address major issues: the importance of democracy as an ongoing struggle, the meaning of educating students to govern, and the imperative of creating pedagogical conditions in which political citizens can be educated within a politics of difference that supports rather than opposes the reconstruction of a radical democracy.

Notes

1. Dick Hebdige provides a sense of the range of meanings, contexts, and objects that can be associated with the postmodern: "the decor of a room, the design of a building, the diegesis of a film, the construction of a record, or a 'scratch' video, a TV commercial, or an arts documentary, or the 'intertextual' relations between them, the layout of a page in a fashion magazine or critical journal, an antiteleological tendency within epistemology, the attack on the 'metaphysics of presence,' a general attenuation of feeling, the collective chagrin and morbid projections of a post-War generation of Baby Boomers confronting disillusioned middle age, the 'predicament' of reflexivity, a group of rhetorical tropes, a proliferation of surfaces, a new phase in commodity fetishism, a fascination for 'images,' codes and styles, a process of cultural, political or existential fragmentation and/or crisis, the 'de-centering' of the subject, an 'incredulity towards metanarratives,' the replacement of unitary power axes by a pluralism of power/discourse formations, the 'implosion,' the collapse of cultural hierarchies, the dread engendered by the threat of nuclear self-destruction, the decline of the University, the functioning and effects of the new miniaturized technologies, broad societal and economic shifts into a 'media,' 'consumer' or 'multinational' phase, a sense (depending on whom you read) of 'placelessness' or the abandonment of placelessness ('critical regionalism') or (even) a generalized substitution of spatial for temporal co-ordinates." ("Postmodernism" 78)

2. The now classic defense of modernity in the postmodern debate can be found in Habermas ("Modernity"; *Discourse*). For more extensive analyses of modernity, see Berman (*Air*); Lunn; Bernstein; Frisby; Kolb; Connolly; Larsen. An interesting comparison of two very different views on modernity can be found in Berman ("Why Modernism") and Richard.

3. A representative sample of postmodern feminist works includes: Benhabib and Cornell; Diamond and Quinby; Flax, "Postmodernism"; Hutcheon, *Politics;* E. Kaplan; Morris; Nicholson.

Works Cited

Alcoff, L. "Cultural Feminism vs. Poststructuralism: The Identity Crisis in Feminist Theory." *Signs* 13.3 (1988): 405–36.

Anderson, P. "Modernity and Revolution." *New Left Review* 144 (1984): 96–113.

Appignanensi, L., and G. Bennington, eds. *Postmodernism: ICA Documents 4.* London: Institute of Contemporary Arts, 1986.

Arac, J., ed. *Postmodernism and Politics.* Minneapolis: U of Minnesota P, 1986.

Aronowitz, S. "Postmodernism and Politics." *Social Text* 18 (1987/88): 94–114.

_____, and H. A. Giroux. "Schooling, Culture, and Literacy in the Age of Broken Dreams." *Harvard Educational Review* 58.2 (1988): 172–94.

_____, and _____. *Postmodern Education: Politics, Culture, and Social Criticism.* Minneapolis: U of Minnesota P, 1991.

Barthes, R. *Critical Essays.* New York: Hill and Wang, 1972.

Bartky, S. L. "Foucault, Femininity, and the Modernization of Patriarchal Power." Diamond and Quinby. 61–86.

Baudrillard, J. "Modernity." *Canadian Journal of Political and Social Theory* 11.3 (1987): 63–72.

Benhabib, S., and D. Cornell. *Feminism as Critique.* Minneapolis: U of Minnesota P, 1987.

Berman, M. *All That Is Solid Melts into Air: The Experience of Modernity.* New York: Simon & Schuster, 1982.

_____. "Why Modernism Still Matters." *Tikkun* 4.1 (1988): 11–14, 81–86.

Bernstein, R., ed. *Habermas and Modernity.* Cambridge: MIT Press, 1985.

Birke, L. *Women, Feminism, and Biology: The Feminist Challenge.* New York: Methuen, 1986.

Calinescu, M. *Five Faces of Modernity: Modernism, Avant-Garde, Decadence, Kitsch, Post-modernism.* Durham: Duke UP, 1987.

Cherryholmes, C. *Power and Criticism: Poststructural Investigations in Education.* New York: Teachers College P, 1988.

Christian, B. "The Race for Theory." *Cultural Critique* 6 (1987): 51–64.

Clifford, J. *The Predicament of Culture: Twentieth Century Ethnography, Literature, and Art.* Cambridge: Harvard UP, 1988.

_____, and G. Marcus, eds. *Writing Culture: The Poetics and Politics of Ethnography.* Berkeley: U of California P, 1986.

Collins, J. *Uncommon Cultures: Popular Culture and Post-Modernism.* New York: Routledge, 1989.

Connolly, W. *Political Theory and Modernity.* New York: Basil Blackwell, 1988.

Connor, S. *Postmodernist Culture: An Introduction to Theories of the Contemporary.* New York: Basil Blackwell, 1989.

Crimp, D. "On the Museum's Ruin." Foster. 43–56.

Derrida, J. *Of Grammatology.* Trans. G. Spivak. Baltimore: Johns Hopkins UP, 1976.

Diamond, I., and L. Quinby. "American Feminism and the Language of Control." Diamond and Quinby, eds. *Feminism and Foucault: Reflections on Resistance.* Boston: Northeastern UP, 1988. 193–206.

Dewey, J. *Democracy and Education.* New York: Macmillan, 1916.

Eagleton, T. "The Subject of Literature." *Cultural Critique* 2 (1985/86): 95–104.

Ebert, T. "The Romance of Patriarchy: Ideology, Subjectivity, and Postmodern Feminist Cultural Theory." *Cultural Critique* 10 (1988): 19–57.

Epstein, B. "Rethinking Social Movement Theory." *Socialist Review* 20.1 (1990): 35–65.

Flax, J. "Reply to Tress." *Signs* 14.1 (1988): 201–03.

_____. "Postmodernism and Gender Relations in Feminist Theory." Malson et al. 51–73.

Foster, H. "Postmodernism: A Preface." Foster, ed. *The Anti-Aesthetic: Essays on Postmodern Culture.* Port Townsend: Bay, 1983. ix-xvi.

Foucault, M. *Language, Counter-Memory, Practice: Selected Essays and Interviews.* Ed. D. Bouchard. Ithaca: Cornell UP, 1977.

_____. *Power and Knowledge: Selected Interviews and Other Writings.* Ed. G. Gordon. New York: Pantheon, 1977.

_____. *Discipline and Punish: The Birth of the Prison.* New York: Vintage, 1979.

_____. *The History of Sexuality.* Vol. I: *An Introduction.* New York: Vintage, 1980.

Fraser, N. "What Is Critical About Critical Theory? The Case of Habermas and Gender." *New German Critique* 12.2 (1985): 97–131.

_____. *Unruly Practices.* Minneapolis: U of Minnesota P, 1989.

_____, and L. Nicholson. "Social Criticism Without Philosophy: An Encounter Between Feminism and Postmodernism." Ross. 83–104.

Frisby, D. *Fragments of Modernity.* Cambridge: MIT Press, 1986.

Giddens, A. *The Consequences of Modernity.* Stanford: Stanford UP, 1990.

Giroux, H. *Schooling and the Struggle for Public Life.* Minneapolis: U of Minnesota P, 1988.

_____, and R. Simon. *Popular Culture, Schooling, and Everyday Life.* Granby: Bergin and Garvey, 1989.

Grossberg, L. "On Postmodernism and Articulation: An Interview with Stuart Hall." *Journal of Communication* 10.2 (1986): 45–60.

Groz, E. A., et al., eds. *Futur*fall: Excursions into Postmodernity.* Sydney: Power Institute of Fine Arts, 1986.

Grumet, M. *Bitter Milk: Women and Teaching.* Amherst: U of Massachusetts P, 1988.

Habermas, J. *Communication and the Evolution of Society.* Boston: Beacon, 1979.

_____. "Modernity versus Postmodernity." *New German Critique* 8.1 (1981): 3–18.

_____. "The Entwinement of Myth and Enlightenment." *New German Critique* 9.3 (1982): 13–30.

_____. "Modernity—An Incomplete Project." Foster. 3–16.

_____. *The Philosophical Discourse of Modernity.* Trans. F. Lawrence. Cambridge: MIT Press, 1987.

Hannam, M. "The Dream of Democracy." *Arena* 90 (1990): 109–16.

Haraway, D. "Situated Knowledges: The Science Question in Feminism and the Privilege of Partial Perspective." *Feminist Studies* 14.3 (1989): 575–99.

Harding, S. *The Science Question in Feminism.* Ithaca: Cornell UP, 1986.

Hartsock, N. "Rethinking Modernism: Minority vs. Majority Theories." *Cultural Critique* 7 (1987): 187–206.

Hebdige, D. "Postmodernism and 'The Other Side.'" *Journal of Communication Inquiry* 10.2 (1986): 78–99.

_____. *Hiding in the Light.* New York: Routledge, 1989.

Hicks, E. "Deterritorialization and Border Writing." Merrill. 47–58.

Hirsch, E. D., Jr. *Cultural Literacy: What Every American Needs to Know.* Boston: Houghton Mifflin, 1987.

hooks, b. *Talking Back.* Boston: South End, 1989.

Hutcheon, L. "Postmodern Problematic." Merrill. 1–10.

_____. *The Politics of Postmodernism.* New York: Routledge, 1989.

Huyssen, A. *After the Great Divide.* Bloomington: Indiana UP, 1986.

Jagger, A. M. *Feminist Politics and Humanist Nature.* Totowa: Rowman & Allanheld, 1983.

Kaplan, C. "Deterritorializations: The Rewriting of Home and Exile in Western Feminist Discourse." *Cultural Critique* 6 (1987): 187–98.

Kaplan, E. Introduction. Ed. E. Kaplan, *Postmodernism and Its Discontents, Theories, Practices.* London: Verso, 1988.

Kearney, R. *The Wake of Imagination.* Minneapolis: U of Minnesota P, 1988.

Keller, E. F. *Gender and Science.* New Haven: Yale UP, 1985.

Kellner, D. "Postmodernism as Social Theory: Some Challenges and Problems." *Theory, Culture and Society* 5.2/3 (1988): 239–69.

Kolb, D. *The Critique of Pure Modernity: Hegel, Heidegger, and After.* Chicago: U of Chicago P, 1986.

Kristeva, J. "Oscillation Between Power and Denial." Eds. E. Marks and I. de Courtivron. *New French Feminisms.* New York: Schocken, 1981. 165–67.

Kroker, A., and D. Cook. *The Postmodern Scene: Excremental Culture and Hyper-Aesthetics.* Montreal: New World Perspectives, 1986.

Lacan, J. *Speech and Language in Psychoanalysis.* Trans. A. Wilden. Baltimore: Johns Hopkins UP, 1968.

Laclau, E. "Politics and the Limits of Modernity." Ross. 63–82.

_____. "Building a New Left: An Interview with Ernesto Laclau." *Strategies* 1.1 (1988): 10–28.

_____, and C. Mouffe. *Hegemony and Socialist Strategy.* London: Verso, 1985.

Larsen, N. *Modernism and Hegemony: A Materialist Critique of Aesthetic Agencies.* Minneapolis: U of Minnesota P, 1990.

Lash, S., and J. Urry. *The End of Organized Capitalism.* Madison: U of Wisconsin P, 1987.

Lather, P. "Postmodernism and the Politics of Enlightenment." *Educational Foundations* 3.3 (1989): 7–28.

de Lauretis, T. *Alice Doesn't: Feminism, Semiotics, Cinema.* Bloomington: Indiana UP, 1984.

_____. "Feminist Studies/Critical Studies: Issues, Terms, Contexts." *Feminist Studies/Critical Studies.* Ed. T. de Lauretis. Bloomington: Indiana UP, 1986. 1–19.

_____. *Technologies of Gender.* Bloomington: Indiana UP, 1987.

Lipsitz, G. *Time Passages: Collective Memory and American Popular Culture.* Minneapolis: U of Minnesota P, 1990.

Lunn, E. *Marxism and Modernism.* Berkeley: U of California P, 1982.

Lyotard, J. *The Postmodern Condition.* Minneapolis: U of Minnesota P, 1984.

Malson, M., et al. Introduction. *Feminist Theory in Practice and Process.* Eds. M. Malson, et al. Chicago: U of Chicago P, 1989. 1–13.

McCarthy, T. Introduction. Habermas 1987. vii–xvii.

McLaren, P., and R. Hammer. "Critical Pedagogy and the Postmodern Challenge: Toward a Critical Postmodernist Pedagogy of Liberation." *Educational Foundations* 3.3 (1989): 29–62.

McRobbie, A. "Postmodernism and Popular Culture." Appignanensi and Bennington. 54–58.

Merrill, R. "Toward Ethics/Aesthetics: A Post-Modern Position." *Ethics/Aesthetics: Post-Modern Positions.* Ed. R. Merrill. Washington: Maisonneuve, 1988.

Michnik, A. "Notes on the Revolution." *The New York Times Magazine* (11 March 1990): 38–45.

Minh-ha, T. *Women, Native, Other: Writing Postcoloniality and Feminism.* Bloomington: Indiana UP, 1989.

Morris, M. *The Pirate's Fiancee: Feminism, Reading, Postmodernism.* London: Verso, 1988.

Mouffe, C. "Radical Democracy: Modern or Postmodern?" Ross. 31–45.

_____. "Toward a Radical Democratic Citizenship." *Democratic Left* 17.2 (1989): 6–7.

Newman, C. *The Post-Modern Aura: The Age of Fiction in an Age of Inflation.* Evanston: Northwestern UP, 1985.

_____. "Revising Modernism, Representing Postmodernism." Appignanensi and Bennington. 32–51.

Nicholson, L. *Feminism/Postmodernism.* New York: Routledge, 1990.

Oreskes, M. "America's Politics Lose Way as Its Vision Changes World." *The New York Times* CXXXIX.48,178 (18 March 1990): 1, 16.

Owens, C. "The Discourse of Others: Feminists and Postmodernism." Foster. 57–82.

Peller, G. "Reason and the Mob: The Politics of Representation." *Tikkun* 2.3 (1987): 28–31, 92–95.

Penley, C. *The Future of an Illusion: Film, Feminism, and Psychoanalysis.* Minneapolis: U of Minnesota P, 1989.

Popkewitz, T. "Culture, Pedagogy, and Power: Issues in the Production of Values and Colonialization." *Journal of Education* 170.2 (1988): 77–90.

Poster, M. *Critical Theory and Poststructuralism.* Ithaca: Cornell UP, 1989.

Richard, N. "Postmodernism and Periphery." *Third Text* 2 (1987/88): 5–12.

Rorty, R. "Habermas and Lyotard on Postmodernity." Bernstein. 161–76.

Rosaldo, R. *Culture & Truth: The Remaking of Social Analysis.* Boston: Beacon, 1989.

Ross, A., ed. *Universal Abandon? The Politics of Postmodernism.* Minneapolis: U of Minnesota P, 1988.

Roth, R. "The Colonial Experience and Its Postmodern Fate." *Salmagundi* 84 (1988): 248–65.

Ryan, K. *Politics and Culture: Working Hypotheses for a Post-Revolutionary Society.* Baltimore: Johns Hopkins UP, 1989.

Scott, J. W. *Gender and the Politics of History.* New York: Columbia UP, 1988.

Sculley, J. *Line Break: Poetry as Social Practice.* Seattle: Bay, 1988.

Shapiro, S. *Between Capitalism and Democracy.* Westport: Bergin and Garvey, 1990.

Showalter, E. "Introduction: The Rise of Gender." *Speaking of Gender.* Ed. E. Showalter. New York: Routledge, 1989. 1–13.

Simon, R. *Teaching Against the Grain.* Westport: Bergin and Garvey, forthcoming.

Spivak, G. *In Other Worlds: Essays in Cultural Politics.* New York: Methuen, 1987.

Thompson, E. P. "History Turns on a New Hinge." *The Nation* (29 January 1990): 117–22.

Tyler, S. *The Unspeakable: Discourse, Dialogue, and Rhetoric in the Postmodern World.* Madison: U of Wisconsin P, 1987.

Warren, M. *Nietzsche and Political Thought.* Cambridge: MIT Press, 1988.

Welch, S. D. *Communities of Resistance and Solidarity: A Feminist Theology of Liberation.* Maryknoll: Orbis, 1985.

9 *Insurgent Multiculturalism and the Promise of Pedagogy*

Introduction

Multiculturalism has become a central discourse in the struggle over issues regarding national identity, the construction of historical memory, the purpose of schooling, and the meaning of democracy. While most of these battles have been waged in the university around curriculum changes and in polemic exchanges in the public media, today's crucial culture wars increasingly are being fought on two fronts. First, multiculturalism has become a "tug of war over who gets to create public culture."[1] Second, the contested terrain of multiculturalism is heating up between educational institutions that do not meet the needs of a massively shifting student population and students and their families for whom schools increasingly are perceived as merely one more instrument of repression.

In the first instance, the struggle over public culture is deeply tied to a historical legacy that affirms American character and national identity in terms that are deeply exclusionary, nativist, and racist. Echoes of this racism can be heard in the voices of public intellectuals such as George Will, Arthur Schlesinger Jr, and George Gilder. Institutional support for such racism can be found in neoconservative establishments such as the Olin Foundation and the National Association of Scholars.

In the second instance, academic culture has become a contested space primarily because groups that have been traditionally excluded from the public school curriculum and from the ranks of higher education are now becoming more politicized and are attending higher education institutions in increasing numbers. One consequence of this developing politics of difference has been a series of struggles by subordinate groups over access to educational resources, gender and racial equity, curriculum content, and the disciplinary-based organization of academic departments.

While it has become commonplace to acknowledge the conflicting meanings of multiculturalism, it is important to acknowledge that in its conservative and liberal forms multiculturalism has placed the related problems of white racism, social justice, and power off limits, especially as these might be addressed as part of a broader set of political and pedagogical concerns. In what follows, I want to reassert the importance of making the pedagogical more political. That is, I want to analyze how a broader definition of pedagogy can be used to address how the production of knowledge, social identities, and social relations might challenge the racist assumptions and practices that inform a variety of cultural sites, including but not limited to the public and private spheres of schooling. Central to this approach is an attempt to define the pedagogical meaning of what I will call an insurgent multiculturalism. This is not a multiculturalism that is limited to a fascination with the construction of identities, communicative competence, and the celebration of tolerance. Instead, I want to shift the discussion of multiculturalism to a pedagogical terrain in which relations of power and racialized identities become paramount as part of a language of critique and possibility.

In part, this suggests constructing "an educational politics that would reveal the structures of power relations at work in the racialization of our social order" while simultaneously encouraging students to "think about the invention of the category of whiteness as well as that of blackness and, consequently, to make visible what is rendered invisible when viewed as the normative state of existence: the (white) point in space from which we tend to identify difference."[2] As part of a language of critique, a central concern of an insurgent multiculturalism is to strip white supremacy of its legitimacy and authority. As part of a project of possibility, an insurgent multiculturalism is about developing a notion of radical democracy around differences that are not exclusionary and fixed, but that designate sites of struggle that are open, fluid, and that will provide the conditions for expanding the heterogeneity of public spaces and the possibility for "critical dialogues across different political communities and constituencies."[3]

Multiculturalism and White Racism

If . . . one managed to change the curriculum in all the schools so that [Afro-Americans] learned more about themselves and their real contributions to this culture, you would be liberating not only [Afro-Americans], you'd be liberating white people who know nothing about their own history. And the reason is that if you are compelled to lie about one aspect of anybody's history, you must lie about it all. If you have to lie about my real role here, if you have to pretend that I hoed all that cotton just because I loved you, then you have done something to yourself. You are mad.[4]

What James Baldwin, the renowned Afro-American novelist, is suggesting in the most immediate sense is that issues concerning multiculturalism are fundamentally about questions of race and identity. A more penetrating analysis reveals that multiculturalism is not only about the discourse of racialized identities, but is also fundamentally about the issue of whiteness as a mark of racial and gender privilege. For example, Baldwin argues that multiculturalism cannot be reduced to an exclusive otherness that references Afro-Americans, Hispanics, Latinos, or other suppressed "minorities," as either a problem to be resolved through the call for benevolent assimilation or as a threat to be policed and eliminated. For Baldwin, multiculturalism is primarily about whiteness and its claims to a self-definition that excludes the messy relations of race, ethnicity, power, and identity. Baldwin highlights how differences in power and privilege authorize who speaks, how fully, under what conditions, against what issues, for whom, and with what degree of consistent, institutionalized support. In this sense, multiculturalism raises the question of whether people are speaking within or outside a privileged space, and whether such spaces provide the conditions for different groups to listen to each other differently to address how the racial economies of privilege and power work in American society.

I want to argue that educators need to rethink the politics of multiculturalism as part of a broader attempt to engage the world of public and global politics. This suggests challenging the narratives of national identity, culture, and ethnicity as part of a pedagogical effort to provide dominant groups with the knowledge and histories to examine, acknowledge, and unlearn their own privilege. But more is needed in this view of multiculturalism than deconstructing the centers of colonial power and undoing the master narratives of racism. A viable multicultural pedagogy and politics must also affirm cultural differences while simultaneously refusing to essentialize and grant immunity to those groups that speak from subordinate positions of power. As Gerald Graff and Bruce Robbins point out, the most progressive aspect of multiculturalism "has been not to exalt group 'particularism' but to challenge it, to challenge the belief that blackness, femaleness, or Africanness are essential, unchanging qualities."[5]

Within the current historical conjuncture, the struggles over national identity, race, and what it means to be an "American" have taken place largely within discussions that focus on questions of self- and social representation. While a politics of representation is indispensable in creating a multicultural and multiracial society, educators must also address the systemic, structural changes that are needed to produce such a social order. In part, this demands an approach to multiculturalism that addresses "the context of massive black unemployment, overcrowded schools, a lack of recreational facilities, dilapidated housing and racist policing."[6] Cornel West builds upon this position by arguing that white America needs to address the nihilism that permeates black communities in the United States. He defines such nihilism as "the lived experience of coping with a life of horrifying meaninglessness, hopelessness, and (most important) lovelessness."[7] In this scenario, the black community is depicted as a culture that has lost the moral strength, hope, and resistance once provided by the institutions of black civil society: "black families, neighborhoods, schools, churches, mosques."[8]

I want to extend West's argument and suggest that if the depiction of black nihilism is not to reproduce the culture of poverty thesis made popular among conservatives, then educators must attempt to understand how white institutions, ethnicity, and public life is structured through a nihilism that represents another type of moral disorder, impoverishment of the spirit, and decline of public life. In this analysis, cultural criticism moves from a limited emphasis on the effects of racism and the workings of black nihilism to the origins of racism in the political, social, and cultural dynamics of white "supremacy." More specifically, a critical multiculturalism must shift attention away from an exclusive focus on subordinate groups, especially since such an approach tends to highlight their deficits, to one that examines how racism in its various forms is produced historically, semiotically, and institutionally at various levels of society. This is not meant to suggest that blacks and other subordinate groups do not face problems that need to be addressed in the discourse of multiculturalism. On the contrary, it means that a critical analysis of race must move beyond the discourse of blaming the victim in which whites view multiculturalism as a code word for black lawlessness and other "problems" blacks create for white America. Viewing black people in this manner reveals not only white supremacy as the discursive and institutional face of racism, but it also presents us with the challenge of addressing racial issues not as a dilemma of black people but as a problem endemic to the legacy colonialism rooted in "historical inequalities and longstanding cultural stereotypes."[9]

In opposition to a quaint liberalism, a critical multiculturalism means more than simply acknowledging differences and analyzing stereotypes; more fundamentally, it means understanding, engaging, and transforming the diverse histories, cultural narratives, representations, and institutions that produce racism and other forms of discrimination. As bell hooks points out, for too long white people have imagined that they are invisible to black people. Not only does whiteness in this formulation cease to mark the locations of its own privileges, it reinforces relations in which blacks become invisible in terms of how they name, see, experience, and bear the pain and terror of whiteness. hooks puts it succinctly:

> In white supremacist society, white people can "safely" imagine that they are invisible to black people since the power they have historically asserted, and even now collectively assert over black people, accorded them the right to control the black gaze. . . . [And yet] to name that whiteness in the black imagination is often a representation of terror. One must face written histories that erase and deny, that reinvent the past to make the present vision of racial harmony and pluralism more plausible. To bear the burden of memory one must willingly journey to places long uninhabited, searching the debris of history for traces of the unforgettable, all knowledge of which has been suppressed.[10]

It is worth noting that many educational commentators who address the issue of multiculturalism have ruled out any discussion of the relationship between race and class and how they are manifested within networks of hierarchy and subordination in and out of the schools. This particular silence, coupled with the popular perception bolstered by the media that recent racial disturbances and uprisings such as the rape of the female jogger in Central Park, the murder of Michael Jordan's father, and the LA uprising can be explained by pointing to those involved as simply thugs, looters, and criminals, makes it clear why the multicultural peril is often seen as a black threat; it suggests what such a belief shares with the dominant ideological view of the "other" as a disruptive outsider. In this scenario, multiculturalism is seen as an impediment rather than an essential condition for the survival of democratic public life.

To understand fully the conservative response to multiculturalism, it is crucial to situate the debates around the politics of cultural difference within the broader assault on democracy that has taken place in the last decade. But before I address this issue, I want to suggest that public schooling and higher education are crucial sites in which the relationship between multiculturalism and democracy should be acknowledged and incorporated into the curriculum. A democratic or insurgent multiculturalism is one that offers a new language for students and others to move between disciplinary borders and to travel within zones of cultural difference. This is a language that challenges the boundaries of cultural and racial difference as sites of exclusion and discrimination while simultaneously rewriting the script of cultural difference as part of a broader attempt to expand and deepen the imperatives of a multicultural and multiracial democracy.

An insurgent multiculturalism takes as its starting point the question of what it means for educators and cultural workers to treat schools and other public sites as border institutions in which teachers, students, and others engage in daily acts of cultural translation and negotiation. For it is within such institutions that students and teachers are offered the opportunity to become border crossers, to recognize that schooling is really an introduction to how culture is organized, a demonstration of who is authorized to speak about particular forms of culture, what culture is considered worthy of valorization, and what forms of culture are considered invalid and unworthy of public esteem. Drawing upon Homi Bhabha, I want to contend that schools, in part, need to be understood as sites engaged in the "strategic activity of 'authorizing' agency," of exercising authority "to articulate and regulate incommensurable meanings and identities."[11] Within this perspective, pedagogy is removed from its exclusive emphasis on management and is defined as a form of political leadership and ethical address. The pedagogical imperative here is to weigh cultural differences against the implications they have for practices that disclose rather than mystify, democratize culture rather than close it off, and provide the conditions for people to believe that they can take risks and change existing power relations. Translated into a critical pedagogical practice, multiculturalism pluralizes the spaces for exchange, understanding, and identity formation among a variety of dominant and subordinate groups. It is precisely because of the possibility of rewriting dominant cultural narratives and social relations that multiculturalism appears so threatening to conservatives and liberals. One of the most frank expressions of this position came from the 1975 Trilateral Commission report *The Crisis of Democracy* which boldly alleged that a substantive democracy represents an unwarranted challenge to government authority and existing configurations of power. Viewed in this context, the current assault on multiculturalism must be understood as a part of a broader assault on democracy itself.

Multiculturalism and the Perils of Democracy

Within the last decade, cultural authority and legislative policy have combined to extend massively the influence of domination to increasing numbers of subordinate groups in America. In the face of escalating poverty, increasing racism, growing unemployment among "minorities," and the failure of an expanding number of Americans to receive adequate health care and education, the Reagan/Bush administrations invoked a wooden morality coupled with a disdain for public life by blaming the nation's ills on the legislation of the Great Society, TV sitcom characters such as Murphy Brown, and the alleged breakdown of family values. Within this scenario, poverty is caused by the poverty of values, racism is seen as a "black" problem (lawlessness), and social decay is rectified by shoring up the nuclear family and social relations of the alleged free market.

Abandoning its responsibility for political and moral leadership, the federal government, during the last decade, reduced its intervention in public life to waging war against Iraq, using taxpayers' money to bail out corrupt bankers, and slashing legislation that would benefit the poor, the homeless, and the disadvantaged. There is a tragic irony at work when a government can raise 500 billion dollars to bail out corrupt bankers and 50 billion to fight a war in Iraq (put in perspective, the combined costs of these adventures exceeds the cost of World War II, including veterans benefits) while at the same time that same government cuts back food stamp and school lunch programs in a country in which nearly one out of every four children under six live in poverty. But there is more at stake here than simply the failure of moral and political leadership. The breadth and depth of democratic relations are being rolled back at all levels of national and daily life. For example, this is seen in the growing disparity between the rich and poor, the ongoing attacks by the government and courts on civil rights and the welfare system, and the proliferating incidents of racist harassment and violence on college and public school sites.

The retreat from democracy is evident also in the absence of serious talk about how as a nation, we might educate existing and future generations of students in the language and practice of moral compassion, critical agency, and public service. The discourse of leadership appears trapped in a terminology in which the estimate of a good society is expressed in indices that measure profit margins and the Dow Jones Average. Missing in this vocabulary is a way of nourishing and sustaining a popular perception of democracy as something that needs to be constantly struggled for in public arenas such as the schools, churches, and other sites which embody the promise of a multiracial and multicultural democracy.

This current assault on democratic public life has taken a new turn in the last few years. At one level, American conservatives have initiated a long-term project of discrediting and dismantling those institutions, ideologies, and practices that are judged incompatible with the basic ideology of the market place with its unswerving commitment to the principles of individualism, choice, and the competitive ethic. Accompanying this attempt has been a parallel effort to reprivatize and deregulate schools, health care, the welfare system, and other public services and institutions.

Part of the attempt to rewrite the terms of a discourse of democratic public life can be seen in the emergence of a new breed of intellectuals, largely backed by conservative think tanks such as the Madison Group, the Hoover Institute, Heritage Foundation, and a host of other conservative foundations. With access to enormous cultural resources infused by massive financial backing from the Olin, Scaife, and Smith Richardson foundations, right-wing think tanks have begun to mount mammoth public campaigns to promote their cultural revolution. Many of the major right-wing intellectuals who have helped to shape popular discourse about educational reform in the last decade have received extensive aid from the conservative foundations. These include intellectuals such as Diane Ravitch, Chester Finn Jr, Dinish D'Souza, and Thomas Sowell; all of whom have targeted public schools and higher education as two principal spheres of struggle over issues of curricula reform, privatization, choice, and difference. To understand the model of leadership these intellectuals provide, it is important to examine how some of their underlying ideological concerns relate to the broader issues of democracy, race, and public accountability.

For many conservatives, the utopian possibility of cultural democracy has become dangerous at the current historical conjuncture for a number of reasons. Most important, cultural democracy encourages a language of critique for understanding and transforming those relations that trap people in networks of hierarchy and exploitation. That is, it provides normative referents for recognizing and assessing competing political vocabularies, the visions of the future they presuppose, and the social identities and practices they produce and legitimate. Clearly, such a position poses a challenge to right-wing educators whose celebration of choice and the logic of the market place often abstracts freedom from equality and the imperatives of citizenship from its historical grounding in the public institutions of modern society.

In fact, many conservatives have been quite aggressive in rewriting the discourse of citizenship *not* as the practice of social responsibility but as a privatized act of altruism, self-help, or philanthropy. It is crucial to recognize that within this language of privatization, the disquieting, disrupting, interrupting difficulties of sexism, crime, youth unemployment, AIDS, and other social problems, and how they bear down on schools and subordinated groups, are either ignored or summarily dismissed as individual problems caused, in part, by the people who are victimized by them. This position accentuates individual character flaws and behavioral impediments to economic and social mobility to elide the political and economic conditions that produce the context of victimization and the systemic pressures and limits that must be addressed to overcome it. By focusing on the privatized language of individual character, conservatives erase the moral and political obligation of individuals, groups, and institutions to recognize their complicity in creating the racial problems that multicultural critics have addressed. In this scenario, we end up with a vision of leadership in which individuals act in comparative isolation and without any sense of public accountability. This is why many right-wing educators praise the virtues of the competition and choice but rarely talk about how money and power, when unevenly distributed, influence "whether people have the means or the capacity" to make or act on choices that inform their daily lives.[12]

Choice in this case serves to rewrite the discourse of freedom within a limited conception of individual needs and desires. What disappears from this view of leadership is the willingness to recognize that the fundamental issues of citizenship, democracy, and public life can neither be understood nor addressed solely within the restricted language of the marketplace or choice. Choice and the market are not the sole conditions of freedom, nor are they adequate to constituting political subjects within the broader discourses of justice, equality, and community. In fact, no understanding of community, citizenship, or public culture is possible without a shared conception of social justice, yet it is precisely the notion of social justice that is missing in mainstream discussions of multiculturalism and school reform.

Conservatives not only view multiculturalism as a threat to national identity, they have actively attempted to remove it from the language of community and social justice. Rather than asserting the primacy of the ethical in responding to the suffering of subordinated groups in America's schools and other social institutions, conservatives have developed educational and public policies that expand cost-benefit analyses and market relations at the expense of addressing major social problems such as racism, poverty, crime, and unemployment. For example, it is worth noting that 45 per cent of all "minority" children live in poverty while the dropout rate among "minority" students has attained truly alarming proportions, reaching as high as 70 per cent in some major urban areas. These problems are compounded by an unemployment rate among black youth that is currently 38.4 per cent. In the face of these problems, conservatives are aggressively attempting to enact choice legislation that would divert funds away from the public schools to private schools. Against these efforts, it is worth noting, as Peter Drier points out, that:

> since 1980 the federal government has slashed successful urban programs—public works, economic development, health and nutrition,

schools, housing, and job training—by more than 70 per cent. . . . In 1980, federal dollars accounted for 14.3 per cent of city budgets; today, the federal share is less than five per cent. . . . To avert fiscal collapse, many cities have been closing schools, hospitals, police and fire stations; laying off of essential employees; reducing such basic services as maintenance of parks and roads; neglecting housing and health codes, and postponing or canceling capital improvements.[13]

The claim by conservatives that these problems can be solved by raising test scores, promoting choice, developing a national curriculum, and creating a uniform standard of national literacy is cruel and mean-spirited. But, of course, this is where the discourse of critical democracy becomes subversive; it makes visible the political and normative considerations that frame such reforms. It also offers a referent for analyzing how the language of excessive individualism and competitiveness serves to make social inequality invisible, promoting an indifference to human misery, exploitation, and suffering. Moreover, it suggests that the language of excellence and individualism when abstracted from considerations of equality and social justice serves to restrict rather than animate the possibilities of democratic public life. Increasingly, conservatives also have used the language of individual rights; that is, the right of individuals to think and act as they please, to attack any discourse or program that questions the existence of social inequalities. As Joan Scott points out, there is more at stake here than what the conservatives call the existence of dangerous orthodoxies in the university.

> We are experiencing another phase of the ongoing Reagan-Bush revolution which, having packed the courts and privatized the economy, now seeks to neutralize the space of ideological and cultural nonconformity by discrediting it. This is the context within which debates about political correctness and multiculturalism have taken shape.[14]

Rather than engage the growing insistence on the part of more and more groups in this country to define themselves around the specificity of class, gender, race, ethnicity, or sexual orientation, conservatives have committed themselves simply to resisting and subverting these developments. While conservatives rightly recognize that struggles over the public school curriculum and the canon in higher education are fueled, in part, over anxiety about the issue of national identity, they engage this issue from a largely defensive posture and in doing so appear to lack any understanding of how the curriculum itself is implicated in producing relations of inequality, domination, and oppression. For example, even moderate liberals who adopt a conservative stance on multicultural issues resort to rhetorical swipes that share ideological ground with nativist writing against Catholics and immigrants in the 1920s. For example, Schlesinger refers to the multiculturalists in the United States as part of an "ethnic upsurge" that threatens to become a full-fledged counterrevolution against the alleged common culture and the "American ideal of assimilation."[15] Schlesinger is quite clear, as are many of his conservative allies, that as soon as public schools refuse to serve as vehicles for cultural assimilation, they have betrayed their most important historically-sanctioned role. Unfortunately, Schlesinger does not see anything wrong with the schools producing social identities in which cultural differences are seen as a deficit rather than a strength. That the assimilation model of schooling maintains its hegemony through the racist, class-specific dynamics of tracking and cultural discrimination appears to Schlesinger to be unworthy of critical attention. When critical multiculturalists criticize how the curriculum through a process of exclusion and inclusion privileges some groups over others, such critics are summarily dismissed as being political, partisan, and radically anti-American by critics such as Schlesinger.

It is difficult to imagine what is either unpatriotic or threatening about subordinate groups attempting to raise questions such as: "Whose experiences, histories, knowledge, and arts are represented in our educational and cultural institutions? How fully, on whose terms, and with what degree of ongoing, institutionalized participation and power?"[16] Nor in a democratic society should subordinate groups attempting to fashion a pedagogy and politics of inclusion and cultural democracy be derisively labeled as particularistic because they have raised serious questions regarding how the canon and public school curriculum work to secure specific forms of cultural authority or how the dynamics of cultural power works to silence and marginalize specific groups of students. Responding to these concerns, academic conservatives such as William Kerrigan simply recycle their own beliefs about the superiority of the established canon without revealing the slightest element of self criticism. Kerrigan argues that "an undergraduate education that *saddles* (my emphasis) students with 'cultural diversity' requirements encourages them to flit incoherently from this concentration to that major."[17] That the knowledge that constitutes the academic disciplines is neither universal nor the highest expression of scholarship given its exclusion of women and "minorities" does not seem to bother Kerrigan. In this case, the claims that subordinate groups make upon the shaping of cultural memory and the promise of democratic pluralism are dismissed by Kerrigan through the arrogant, self-serving assertion that "educators have become pathologically sensitive to complaints of ethnocentrism. Rather than elevating the minds of students from historically oppressed groups, the whole educational system is sinking."[18] This emerging critique of schools and other cultural institutions is based on the elitist and racist assumptions that the enemy of democracy is not intolerance, structured inequality, and social injustice, but cultural differences.

In treating cultural narrative and national history in fixed and narrow terms, conservatives relinquish one of the most important defining principles of any democracy; that is, they ignore the necessity of a democratic society to rejuvenate itself by constantly reexamining the strengths and limits of its traditions. In the absence of a critical encounter with the past and a recognition of the importance of cultural diversity, multiculturalism becomes acceptable only if it is reduced to a pedagogy of reverence and transmission rather than a pedagogical practice that puts people in dialogue with each other as part of a broader attempt to fashion a renewed interest in cultural democracy and the creation of engaged and critical citizens. Bhikhu Parekh rightly argues that such an uncritical stance defines what he calls demagogic multiculturalism. For Parekh, the traditionalists' refusal of cultural hybridity and differences and the fixity of identity and culture promotes a dangerous type of fundamentalism. He writes:

> When a group feels besieged and afraid of losing its past in exchange for a nebulous future, it lacks the courage to critically reinterpret its fundamental principles, lest it opens the door to "excessive" reinterpretation. It then turns its fundamentals into fundamentalism, it declares them inviolate and reduces them to a neat and easily enforceable package of beliefs and rituals.[19]

Parekh's fear of demagogic multiculturalism represents a pedagogical problem as much as it does a political one. The political issue is exemplified in the conservative view that critical multiculturalism with its assertion of multiple identities and diverse cultural traditions represents a threat to democracy. As I have mentioned previously, the fatal political transgression committed here lies in the suggestion that social criticism itself is fundamentally at odds with democratic life. Indeed, this is more than mere rhetoric, it is a challenge to the very basic principles that inform a democratic society. Pedagogically, demagogic multiculturalism renders any debate about the relationship between democracy and cultural difference moot. By operating out of a suffocating binarism that pits "us" against "them" conservatives annul the possibility for dialogue, education, understanding, and negotiation. In other words, such a position offers no language for contending with cultures whose boundaries cross over into diverse spheres that are fluid and saturated with power. How this type of fundamentalism will specifically impact the schools can be seen in the increased calls for censorship as well as in the bleaching of the curriculum to exclude or underrepresent the voices and histories of various subordinate groups.

Instead of responding to the increasing diversity of histories, ethnicities, and cultures complexly layered over time, dominant institutions and discourses appear increasingly indifferent to the alarming poverty, shameful school dropout rate, escalating unemployment and a host of other problems that accentuate the alienation, inequality, and racial segregation that fuel the sense of desperation, hopelessness, and disempowerment felt by many "minorities" in the United States. It appears morally careless and politically irresponsible to define multiculturalism as exclusively disruptive and antithetical to the most fundamental aspects of American democracy. Such a position fails to explore the potential that multiculturalism has as a critical referent for linking diversity and cultural democracy while simultaneously serving to ignore the social, economic, and political conditions that have spurned the current insurgency among "minorities" and others around the issue of multiculturalism.

Toward an Insurgent Multiculturalism

To make a claim for multiculturalism is not . . . to suggest a juxtaposition of several cultures whose frontiers remain intact, nor is it to subscribe to a bland "melting-pot" type of attitude that would level all differences. It lies instead, in the intercultural acceptance of risks, unexpected detours, and complexities of relation between break and closure.[20]

Multiculturalism like any other broadly signifying term is multiaccentual and must be adamantly challenged when defined as part of the discourse of domination or essentialism. The challenge the term presents is daunting given the way in which it has been appropriated by various mainstream and orthodox positions. For example, when defined in corporate terms it generally is reduced to a message without critical content. Liberals have used multiculturalism to denote a pluralism devoid of historical contextualization and the specificities of relations of power or they have depicted a view of cultural struggle in which the most fundamental contradictions "implicating race, class, and gender can be harmonized within the prevailing structure of power relations."[21] For many conservatives, multiculturalism has come to signify a disruptive, unsettling, and dangerous force in American society. For some critics, it has been taken up as a slogan for promoting an essentializing identity politics and various forms of nationalism. In short, multiculturalism can be defined through a variety of ideological constructs, and signifies a terrain of struggle around the reformation of historical memory, national identity, self- and social representation, and the politics of difference.

Multiculturalism is too important as a political discourse to be exclusively appropriated by liberals and conservatives. This suggests that if the concept of multiculturalism is to become useful as a pedagogical concept, educators need to appropriate it as more than a tool for critical understanding and the pluralizing of differences; it must also be used as an ethical and political referent which allows teachers and students to understand how power works in the interest of dominant social relations, and how such relations can be challenged and transformed. In other words, an insurgent multiculturalism should promote pedagogical practices that offer the possibility for schools to become places where students and teachers can become border crossers engaged in critical and ethical reflection about what it means to bring a wider variety of cultures into dialogue with each other, to theorize about cultures in the plural, within rather than outside "antagonistic relations of domination and subordination."[22]

In opposition to the liberal emphasis on individual diversity, an insurgent multiculturalism also must address issues regarding group differences and how power relations function to structure racial and ethnic identities. Furthermore, cultural differences cannot be merely affirmed to be assimilated into a common culture or policed through economic, political, and social spheres that restrict full citizenship to dominant groups. If multiculturalism is to be linked to renewed interests in expanding the principles of democracy to wider spheres of application, it must be defined in pedagogical and political terms that embrace it as a referent and practice for civic courage, critical citizenship, and democratic struggle. Bhikhu Parekh provides a definition that appears to avoid a superficial pluralism and a notion of multiculturalism that is structured in dominance. He writes:

> Multiculturalism doesn't simply mean numerical plurality of different cultures, but rather a community which is creating, guaranteeing, encouraging spaces within which different communities are able to grow at their own pace. At the same time it means creating a public space in which these communities are able to interact, enrich the existing culture and create a new consensual culture in which they recognize reflections of their own identity.[23]

In this view, multiculturalism becomes more than a critical referent for interrogating the racist representations and practices of the dominant culture, it also provides a space in which the criticism of cultural practices is inextricably linked to the production of cultural spaces marked by the formation of new identities and pedagogical practices that offers a powerful challenge to the racist, patriarchal, and sexist principles embedded in American society and schooling. Within this discourse, curriculum is viewed as a hierarchical and representational system that selectively produces knowledge, identities, desires, and values. The notion that curriculum represents knowledge that is objective, value free, and beneficial to all students is challenged forcefully as it becomes clear that those who benefit from public schooling and higher education are generally white, middle-class students whose histories, experiences, language, and knowledge largely conform to dominant cultural codes and practices. Moreover, an insurgent multiculturalism performs a theoretical service by addressing curriculum as a form of cultural politics which demands linking the production and legitimation of classroom knowledge, social identities, and values to the institutional environments in which they are produced.

As part of a project of possibility, I want to suggest some general elements that might inform an insurgent multicultural curriculum. First, a multicultural curriculum must be informed by a new language in which cultural differences are taken up not as something to be tolerated but as essential to expanding the discourse and practice of democratic life. It is important to note that multiculturalism is not merely an ideological construct, it also refers to the fact that by the year 2010, people of color will be the numerical majority in the United States. This suggests that educators need to develop a language, vision, and curriculum in which multiculturalism and democracy become mutually reinforcing categories. At issue here is the task of reworking democracy as a pedagogical and cultural practice that contributes to what John Dewey once called the creation of an articulate public. Manning Marable defines some of the essential parameters of this task.

> Multicultural political democracy means that this country was not built by and for only one group—Western Europeans; that our country does not have only one language—English; or only one religion—Christianity; or only one economic philosophy—corporate capitalism. Multicultural democracy means that the leadership within our society should reflect the richness, colors and diversity expressed in the lives of all of our people. Multicultural democracy demands new types of power sharing and the reallocation of resources necessary to great economic and social development for those who have been systematically excluded and denied.[24]

Imperative to such a task is a reworking of the relationship between culture and power to avoid what Homi Bhabha has called "the subsumption or sublation of social antagonism . . . the repression of social divisions . . . and a representation of the social that naturalizes cultural difference and turns it into a 'second'-nature argument."[25]

Second, as part of an attempt to develop a multicultural and multiracial society consistent with the principles of a democratic society, educators must account for the fact that men and women of color are disproportionately underrepresented in the cultural and public institutions of this country. Pedagogically this suggests that a multicultural curriculum must provide students with the skills to analyze how various audio, visual, and print texts fashion social identities over time, and how these representations serve to reinforce, challenge, or rewrite dominant moral and political vocabularies that promote stereotypes that degrade people by depriving them of their history, culture, and identity.

This should not suggest that such a pedagogy should solely concentrate on how meanings produce particular stereotypes and the uses to which they are put. Nor should a multicultural politics of representation focus exclusively on producing positive images of subordinated groups by recovering and reconstituting elements of their suppressed histories. While such approaches can be pedagogically useful, it is crucial for critical educators to reject any approach to multiculturalism that affirms cultural differences in the name of an essentialized and separatist identity politics. Rather than recovering differences that sustain their self-representation through exclusions, educators need to demonstrate how differences collide, cross over, mutate, and transgress in their negotiations and struggles. Differences in this sense must be understood not through the fixity of place or the romanticization of an essentialized notion of history and experience but through the tropes of indeterminacy, flows, and translations. In this instance, multiculturalism can begin to formulate a politics of representation in which questions of access and cultural production are linked to what people do with the signifying regimes they use within historically-specific public spaces.

While such approaches are essential to giving up the quest for a pure historical tradition, it is imperative that a multicultural curriculum also focus on dominant, white institutions and histories to interrogate them in terms of their injustices and their contributions for "humanity." This means, as Cornel West points out, that

> to engage in a serious discussion of race in America, we must begin not with the problems of black people but with the flaws of American society— flaws rooted in historical inequalities and longstanding cultural stereotypes. . . . How we set up the terms for discussing racial issues shapes our perception and response to these issues. As long as black people are viewed as "them," the burden falls on blacks to do all the "cultural" and "moral" work necessary for healthy race relations. The implication is that only cer-

tain Americans can define what it means to be American—and the rest must simply "fit in."[26]

In this sense, multiculturalism is about making whiteness visible as a racial category; that is, it points to the necessity of providing white students with the cultural memories that enable them to recognize the historically- and socially-constructed nature of their own identities. Multiculturalism as a radical, cultural politics should attempt to provide white students (and others) with the self-definitions upon which they can recognize their own complicity with or resistance to how power works within and across differences to legitimate some voices and dismantle others. Of course, more is at stake here than having whites reflect critically on the construction of their own racial formation and their complicity in promoting racism. Equally important is the issue of making all students responsible for their practices, particularly as these serve either to undermine or expand the possibility for democratic public life.

Third, a multicultural curriculum must address how to articulate a relationship between unity and difference that moves beyond simplistic binarisms. That is, rather than defining multiculturalism against unity or simply for difference, it is crucial for educators to develop a unity-in-difference position in which new, hybrid forms of democratic representation, participation, and citizenship provide a forum for creating unity without denying the particular, multiple, and the specific. In this instance, the interrelationship of different cultures and identities become borderlands, sites of crossing, negotiation, translation, and dialogue. At issue is the production of a border pedagogy in which the intersection of culture and identity produces self-definitions that enable teachers and students to authorize a sense of critical agency. Border pedagogy points to a self/other relationship in which identity is fixed as neither Other nor the same; instead, it is both and, hence, defined within multiple literacies that become a referent, critique, and practice of cultural translation, a recognition of no possibility of fixed, final, or monologically authoritative meaning that exists outside of history, power, and ideology.

Within such a pedagogical cartography, teachers must be given the opportunity to cross ideological and political borders as a way of clarifying their own moral vision, as a way of enabling counterdiscourses, and, as Roger Simon points out, as a way of getting students "beyond the world they already know in order to challenge and provoke their inquiry and challenge of their existing views of the way things are and should be."[27]

Underlying this notion of border pedagogy is neither the logic of assimilation (the melting pot) nor the imperative to create cultural hierarchies, but the attempt to expand the possibilities for different groups to enter into dialogue to understand further the richness of their differences and the value of what they share in common.

Fourth, an insurgent multiculturalism must challenge the task of merely re-presenting cultural differences in the curriculum; it must also educate students of the necessity for linking a justice of multiplicity to struggles over real material conditions that structure everyday life. In part, this means understanding how structural imbalances in power produce real limits on the capacity of subordinate groups to exercise a sense of agency and struggle. It also means analyzing specific class, race, gender, and other issues as social problems rooted in real material and institutional factors that produce specific forms of inequality and oppression. This would necessitate a multicultural curriculum that produces a language that deals with social problems in historical and relational terms, and uncovers how the dynamics of power work to promote domination within the school and the wider society. In part, this means multiculturalism as a curricula discourse and pedagogical practice must function in its dual capacity as collective memory and alternative reconstruction. History, in this sense, is not merely resurrected but interrogated and tempered by "a sense of its liability, its contingency, its constructedness."[28] Memory does not become the repository of registering suppressed histories, albeit critically, but of reconstructing the moral frameworks of historical discourse to interrogate the present as living history.

Finally, a multicultural curriculum must develop, in public schools and institutions of higher education, contexts that serve to refigure relations between the school, teachers, students, and the wider community. For instance, public schools must be willing to develop a critical dialogue between the school and those public cultures within the community dedicated to producing students who address the discourse and obligations of power as part of a larger attempt at civic renewal and the reconstruction of democratic life. At best, parents, social activists, and other socially-concerned community members should be allowed to play a formative role in crucial decisions about what is taught, who is hired, and how the school can become a laboratory for learning that nurtures critical citizenship and civic courage. Of course, the relationship between the school and the larger community should be made in the interest of expanding "the social and political task of transformation, resistance, and radical democratization."[29] In both spheres of education, the curriculum needs to be decentralized to allow students to have some input into what is taught and under what conditions. Moreover, teachers need to be educated to be border crossers, to explore zones of cultural difference by moving in and out of the resources, histories, and narratives that provide different students with a sense of identity, place, and possibility. This does not suggest that educators become tourists traveling to exotic lands; on the contrary, it points to the need for them to enter into negotiation and dialogue around issues of nationality, difference, and identity so as to be able to fashion a more ethical and democratic set of pedagogical relations between themselves and their students while simultaneously allowing students to speak, listen, and learn differently within pedagogical spaces that are safe, affirming, questioning, and enabling.

In this instance, a curriculum for a multicultural and multiracial society provides the conditions for students to imagine beyond the given and to embrace their identities critically as a source of agency and possibility. In addition, an insurgent multiculturalism should serve to redefine existing debates about national identity while simultaneously expanding its theoretical concerns to more global and international matters. Developing a respect for cultures in the plural demands a reformulation of what it means to be educated in the United States and what such an education implies for the creation of new cultural spaces that deepen and extend the possibility of democratic public life. Multiculturalism insists upon challenging old orthodoxies and reformulating new projects of possibility. It is a challenge that all critical educators need to address.

Notes

1. Alice Kessler-Harris, "Cultural Locations: Positioning American Studies in the Great Debate," *American Quarterly*, 44, 3 (1992), p. 310.

2. Hazel Carby, "The Multicultural Wars," in *Black Popular Culture*, ed. Gina Dent (Seattle: Bay Press, 1992), pp. 193–4.

3. Kobena Mercer, "Back to my Routes: A Postscript on the 80s," *Ten.8*, 2, 3 (1992), p. 33.

4. James Baldwin, "A Talk to Teachers," in *Multicultural Literacy: Opening the American Mind*, eds Rick Simonson and Scott Waler (Saint Paul, MN: Graywolf Press, 1988), p. 8.

5. Gerald Graff and Bruce Robbins, "Cultural Criticism," in *Redrawing the Boundaries*, eds Stephen Greenblat and Giles Gunn (New York: MLA, 1992), p. 435.

6. Alan O'Connor, "Just Plain Home Cookin'," *Borderlines*, 20/21 (Winter 1991), p. 58.

7. Cornel West, *Race Matters* (Boston: Beacon Press, 1993), p. 14.

8. Ibid., p. 16.

9. Cornel West, "Learning to Talk of Race," *The New York Times Magazine*, 6 (August 2, 1992), p. 24.

10. bell hooks, *Black Looks: Race and Representation* (Boston: South End Press, 1992), p. 168.

11. Homi K. Bhabha, "The Postcolonial Critic—Homi Bhabha interviewed by David Bennett and Terry Collits," *Arena*, 96 (1991), pp. 50–1.

12. Stuart Hall and David Held, "Citizens and Citizenship," in *New Times: The Changing Face of Politics in the 1990s,* eds Stuart Hall and Martin Jacques (London: Verso, 1989), p. 178.

13. Peter Drier, "Bush to the Cities: Drop Dead," *The Progressive* (July 1992), p. 22.

14. Joan Scott, "Multiculturalism and the Politics of Identity," *October,* 61 (Summer 1992), p. 13.

15. Arthur Schlesinger Jr, *The Disuniting of America* (Knoxville, TN: Whittle District Books, 1992), pp. 21, 78.

16. James Clifford, "Museums in the Borderlands," in *Different Voices,* ed. Association of Art Museum Directors (New York: Association of Art Museum Directors, 1992), p. 119.

17. William Kerrigan, "The Falls of Academe," in *Wild Orchids and Trotsky,* ed. Mark Edmundson (New York: Penguin Books, 1993), p. 166.

18. Ibid., p. 167.

19. Homi K. Bhabha and Bhikhu Parekh, "Identities on Parade: A Conversation," *Marxism Today* (June 1989), p. 3

20. Trinh T. Minh-Ha, *Woman, Native, Other: Writing Postcoloniality and Feminism* (Bloomington: Indiana University Press, 1989), p. 232.

21. E. San Juan Jr, *Racial Formations/Critical Transformations: Articulations of Power in Ethnic and Racial Studies in the United States* (Atlantic Highlands, NJ: Humanities Press, 1992), p. 101.

22. Hazel Carby, "Multi-Culture," *Screen Education,* 34 (Spring 1980), p. 65.

23. Bhabha and Parekh, "Identities on Parade: A Conversation," p. 4.

24. Manning Marable, *Black America: Multicultural Democracy* (Westfield, NJ: Open Media, 1992), p. 13.

25. Homi K. Bhabha, "A Good Judge of Character: Men, Metaphors, and the Common Culture" in *Race-ing Justice, Engendering Power: Essays on Anita Hill, Clarence Thomas, and the Construction of Social Reality,* ed Toni Morrison (New York: Pantheon, 1992), p. 242.

26. Cornel West, "Learning to Talk of Race," p. 24.

27. Roger I. Simon, *Teaching Against the Grain* (New York: Bergin and Garvey Press, 1992), p. 17.

28. Henry Louis Gates Jr, "The Black Man's Burden," *Black Popular Culture,* ed. Gina Dent (Seattle: Bay Press, 1992), p. 76.

29. Judith Butler, "Contingent Foundations: Feminism and the Question of Postmodernism'," in *Feminists Theorize the Political,* eds Judith Butler and Joan Scott (New York: Routledge, 1992), p. 13.

 # Public Intellectuals and the Culture of Reaganism in the 1990s

*There is a genuine crisis in education and public life
over whether we really are a civilization and whether
there is anything in the American past worth
transmitting. In schools around the country,
Thanksgiving and other national holidays that once
bound us together have been transformed—with dreary
uniformity—into "multicultural holidays," when
children are asked to celebrate nothing more than their
own ethnicity—and, by implication, their own egos.*[1]

—Newt Gingrich

Schooling and the Culture of Reaganism

Newt Gingrich's comments exemplify for me the legacy of a historical era that has been labeled as the culture of Reaganism.[2] I mention this historical period, beginning with the election of Ronald Reagan to the presidency in the 1980s and continuing into the 1990s, because it inaugurated a fundamental shift in the political and cultural realignments that has had a major impact on American public life since the 1980s.[3] The culture of Reaganism provided the historical, political, and social context that has most deeply affected the various theoretical interventions I have made as a critical educator over the past sixteen years. The problems I have addressed regarding schooling and public life, the role of teachers as intellectuals, and the cultural politics of the curriculum have been forged in a language and set of assumptions shaped by the politics, institutional pressures, and policies that have dominated this historical era.[4] My point here, of course, is that the act of theorizing cannot be abstracted from the conditions we inherit or from the problems that emerge in the face of specific historical conditions.

Moreover, I have always been less concerned with developing a body of scholarly work that simply sniped at those who loosely shared a similar ideological view of the world than with addressing, in a language of critique and possibility, those political, theoretical, and cultural forces that pose the greatest challenge to public schooling as a site for teaching students to take seriously civic responsibility and the imperatives of a vital democracy.

Gingrich's comment also presupposes a neoconservative view of schooling, cultural difference, and public life that has dominated the country since the Reagan era. During this period youth, in particular, have experienced massive changes in nuclear family life, caused by rising poverty rates, the flight of capital from urban centers, and the dismantling of policies designed to protect the poor, children, and the elderly. Furthermore, the forces of economic restructuring and deindustrialization have largely replaced the manufacturing sector with a proliferation of low-skill jobs and have contributed to rising unemployment rates among young people, especially poor, urban black youth. More specifically, in the past sixteen years, we have witnessed a resurgent racism accompanied by an erosion of the safety nets designed to protect children from poverty, disease, and homelessness. One tragic legacy of Reagan's cultural revolution is that youth, especially poor urban youths, have become scapegoats in the neoconservative attack on welfare, civil rights laws, and health care policies. Demonized in the press as thugs and criminals, young black males in particular have been blamed for the breakdown of public civility while young, unwed mothers have been targeted as the source of all social evils in American society.[5] Beneath the moral panic, in the atmosphere of which youth is blamed for the deterioration of public life, lies a different reality:

> In post-Vietnam America, young people have experienced an erosion in their cultural prestige, their impact as a social force has diminished, they are losing ground in their rights and civil liberties. The nature of the nuclear family, the global economy and the world stage is in rapid transition. The American working class is disappearing as a social entity. There now exists a permanent subclass of American citizens we call "the homeless." Half the kids in America don't go to college, and the ones who do spend six years getting degrees, after which they cannot find jobs, or afford housing, health care or cars.[6]

American youth and public schools have not fared well under Reaganism. By calling into question the link between schooling and equity, conservatives have redefined the role of education in terms of privatization and standardization. Neoconservatives have attempted to make the public school an adjunct of the corporation, offering its services to the highest corporate bidder. Within this discourse, there is little room for linking equity with excellence, engaging the role that teachers might play as critical intellectuals, or decentering power in the classroom so as to educate students about the relations between and values of civic and social responsibility. The excerpt from Newt Gingrich's *To Renew America* barely conceals the neoconservative view of national identity that, in its ethnocentrism and monoculturalism, is scornful toward minorities, urban youth, cultural differences, and the democratic possibilities of public schooling.[7] Within this cultural and political hegemonic bloc, there has been a consistent attempt to remove schools from their role in educating students as social subjects who can take up the burdens and responsibilities of democratic public life. Instead, neoconservatives have largely defined education using a monocultural and commercial logic by which pedagogy serves primarily to produce consumers.

The rejection of school as a democratic public sphere has gone hand in hand with the expanding emphasis on defining young people in terms of market values—as either consumers or commodities. When not demonized, youths are viewed as merely filling market niches in a commercial culture that uses mass media, especially television, to sell young children and adolescents toys, clothes, and every other conceivable product.[8] Over the last sixteen years, many conservatives have relied upon the marketplace as a model when shaping and influencing school policy. Corporations such as Whittle Communications have intervened in developing school curricula and have played a major role in contracting services from public school districts. Furthermore, there is an increasing trend toward private corporation management of public school systems on a for-profit basis. According to The Education Industry Directory, the for-profit education market represents a potential $600 billion investment opportunity and currently provides $30 billion in revenue for corporate interests.[9] Conservatives in the past decade and a half have also initiated policies advocating vouchers, privatization, and charter schools. The first casualties in this scenario have been teachers' unions, teacher autonomy, and children attending schools in economically depressed areas.

Opposing this conservative trend in education, I have attempted in my work to insert the political back into educational discourse by focusing on the relationship between schools and society and knowledge and power and on the need for teachers to work for a democratic and ethical project. Although it is impossible to sum up in one chapter the different trajectories my work has taken over time, I will emphasize my finding that what is at stake in the neoconservative attack on education is the role that the university and other schools might play as crucial public spheres, on the one hand, and what the responsibility of the academic as a public intellectual might be on the other. I will focus on both of these issues as they apply to higher education, but I think that many of the points to be developed could be applied just as readily to public schooling.

Higher Education Under Assault

In the past fifteen years, the debate about the role that university educators might play as critically engaged public intellectuals has grown increasingly hostile. This is most evident in the barrage of attacks initiated in the popular press and by right-wing critics against multiculturalism, political correctness, and a variety of other forces that are allegedly undermining what the well-known journalist George Will has called "the common culture that is the nation's social cement."[10]

In their attack on the university, and by default public schooling, neoconservatives imply that the university should not assume the role of a public sphere in which critics actively engage in addressing either the problems of the society or global issues. For neoconservative hardliners such as Chester Finn, William Bennett, and other contributors to the *National Review*, the *New Republic*, *Education Week*, and similar publications, this position translates into the unproblematic assumption that social criticism has no place in the university and that those who engage in it represent either a new form of cultural barbarism or a version of political correctness that has no place in higher education.[11] Moderate conservatives and liberals take the more cautious position that universities should simply impart knowledge that withstands current political and cultural affairs. Others, such as Hilton Kramer, go so far as to deny both the relevance of the university as a public sphere and the assumption that academics can operate as public intellectuals. He writes, "The Great Mistake is to identify public intellectuals with academics. Most of the serious intellectual discourse for some time has not come out of the academy. The academy is intellectually dead."[12]

The crisis over whether the university should be a critical public sphere is also evident in the rhetoric of a currently popular group of diverse public intellectuals located in and supported financially by the government, private foundations, and the popular press. Politicians such as former Secretary of Education William Bennett are now touted as exemplary intellectuals who will restore a traditional moral foundation to the commanding institutions of civic life. In Bennett's worldview, public culture is modeled on civic virtues found in the ninteenth-century McGuffey Readers, and responsible citizenship is embodied in the Hollywood film character Forrest Gump.

In the sphere of mass culture, many journalists—apparently resentful that academics are addressing vital public issues—have invoked populist notions of clarity and "truthfulness" to reaffirm themselves as the "real" voices of the people. One rather grotesque example is the reactionary TV talk show figure Rush Limbaugh. What these conservatives share—beyond their common battle against the perils of deconstruction, postmodernism, cultural studies, black studies, gender studies, gay and lesbian studies, poststructuralism, and other theoretical insurgencies—is the deep rooted belief that university academics have no role as critical public intellectuals.

Although the theoretical particulars are different, a similar critique of intellectuals in the university has emerged among a number of progressive theoreticians. One popular example can be found in Russell Jacoby's *The Last Intellectuals,* which considers the decline of public culture in the United States and the rise of academic intellectuals who allegedly write in arcane languages and largely forsake any viable political intervention into public life.[13] In this view, critical thought nurtured in the halls of higher education offers little in the way of understanding or promoting social struggle. For Jacoby, the only real public intellectuals were such nonacademics as Edmund Wilson, Lewis Mumford, Dwight MacDonald, and others who lived in such urban centers as Greenwich Village and wrote for magazines such as the *Partisan Review.* According to Jacoby, their breed has been replaced by academics who are nothing more than classroom technicians, speaking and writing in specialized languages that cut them off from vital public audiences and issues. Although it is true that the university harbors academics whose work often degenerates into an abstract and empty formalism, such a charge too easily slips into an overgeneralized critique that ignores the important work being done by educators at all levels of schooling, whose "principal occupation is studying, reading, teaching, writing, publishing, [and] addressing the public" and who help students think critically "about the affairs of this world and the broader context of things."[14] The backlash against critical intellectuals and educators has gained substantial currency under Reaganism and with the increasing rise of corporate culture in the United States; it is indicative of one dimension of the crisis that higher education is facing.

Higher Education as a Public Sphere

I believe that higher education must be defended as a vital public sphere in its own right—that is, as a public sphere whose moral and pedagogical dimensions help renew civic life. The university influences large numbers of people not only in terms of what they learn and how they locate themselves in the context and content of specific knowledge forms but also in terms of their impact on a variety of institutions in public life.[15] For example, if cultural critics were more attentive to what is taught in professions such as nursing, social work, and education, they might become more aware of the effect of such teaching on the thousands of teachers, health workers, and community members who do battle on the health care, social service, and the public school fronts. Public schools, for instance, surely can be said to comprise a major public sphere; yet hardly a word is uttered by radical or conservative critics about the crucial relationship between such schools and institutions of higher learning. Perhaps the more important question here is, What silences will have to endure in the debate on higher education before academic intellectuals are dismissed as irrelevant, even though much of the work that goes on in institutions of higher education directly impacts thousands of students whose work concerns public issues and the renewal of civil society.

To elaborate further on the university as a crucial public sphere and the role of teachers as public intellectuals, I will analyze how some cultural studies scholars have attempted to address some of the same issues that conservatives and liberals have used to criticize higher education. In addition, I will argue that the absence of any serious discussion of pedagogy in cultural studies and in the debates about higher education has narrowed significantly the possibilities for redefining the role of educators as public intellectuals and of students as critical citizens capable of governing rather than simply being governed. Schools in this view become more than museums, Sunday schools, or corporate training centers.[16] More specifically, I will stress the importance of pedagogy in the further development of cultural studies, the broader attempt to reform higher education, and the effort to educate youth not merely to adapt to the existing demands of the work force but to be critical cultural workers, willing to fight for a democratic society. With this in mind, I want to turn to the issue of cultural studies.

Rethinking the Importance of
Cultural Studies for Educators

Employing diverse discourses and forms of cultural criticism, cultural studies provides a theoretical service to educators and others in the following ways. First, it broadens our understanding of how politics and power work through institutions, language, representations, and culture, across diverse economies of desire, time, and space. In its critical analysis of culture and power, cultural studies has consistently emphasized the interrelations of theory and context-specific studies to address issues ranging from adult literacy, class analysis, and youth subcultures to feminism, racism, popular culture, and identity politics.

Second, cultural studies has reinvigorated academia with its transdisciplinary and transcultural approach to scholarship. It has echoed Walter Benjamin's call upon intellectuals to assume responsibility for translating theory back into a constructive practice that transforms the everyday terrain of cultural and political power. Pushing the boundaries of traditional disciplines and the frontiers of intellectual life, cultural studies presses "for new questions, new models, and new ways of study, testing the fine line between intellectual rigor and social relevance."[17]

Third, cultural studies provide theoretical frameworks for analyzing how power works through the popular and everyday to produce knowledge, social identities, and maps of desire. Crucial here is the ongoing theoretical and pedagogical work of understanding how the new electronic media deploy images, sounds, and other representational practices that are redefining the production of knowledge, reason, and new forms of global culture. Abandoning the elitist distinction between high and popular culture, cultural studies has provided a theoretical service by making the objects of everyday life legitimate sources of social analysis. Moreover, its emphasis on how meaning and power circulate in the realm of the popular has not only challenged overdetermined theories of domination by focusing on the ways in which resistance maybe construed by popular culture; it has also focused new attention on the ways in which dominant intellectual and institutional forces police, contain, and address meaning as a site for a variety of social struggles.[18]

Fourth, in opposition to vanguard and elitist notions of the intellectual, cultural studies views intellectual work as tempered by humility, highlights its moral focus on suffering, and points to the need for public intellectuals to go beyond critique to offer alternative visions and policies. On one level, cultural studies is important because it takes on the task of establishing and struggling over institutional spaces and practices that might produce public intellectuals. But the determination to provide institutional spaces in which public intellectuals have a voice is matched by a cautious pedagogical regard for striking a critical balance between producing rigorous intellectual work, on the one hand, and exercising authority that is firm rather than rigid and self-critical and concretely utopian rather than repressive and doctrinaire, on the other. Stuart Hall is helpful here. He argues that in insisting on the vocation of intellectual life, cultural workers must "address the central, urgent, and disturbing questions of a society and a culture in the most rigorous intellectual way we have available. Such a vocation is, above all, one of the principal functions of a university, though university scholars are not always happy to be reminded of it."[19]

For educators, cultural studies offers a broader understanding of how power inserts itself into the cultural realm; it also raises important questions about the vocation of intellectual work, the relevance of interdisci-plinary inquiry, and the centrality of popular culture as a realm of criti-cal analysis. But if educators are to not merely appropriate but take in-spiration from cultural studies as a form of cultural criticism and pedagogical work, we will have to deepen and extend the democratic possibilities in this field as well as address some of its glaring absences. To be more specific, I believe that cultural studies has not adequately developed a notion of the political as part of a wider project for social re-construction and progressive change. That is, it has failed to unite its dif-ferent theoretical considerations into a shared notion of public struggle and social justice for a comprehensive democratic politics. Although is-sues of racism, class, gender, textuality, national identity, subjectivity, and media culture must remain central to any cultural studies dis-course, the issue of radical democracy must be located at the center of its politics. This is particularly important for educators who wish to ar-ticulate the dynamics and possibilities of schooling in larger public dis-courses.

By using radical democracy as a political, social, and ethical referent in redefining education for a world made up of multiple and fractured public cultures, cultural studies confronts the need for constructing a new ethical and political language to describe the problems and chal-lenges of a newly constituted global public. Within this postmodern pol-itics of difference and the increasingly dominant influence of globaliza-tion, cultural studies needs to become sufficiently attentive to restoring the language of ethics, agency, power, and identity in the wider effort to revitalize democratic public life.

At stake here is the necessity for cultural studies to provide some com-mon ground on which traditional binarisms of margin/center, unity/difference, local/national, and public/private can be reconsti-tuted through more complex representations of identification, belong-ing, and community. Cultural studies must continue to develop new theoretical frameworks for challenging the way we think about the dy-namics and effects of cultural and institutional power. This requirement, in turn, suggests the need for a discourse of ruptures, shifts, flows, and unsettlement—one that functions less as a politics of transgression than as part of a concerted effort to construct a broader vision of political commitment and democratic struggle. Cultural studies in this sense can further expand its theoretical horizons by considering radical democ-racy in a wider discourse of rights and economic equality. In this con-text, cultural studies offers the possibility for extending the democratic principles of justice, liberty, and equality to the widest possible set of so-cial relations and institutional practices that constitute everyday life. Via the issue of radical democracy, cultural studies can forcefully assert its own politics by affirming the importance of the particular and the contingent while acknowledging the shared political values and goals of a democratic society.

In addition, although cultural studies theorists often call for interdisciplinary or transdisciplinary work, they often fail to challenge a major assumption behind disciplinarity: that pedagogy is an unproblematic vehicle for transmitting knowledge. Lost in this notion is a rigorous and critical understanding of pedagogy as a means of questioning the cultural conditions under which knowledge and identities are produced.[20] Unfortunately, unlike early cultural studies theorists such as Raymond Williams, the current crop of theorists inhabiting this diverse field exhibits little concern for the importance of pedagogy as a form of cultural practice and politics. Within this silence lurks the often unconscious privileging of certain forms of academic capital, the seductive rewards of disciplinary policing, a refusal to cross academic borders, and a shoring up of academic careerism, competitiveness, and elitism. It appears that the legacy of the latter still exercises a strong influence on cultural studies, despite its alleged democratization of social knowledge.

The importance of pedagogy to the content and context of cultural studies lies in the relevance it has for illuminating how power and knowledge configure in the production, reception, and transformation of social identities, forms of ethical address, and "desired versions of a future human community."[21] Asserting that all forms of pedagogical authority are partial, critical pedagogy inquires into the relationship between cultural work, authority, experience, and securing particular cultural practices. In a cultural political mode, pedagogy studies the possibilities for social agency expressed in a range of human capacities in light of the social forms that often constrain or enable them.

In this form of pedagogy, intellectuals address what it means to construct social relations that enable students to speak differently so as to affirm and analyze their narratives, marked by consistencies and contradictions. Not only may students who have been traditionally marginalized thus be heard, they may be taken seriously as the implications of their discourse in broader historical and ideological terms are considered.[22] Equally important, however, is the need to provide safe spaces in which students cross ideological and political borders to clarify their own moral visions, engage in counter-discourses, and, as Roger Simon points out, get "beyond the world they already know in order to challenge and provoke their existing views of the way things are and should be."[23]

Whether in schools or in other cultural spheres, public intellectuals must struggle to create the conditions that enable students and others to become cultural producers who can rewrite their own experiences and perceptions by engaging with various texts, ideological positions, and theories. They must construct pedagogical relations in which students learn from each other, learn to theorize rather than simply ingest theories, and begin to address how to decenter the authoritarian power of the classroom. Students must also be given the opportunity to challenge disciplinary borders, create pluralized spaces from which hybridized identities might emerge, take up critically the relationship between language and experience, and appropriate knowledge as part of a broader effort at self-definition and ethical responsibility. What I am suggesting here is that public intellectuals move away from the rigid, ideological parameters of the debate about the curriculum or canon. What is needed is a new language for discussing knowledge and authority and the possibility of giving students a role in deciding what is taught and how it is taught under specific circumstances. The question is not merely, who speaks and under what conditions? It is also about how to see universities (and public schools) as important sites of struggle over what is taught and for control of the conditions of knowledge production itself.

Now, I will shift my frame a bit to focus on some implications of the concerns I have addressed thus far and how they might be connected to developing an academic agenda for public intellectuals in higher education.

Public Intellectuals and the Politics of Education

Institutions of higher education must be seen as deeply moral and political spaces in which intellectuals assert themselves not merely as professional academics but as citizens, whose knowledge and actions presuppose specific visions of public life, community, and moral accountability. This view suggests that higher education be defended through intellectual work that self-consciously recalls the tension between the democratic imperatives or possibilities of public institutions and their everyday realization. For instance, academics might develop their research programs, pedagogy, and conceptual frameworks in connection to cultural work undertaken by the media, labor organizations, or insurgent social movements. Such relationships should allow public intellectuals to speak to a diverse range of audiences from a number of public arenas. At the same time, such connections and alliances should not support the idea that higher education may define its public function simply through its association with other public spheres. First and foremost, it must be defended as a vital public sphere in its own right, one that has deeply moral and educative dimensions that directly impact civic life. This defense must be maintained by academics redefining

their roles as public intellectuals who can move between academic institutions and other public spheres in which knowledge, values, and social
identities are produced.

If the university is to remain a site of critical thinking, collective work,
and social struggle, public intellectuals need to expand its meaning and
purpose. That is, they need to define higher education as a resource vital
to the moral life of the nation, open to working people and communities
whose resources, knowledge, and skills have often been viewed as marginal. The goal here is to redefine the knowledge, skills, research, and social relations constructed in the university in order to more broadly reconstruct a tradition that links critical thought to collective action,
knowledge and power to a profound impatience with the status quo,
and human agency to social responsibility.

Opposing this view, many neoconservatives argue that university
teachers who address public issues out of personal commitment either
violate the spirit of academic professionalism or via ideology left over
from the 1960s, present a dangerous threat to the freedom and autonomy of the university. Irving Kristol implies as much when he charges
that the greatest threat to conservative hegemony comes from the cultural left, which consists of teachers and others "from the so-called helping professions."[24] This position rests on a deep suspicion of any attempt to enable educators to address pressing social issues in
connection with their teaching. Attempting to license and regulate critical pedagogical practice, conservatives argue that universities are apolitical institutions whose primary goal is to create a select strata of technical experts to run the commanding institutions of the state, to prepare
students for the workplace, and to reproduce the alleged common values that define the "American" way of life.[25] In this discourse, politics is
subordinated to management, and political activity is displaced by the
imperatives of objectivity and appropriate academic standards.

Of course, many liberals also have argued that although university
academics have the right to address public issues, they should do so
from the perspective of a particular teaching methodology or pedagogy
rather than from a particular political project. Gerald Graff, for instance,
has called for university educators to teach the conflicts. Graff's position
is that academics who teach about oppression presuppose some prior
agreement among students that it actually exists before it can be discussed. As for those "radical" educators who address issues of human
suffering and other social problems, he believes that they end up speaking to the converted or use their authority to indoctrinate students. His
is more than a cheap theoretical pronouncement; it is an ideologically
loaded assertion based on a confusion between political education and
politicizing education—one that needs further elaboration.[26]

Political education means teaching students to take risks, challenge those with power, honor critical traditions, and be reflexive about how authority is used in the classroom. A politicizing education refuses to address its own political agenda and creates silences through an appeal to a specious methodology, objectivity, or a notion of balance. Politicizing education perpetuates pedagogical terrorism; a political education improves the pedagogical conditions for students to understand how power works on them, through them, and for them in the service of constructing and expanding their roles as critical citizens.

In politicizing education, the language of objectivity and methodology runs the risk of replacing an ethical discourse concerned with the political responsibility of university professors, including the issue of how they might help students identify, engage, and transform relations of power that generate the material conditions of racism, sexism, poverty, and other oppressive conditions.[27] Lacking a political project, the role of the university intellectual is reduced to a technician engaged in formalistic rituals unconcerned with the disturbing and urgent problems that confront the larger society.

In opposition to this view, I will argue that public intellectuals must combine the interdependent roles of critical educator and active citizen. They must find ways to connect the practice of classroom teaching to the operation of power in the larger society. I think Edward Said is on target when he argues that the public intellectual must function within institutions, in part, as an exile, as someone whose "place it is publicly to raise embarrassing questions, to confront orthodoxy and dogma, to be someone who cannot easily be co-opted by governments or corporations."[28] In this perspective, the educator as public intellectual becomes responsible for linking the diverse experiences that produce knowledge, identities, and social values in the university to the quality of moral and political life in the wider society. Vaclav Havel captures this sentiment in arguing that intellectuals have a responsibility to engage in practical politics, to see "things in more global terms. . . . build people-to-people solidarity. . . . foster tolerance, struggle against evil and violence, promote human rights, and argue for their indivisibility."[29]

Intellectuals who feel an increased sense of responsibility for humanity may not be able to and do not necessarily have to explain the problems of the world in terms that purport to be absolute or all encompassing. They also should not limit their responsibility to the university or the media. On the contrary, public intellectuals need to approach social issues with humility, mindful of the multiple connections and issues that tie humanity together; but they need to do so by moving within and across diverse sites of learning as part of an engaged and practical politics that recognizes the importance of "asking questions, making distinctions, restoring to memory all those things that tend to be over-looked or walked past in the rush to collective judgment and action."[30]

Within this discourse, the experiences that constitute the production of knowledge, identities, and social values in the university are inextricably linked to the quality of moral and political life of the wider society. Thus, intellectuals engaged in it must challenge forms of disciplinary knowledge and social relations that promote material and symbolic violence, while remaining deeply critical of their own authority and how it structures classroom relations and cultural practices. In this way, the authority they legitimate in the classroom would become both an object of self-critique and a critical referent for expressing a more "fundamental dispute with authority itself."[31] In addition, as public intellectuals, academics must move beyond recognizing the partiality of their own narratives to address more concretely the ethical and political consequences of the social relations and cultural practices generated by the forms of authority used in the classroom.

As I pointed out earlier in this chapter, if educators are to function as public intellectuals they need to provide the opportunities for students to learn that the relationship between knowledge and power can be emancipatory, that their histories and experiences matter, and that what students say and do counts in their struggle to unlearn dominating privileges, productively reconstruct their relations with others, and transform, when necessary, the world around them. More specifically, such educators need to argue for forms of pedagogy that close the gap between the university and the everyday life. Their curriculum needs to be organized around knowledge of the communities, cultures, and traditions that give students a sense of history, identity, and place. As I suggested in my analysis of cultural studies, I'm calling for transgressing the often rigid division between academic culture and popular/oppositional culture and for expanding pedagogical practice as a form of cultural politics by making all knowledge subject to serious analysis and interrogation—and in so doing, making visible the operations of power that connect such knowledge to specific views of authority and cultural practice.

Educators need to construct pedagogical approaches that do more than make learning context-specific; in effect, they need to challenge the content of the established canon and, similarly, to expand the range of cultural texts that count as "really useful knowledge." As public intellectuals, university teachers need to use electronically mediated knowledge forms that constitute the terrain of popular culture. I refer to the world of media texts—videos, films, music, and other mechanisms of popular culture outside of print. The content of the curriculum should affirm and critically enrich the meaning, language, and knowledge forms that students actually use to negotiate and inform their lives. Academics can in part exercise their role as public intellectuals via such curricula, giving students the opportunity to understand how power is organized through the enormous number of "popular" cultural spheres, ranging from libraries, movie theaters, and schools to high-tech media conglomerates that circulate signs and meanings through newspapers, magazines, advertisements, electronic programming, machines, films, and television programs. University intellectuals must draw a lesson from cultural studies in extending the historical and relational definition of cultural texts while redefining in Toni Morrison's terms how "knowledge, however mundane and utilitarian, plays about in linguistic images and forms cultural practices."[32]

Although it is central for university teachers to enlarge the curriculum to reflect the richness and diversity of the students they actually teach, they also need to decenter the curriculum. That is, students should be actively involved in governance, "including setting learning goals, selecting courses, and having their own, autonomous organizations, including a free press."[33] Not only does the distribution of power among teachers, students, and administrators provide the conditions for students to become agents in their learning process, it also provides the basis for collective learning, civic action, and ethical responsibility. Moreover, student agency emerges from a pedagogy of lived experience and struggle, not from mere formalistic mastery of an academic subject.

In addition, as public intellectuals, university teachers need to make cultural difference a defining principle of knowledge production, development, and research. In an age of shifting demographics, large-scale immigration, and multiracial communities, university teachers must make a firm commitment to cultural difference as central to the relationship between schooling and citizenship. Doing so means dismantling and deconstructing the legacy of nativism and racial chauvinism that has informed the rhetoric of school reform for the last decade.[34]

The Reagan and Bush eras witnessed a full-fledged attack on the rights of minorities, civil rights legislation, and affirmative action, accompanied by the legitimation of curriculum reforms pandering to ethnocentric interests. University educators can affirm their commitment to democratic public life and cultural democracy by struggling in and out of the classroom in solidarity with other activists to reverse these policies and make schools more attentive to the cultural resources that students bring with them at all levels of schooling. For instance, they can work to develop legislation that protects the civil rights of all groups. Equally important, the university teachers should take the lead in encouraging programs that open school curricula to the narratives of cultural difference, without falling into the trap of merely romanticizing the experience of Otherness. At stake is the development of an educational policy that places university education in a broader ethical and political discourse, one that both challenges and transforms those curricula reforms of the past decade that are profoundly racist in context and content. In part, such a policy would change the terms of the debate over the relationship between schooling and national identity, moving away from an assimilationist ethic and the profoundly ethnocentric fantasy of a common culture to a view of national identity that includes diverse traditions, histories, and the expansion of democratic public life.

During the past fifteen years, I have been building upon my earlier studies of teachers as intellectuals in an attempt to reclaim a critical relationship between pedagogy and politics on the one hand and democracy and schooling on the other. At the risk of being too bold, I have suggested that educators need to become provocateurs; they need to take a stand while refusing to be involved in either a cynical relativism or doctrinaire politics. In part, I mean that central to intellectual life is the pedagogical and political imperative that academics engage in rigorous social criticism while becoming a stubborn force for challenging false prophets, deconstructing social relations that promote material and symbolic violence, and speaking the "truth" to dominant forms of power and authority. At the same time, as I mentioned earlier such intellectuals must be deeply critical of their own authority and how it structures classroom relations and cultural practices.[35]

In critiquing one's own experiences, it is imperative to guard against a confessionalism by which the interrogation becomes tantamount to speaking a transparent version of the "truth." Such self-reflexivity must become part of a wider strategy of crossing and transgressing the borders between the self and others, theory and practice, and the university and everyday life.

Finally, as public intellectuals, university educators must bring to bear in their classrooms and other pedagogical sites the courage, analytical tools, moral vision, time, and dedication required to return universities to their most important task: creating a public sphere in which citizens are able to exercise power over their own lives and especially over the conditions of knowledge acquisition. Central to any such effort is the recognition that democracy is not a set of formal rules of participation, but the lived experience of empowerment for the majority. Moreover, the call for universities to operate as democratic public spheres should not be reduced to the call for autonomy for intellectuals or to the demand for equal access to schools, equal opportunity, and measures of equality. Autonomy and equality are crucial elements in the democratization of schools, but they are not the sole elements in this process. Instead, the rallying cry of university educators should concern empowerment for the vast majority of students in this country who need to be educated in the spirit of a critical democracy.[36] The challenge to educators is ever-present, and they must continue to renew their commitment to the struggle.

Notes

1. Newt Gingrich, *To Renew America* (New York: HarperCollins, 1995), p. 31.

2. On the culture of Reaganism, see Jimmie L. Reeves and Richard Campbell, *Cracked Coverage* (Durham: University of North Carolina Press, 1994); and Herman Gray, *Watching Race* (Minneapolis: University of Minnesota Press, 1995), especially chapter 2.

3. For a brilliant analysis of this issue, see Thomas Byrne Edsall with Mary D. Edsall, *Chain Reaction: The Impact of Race, Rights, and Taxes on American Politics* (New York: Norton, 1992).

4. It is important to acknowledge that members of the right, particularly the neoconservatives associated with the Contract with America, do not speak for all conservatives. I am aware that neoconservatism has many strains and is far from uniform. The assumptions and policies I attribute to neoconservatism represent a loosely defined but largely accepted worldview and not a doctrinaire party line.

5. For a perceptive examination of this issue, see Katha Pollitt, "Devil Women," *New Yorker,* February 26 and March 4, 1996, pp. 58–64.

6. Donna Gaines, "Border Crossing in the U.S.A.," in Andrew Ross and Tricia Ross, eds., *Microphone Fiends* (New York: Routledge, 1994), p. 227. For a more specific indication of how black youth are faring in the age of Bill Clinton and Newt Gingrich, see Andrew Hacker, "The Crackdown on African-Americans," *Nation,* July 10, 1995, pp. 45–49.

7. I take this issue up in Henry A. Giroux, *Living Dangerously: Multiculturalism and the Politics of Culture* (New York: Peter Lang Publishing, 1993).

8. For one excellent source, see Stephen Kline, *Out of the Garden: Toys and Children's Culture in the Age of TV Marketing* (New York: Verso, 1993); see also Henry A. Giroux, *Fugitive Cultures: Race, Violence, and Youth* (New York: Routledge, 1996).

9. Cited in Peter Applebome, "Lure of the Education Market Remains Strong for Business," *New York Times,* January 31, 1996, pp. A1, A15.

10. Cited in Louis Menand, "What Are Universities For?" *Harper's,* December 1991, p. 56.

11. For a representative example of neoconservative attacks on the university along with some responses, see Paul Berman, ed., *Debating P.C.: The Controversy Over Political Correctness on College Campuses* (New York: Laurel, 1992); Michael Keefer, "'Political Correctness': An Annotated List of Readings," *ACCUTE Newsletter,* Fall 1991, pp. 1–13; Patricia Aufderhiede, ed., *Beyond PC: Towards a Politics of Understanding* (St. Paul: Graywolf, 1992). For an example of neoconservative critiques used in the arts, see various articles in Richard Bolton, ed., *Culture Wars: Documents from the Recent Controversies in the Arts* (New York:

New Press, 1992). For a trenchant analysis of the history and nature of the right-wing use of political correctness to attack higher education, see Ellen Messer-Davidow, "Manufacturing the Attack on Liberalized Higher Education," *Social Text* No. 36 (1993), pp. 40–80. The latter piece contains an excellent bibliography. See also Henry A. Giroux, "Pedagogy and Radical Democracy in the Age of 'Political Correctness,'" in David Trend, ed., *Radical Democracy* (New York: Routledge, 1996), pp. 179–193.

12. Cited in Jenny Scott, "Thinking Out Loud: The Public Intellectual Is Born," *New York Times*, August 9, 1994, p. B4.

13. Russell Jacoby, *The Last Intellectuals: American Culture in the Age of Academe* (New York: Basic, 1987).

14. Vaclav Havel, "The Responsibility of Intellectuals," *New York Review of Books* 63:11 (June 22, 1995), p. 36.

15. Analyses of the university as a critical public sphere can be found in Stanley Aronowitz and Henry A. Giroux, *Education Still Under Siege* (Westport: Bergin and Garvey, 1993).

16. Recent examples of theoretical work that attempts to insert the issue of pedagogy back into cultural studies can be found in Henry A. Giroux and Peter McLaren, eds., *Between Borders: Pedagogy and Politics in Cultural Studies* (New York: Routledge, 1994).

17. Stuart Hall, "Race, Culture, and Communications: Looking Backward and Forward at Cultural Studies," *Rethinking Marxism* 5:1 (Spring 1992), p. 11.

18. One of the most forceful expressions of this position can be found in Lawrence Grossberg, *We Gotta Get Out of This Place* (New York: Routledge, 1992); Stuart Hall, "Cultural Studies and Its Theoretical Legacies," in Lawrence Grossberg, et al., eds., *Cultural Studies* (New York: Routledge, 1992), pp. 277–286; and Lawrence Grossberg, "The Formation of Cultural Studies: An American in Birmingham," *Strategies* No. 2 (1989), pp. 114–149.

19. Hall, "Race, Culture, and Communications," p. 11.

20. Of course, such theorists as Gayatri Spivak, Cary Nelson, and Stanley Aronowitz do engage the relationship between cultural studies and pedagogy, but they constitute a small minority in the United States. See Stanley Aronowitz, *Roll Over Beethoven: The Return of Cultural Strife* (Hanover: University Press of New England, 1993). See also a few articles in *Cultural Studies* edited by Grossberg, et al. Also, see various issues of *College Literature* edited by Kostas Myrsiades. It is quite revealing to look into some of the latest books on cultural studies and see no serious engagement of pedagogy as a site of theoretical and practical struggle. For example, see Patrick Brantlinger, *Crusoe's Footprints: Cultural Studies in Britain and America* (New York: Routledge, 1990); Graeme Turner, *British Cultural Studies* (London: Unwin Hyman, 1990); John Clarke, *New Times and Old Enemies* (London: HarperCollins, 1991); Sarah Franklin, Celia Lury, and Jackie Stacey, eds., *Off-Centre: Feminism and Cultural Studies* (London: HarperCollins, 1991); and Simon During, ed., *The Cultural Studies Reader* (New York: Routledge, 1993). In the latter, there is not one chapter on pedagogy.

21. Roger I. Simon, *Teaching Against the Grain* (West Point: Bergin and Garvey Press, 1992), p. 15. Let me add that the term *critical pedagogy* must be used with respectful caution. There are different versions of what constitutes critical peda-

gogy; no generic definition applied. There are also important theoretical insights and practices that weave through various approaches to critical pedagogy. These insights often delineate a common set of problems for critical pedagogy to articulate in relation to particular political projects. These problems include but are not limited to the relationship between knowledge and power, language and experience, ethics and authority, student agency and transformative politics, and teacher location and student formations.

22. For a provocative analysis of the issue of student voice and critical pedagogy, see Chandra Mohanty, "On Race and Voice: Challenges for Liberal Education in the 1990s," *Cultural Critique* No. 14 (1989–1990), pp. 179–208; see also Henry A. Giroux, *Schooling and the Struggle for Public Life* (Minneapolis: University of Minnesota Press, 1988), especially the "Schooling and the Politics of Student Voice," pp. 113–146; for a recent summary and analysis of some of the literature on student voice, see Andy Hargreaves, "Revisiting Voice," *Educational Researcher* 25:1 (January-February, 1996), pp. 12–19.

23. Simon, *Teaching Against the Grain*, p. 47.

24. Irving Kristol, "The New Face of American Politics," *Wall Street Journal*, August 26, 1994, p. A10.

25. For a trenchant analysis of the political correctness movement, which relies on this type of ideological argument, see Aronowitz, *Roll Over Beethoven*, especially chapter 1.

26. I have taken this distinction from Peter Euben, "The Debate over the Canon," *The Civic Arts Review* 1:1 (1994), pp. 14–15.

27. Gerald Graff, "Teaching the Conflicts," in Darryl J. Gless and Barbara Hernstein Smith, eds., *The Politics of Liberal Education* (Durham: Duke University Press, 1992), pp. 57–73.

28. Edward Said, *Representations of the Intellectual* (New York: Pantheon, 1994), p. 11.

29. Havel, "The Responsibility of Intellectuals," p. 37.

30. Said, *Representations of the Intellectual*, pp. 52–53.

31. R. Radhakrishnan, "Canonicity and Theory: Toward a Poststructuralist Pedagogy," in Donald Morton and Mas'ud Zavarzadeh, eds., *Theory/Pedagogy/Politics* (Urbana: University of Illinois Press, 1991), pp. 112–135.

32. Toni Morrison, *Playing in the Dark: Whiteness and the Literary Imagination* (Cambridge: Harvard University Press, 1992), pp. 49–50.

33. Stanley Aronowitz, "A Different Perspective on Educational Equality," *Review of Education/Pedagogy/Cultural Studies* 16:2 (1994), p. 24.

34. Giroux, *Living Dangerously*.

35. R. Radhakrishnan in Morton and Zavarzadeh, eds., *Theory/Pedagogy/Politics*, pp. 112–135.

36. I take this issue up in Giroux, *Schooling and the Struggle for Public Life*.

Credits

Permission to reprint Chapters 1–9 is gratefully acknowledged.

Part 1: Theoretical Foundations for Critical Pedagogy

Chapter 1, "Schooling and the Culture of Positivism: Notes on the Death of History," originally appeared in *Educational Theory* 29, 4 (1979), 263–284.

Chapter 2, "Culture and Rationality in Frankfurt School Thought: Ideological Foundations for a Theory of Social Education," originally appeared in *Theory and Research in Social Education* 9, 4 (1982), 22–56.

Chapter 3, "Ideology and Agency in the Process of Schooling," originally appeared in *Boston University Journal of Education* 165, 1 (Winter 1983), 12–34.

Chapter 4, "Authority, Intellectuals, and the Politics of Practical Learning," originally appeared in *Teachers College Record* 88, 1 (Fall 1986), 22–40.

Part 2: Critical Pedagogy in the Classroom

Chapter 5, "Radical Pedagogy and the Politics of Student Voice," originally appeared in *Interchange* 17, 1 (1986), 48–69. Reprinted with kind permission from Kluwer Academic Publishers.

Chapter 6, "Border Pedagogy in the Age of Postmodernism," originally appeared in *Boston University Journal of Education* 170, 3 (1988) [appeared in October 1989], 166–181.

Chapter 7, "Disturbing the Peace: Writing in the Cultural Studies Classroom," originally appeared in *College Literature* 20, 2 (1993), 13–26.

Part 3: Contemporary Concerns

Chapter 8, "Rethinking the Boundaries of Educational Discourse: Modernism, Postmodernism, and Feminism," originally appeared in *College Literature* 17, 2/3 (1990), 5–50.

Chapter 9, "Insurgent Multiculturalism and the Promise of Pedagogy," originally appeared in David Theo Goldberg, ed., *Multiculturalism: A Reader* (Cambridge, MA: Basil Blackwell, 1994), 325–343.

Chapter 10, "Public Intellectuals and the Culture of Reaganism in the 1990s," is being published for the first time in this book.

About the Book and Author

Henry A. Giroux is one of the most respected and well-known critical education scholars, social critics, and astute observers of popular culture in the modern world. For those who follow his considerably influential work in critical pedagogy and social criticism, this first-ever collection of his classic writings, augmented by a new essay, is a must-have volume that reveals his evolution as a scholar. In it, he takes on three major considerations central to pedagogy and schooling.

The first section offers Giroux's most widely read theoretical critiques on the culture of positivism and technocratic rationality. He contends that by emphasizing the logic of science and rationality rather than taking a holistic worldview, these approaches fail to take into account connections among social, political, and historical forces or to consider the importance of such connections for the process of schooling.

In the second section, Giroux expands the theoretical framework for conceptualizing and implementing his version of critical pedagogy. His theory of border pedagogy advocates a democratic public philosophy that embraces the notion of difference as part of a common struggle to extend the quality of public life. For Giroux, a student must function as a border-crosser, as a person moving in and out of physical, cultural, and social borders. He uses the popular medium of Hollywood film to show students how they might understand their own position as partly constructed within a dominant Eurocentric tradition and how power and authority relate to the wider society as well as to the classroom.

In the last section, Giroux explores a number of contemporary traditions and issues, including modernism, postmodernism, and feminism, and discusses the matter of cultural difference in the classroom. Finally, in an essay written especially for this volume, Giroux analyzes the assault on education and teachers as public intellectuals that began in the Reagan-Bush era and continues today.

Henry A. Giroux is a professor at the School of Education at Pennsylvania State University.

Index

potential and, 75
social, 264
subjective forms of, 140
teaching and, 227
Student voice, 123–124, 141–142
Style, substance and, 49
Subjectivity, 36, 53, 83, 100, 105, 121, 133,
    134, 135, 158, 167, 195, 207, 208, 215,
    220, 261
  changing of, 107
  desire and, 203
  feminism and, 206
  human agency and, 71
  identity and, 203
  intentionality and, 203
  liberal humanist notion of, 203
  objectivity and, 40
  postmodernism and, 202–204, 214
  radical pedagogy and, 81
Subordination, 130, 196, 197, 210, 247
Substance, style and, 49
Surplus repression, concept of, 59–60
Systems management, 16, 19

Teacher voice, 141, 142–143
  schooling and, 142
Teachers
  authority and, 99–100, 103, 104,
    105–106, 111–113
  critical thought and, 24–25
  as cultural workers, 224
  culture of positivism and, 24
  curriculum and, 28–29
  knowledge and, 21, 172–173
  pedagogy and, 150, 158, 171
  social change and, 28
  subjectivity and, 220
  as transformative intellectuals, 103–104,
    111, 112–113, 224, 254
Teaching
  criticism of, 3–4
  democratic struggle and, 227
Technology, 8, 50–51
Textbooks
  analysis of, 22, 65(n5), 88, 135, 137–140
  about pedagogy, 87, 88–89
  for pedagogy, 91
Textuality, 148, 261
Theory, 10, 170
  Frankfurt School and, 41–46
There Ain't No Black in the Union Jack
    (Gilroy), 175

Thompson, E. P., 73
  on politics/democracy, 216–217
Thought
  action and, 43
  as after thought, 49
  experience and, 169
  negative, 60
  objectification of, 25–26
  schooling and, 124–126
  See also Dialectical thought
To Renew America (Gingrich), 256
Totalitarianism, 36, 216, 217
Totality, 204
  negation of, 193–196, 211–212
  postmodern feminism and, 206,
    210–212
Tozer, Steve, on authority/democracy, 101
Traditionalists, 16, 19
Transformation, 95, 158, 161, 227
  counter-memory and, 155
  ideology and, 77
  social and political task of, 171
  teaching for, 103–104
Transformative intellectuals, teachers as,
    103–104, 111, 112–113, 224
Trilateral Commission, report by, 239
Truth, 11, 268
  counter-memory and, 152
  postmodernism and, 195

Unconsciousness, 77
  consciousness and, 81
  ideology and, 75, 78–82
Understanding, 126, 129, 141, 142, 143, 149
  critique and, 45
  enlightenment and, 91
  history and, 40
  observation and, 45
Utopian discourse, 223

Values, 41
  facts and, 11, 40
Victimization, 225, 242
Vienna Circle, 39, 40
Voice
  authorship and, 134
  language and, 134
  politics of, 224
  struggle for, 134, 159
Volosinov, V. V., 73, 86, 87

Warhol, Andy, 49